Streams of Grace

SPIRITUAL MOVEMENTS THAT SHAPED THE CHURCH

Julian Porteous

Modotti Press
AN IMPRINT OF CONNOR COURT PUBLISHING

Published in 2011 by Modotti Press
An imprint of Connor Court Publishing Pty Ltd.

Copyright © Julian Porteous

All rights reserved. No part of this book may be reproduced or transmitted in any form or by any means, electronic or mechanical, including photocopying, recording or by any information storage and retrieval system, without prior permission in writing from the publisher.

Modotti Press
Connor Court Publishing Pty Ltd.
PO Box 7275
Redland Bay QLD 4165

sales@connorcourt.com
www.connorcourt.com

ISBN   9781921421907 (pbk.)

Cover design Ian James

Printed and designed in Australia

"I saw water flowing out from beneath the threshold of the temple toward the east".
Ezekiel 47:1

Contents

    Introduction..1

1. The Church's true Life: its Life in the Spirit....................5
2. Two graces given to the Early Church..........................15
3. The Call to the Desert...31
4. A School for God's Service..41
5. A Land of Saints and Scholars.....................................51
6. The Cistercian Reform..61
7. A Rule of Life for Clergy...69
8. An Evangelical Revival..77
9. An Order of Preachers..87
10. Byzantine Traditions of Prayer....................................95
11. The Jesus Prayer...101
12. The Beguines..111
13. Devotio Moderna..119
14. The Rise of the Mystic...125
15. The Rhineland Mystics..135
16. St Ignatius Loyola – Mental Prayer............................141
17. St Theresa of Avila – States of Prayer........................151
18. Devotion to the Sacred Heart....................................161
19. Devotion to the Blessed Virgin Mary.........................169
20. Streams of Grace Today..179
21. Epilogue...193

    Appendix..195
    Bibliography...207

Introduction

Many have written on the subject of the Catholic spiritual tradition, many more expert than I. I was hesitant to add another book to an already rich library of works. However, my students, seminarians from the Seminary of the Good Shepherd, Homebush in Sydney, urged me to put into book form the series of lectures I gave to them. As Rector from the year 2002 to 2008 I presented a course to the First Year group to introduce them to the tradition of spirituality in the Catholic Church. The course was to assist them as they sought to develop their personal spiritual life. It was they who urged me to produce the lectures in book form. This simple book is the result.

It is written for Catholics who seek to grow in the interior life. It offers an account of the many and varied ways in which people over the centuries have sought a path to a deeper living relationship with God. The words of the psalmist capture well the yearning of the human spirit for union with the divine: "O God, you are my God, for you I long, for you my soul is thirsting."[1]

This book is also testimony to the diverse and wonderful manifestations of the Holy Spirit at work in individual souls and as the transforming influence in the soul of the Church. On a number of occasions Pope Paul VI wrote eloquently about the presence and influence of the Holy Spirit in the life and mission of the Church. He said in one place:

> It is in the "consolation of the Holy Spirit" that the Church increases. The Holy Spirit is the soul of the Church. It is He who explains to the faithful the deep meaning of the teaching of Jesus and of His mystery.[2]

At the heart of the many and varied spiritual movements that

---

[1] The Grail translation of Ps 63:1. This is the version used in the Divine Office. It is a text that becomes part of the "spiritual furniture" of the heart and mind after years of reciting the Divine Office.
[2] *Evangelii Nuntiandi*, n. 75..

have shaped the Catholic Church is the presence and activity of the Holy Spirit. Often the Spirit has acted in surprising and unexpected ways, yet as spiritual movements flourished it has become clearer that they have been critical to maintaining and enriching the calibre of the spiritual life of the Church. These movements often have had saints at their forefront, or have become vehicles for the emergence of great saints. Spiritual movements emerge at particular moments in history and in particular places. We cannot ignore the historical and social context of these movements, nor miss the significance that these movements have on the life of the Church lived most immediately by "ordinary" Catholics. Many movements, as we will see, have shaped the character of Catholic faith and how this faith has come to be expressed in the life of Catholics.

The historical and cultural setting has meant that the movements have been incardinated in quite specific situations, yet they have spread beyond the context in which they were born. This reveals that such moments of grace have a universal and not just localised significance. They speak to the soul of the Church and are the source of regeneration of the spiritual life which is the inner reality of the Church.

The spiritual movements have not just influenced a small number of the spiritual elite, but have become sources of inspiration and fruitfulness for countless thousands. Many of these spiritual movements have become expressed in various writings - sometimes in sermons or sayings, but often in books. Spiritual classics have been read over the centuries and the insights and inspiration of the movement captured in these works have continued to attract many to pursue the interior life and grow in virtue and holiness. The vast library of spiritual writings is the great patrimony of the Church. This resource ensures that graces of earlier times are still accessible and able to inspire peoples of all ages. Spiritual movements may come at a particular historical moment but the legacy lives on in the testimony of the spiritual writings.

The Church has a rich heritage, which sadly, is not known well enough. In recent times many Catholics have been attracted to other Christian Churches particularly those of an evangelical bent. Other

Catholics have turned to Eastern non Christian religions or dabbled in the New Age in an effort to find spiritual nourishment. They have not known of the treasure buried in the heart of the Church.

Presenting the Catholic Spiritual tradition afresh to every age is important. It can enable Catholics to discover what is available to them. It can show them paths for interior nourishment and map out a way to virtue and holiness of life.

The Spirit is always at work in the Church. Our own age has seen the Spirit "blow where he will". There are many positive signs of spiritual resurgence currently in the Church. A Catholic is able to be that wise steward that the Lord spoke about – able to bring out of his storage things both new and old.[3]

Each chapter in this short book explores a spiritual movement within the context of the time. These movements proved to be important moments of spiritual fruitfulness in the particular time and many have continued to make an ongoing contribution to the faith and life of the Church. At the end of each chapter there is a brief quote from material representative of the movement. These "tastes" can help us appreciate the particular flavour of the movement.

May this introductory book help many to recognise more clearly the wonderful ways in which the Holy Spirit has been active in the Church. May this simple book encourage all who seek God within the depths of their lives know something of the paths of the Spirit in the human heart.

Julian Porteous
28 May 2011

---

[3] See Mt 13:52.

1
The Church's true Life: its Life in the Spirit

The Church burst into life when the Holy Spirit came upon the apostles with power at Pentecost. The New Testament writings reveal a particular awareness of the presence and activity of the Holy Spirit in bestowing gifts for building up the Church, as well as graces and charisms[4] that moulded the inner life of individual Christians.

St Paul declares that everyone who has received the Holy Spirit in Christian Baptism is "a son of God" (Rom 8:14). Each believer has the dignity of a personal familial relationship with God. In St Paul's words, we are no longer a slave "bringing fear into your lives" (See Rom 12:1-2), but we have a relationship with God built in love. Indeed "the love of God has been poured into our hearts by the Holy Spirit" (Rom 5:5).

Christians are interested in spiritual things and have an interior spiritual life which is empowered by the presence of the indwelling Spirit. Each Christian lives a spiritual life: "Your interests are not in the unspiritual, but in the spiritual, since the Spirit of God has made his home in you" (Rom 8:9).

---

[4] The Second Vatican Council offered an important contribution to the theology of the Church by addressing the question of charisms. The document on the Church, *Lumen Gentium*, referred to the teaching of St Paul in his first letter to the Corinthians where he speaks of the Holy Spirit "allotting his gifts according as he wills" (1 Cor 11:12). The word "charism" comes from the Greek *charis*, meaning grace, or, free gift. Each Christian receives "grace" at Baptism which is the divine presence nurturing the Christian life. As well as this universal gift, the Holy Spirit gives individuals particular gifts of grace, charisms. This understanding of the action of the Holy Spirit in the life of the Christian lies as a foundation to the emergence of spiritual movements in the Church over its history.

The true history of the Church

Often the history of the Church is evaluated in terms of its political and social presence in the world and its impact on societies and cultures. It is seen as a player in the human drama of history. This is true. The Church is a human and political reality and it has had a profound influence on the direction of human history and the formation of cultures. It will continue to do so. However, to limit the story of the Church only to this dimension of its existence is to fail to appreciate its true presence in the world.

The Church has a rich inner life – the life of the Holy Spirit. It is the presence of the Holy Spirit that makes the Church ever fresh and new in each age. It is the Holy Spirit that renews the youth of the Church "like an eagle." The prophet Isaiah (40:30-31) said "Even youths shall faint and be weary, and young men shall fall exhausted; but they who wait for the Lord shall renew their strength; they shall mount up with wings like eagles; they shall run and not be weary; they shall walk and not faint." This text expresses a significant truth about the spiritual life. The presence of the Holy Spirit is a constant source of rejuvenation of the human spirit. It is also a way in which we can see how the Church over the centuries has never lost its inner vigour. Often when it has seemed that the Church has lost its spiritual energy there has been a fresh manifestation of the Spirit which has engendered new life and vitality. The Church is indeed ever old and ever new.

It is the Holy Spirit who stirs the hearts of believers to new levels of faith, to holiness of life and to heroic virtue. One could say that the true history of the Church is the history of the saints. The work of the Church is particularly accomplished through the lives of those who are closest to God – his saints.

The Holy Spirit has worked in diverse and often unexpected ways to ensure that the Church has the spiritual capacity to meet the particular challenges of different times in its history.

This simple account of the spiritual history of the Church reveals the inner life of the Church over the centuries. This reflection is by no means comprehensive. It takes just a few of the many particular moments of the work of the Holy Spirit in the life of believers. It is an attempt to note some of the wonderful works of God achieved through the action of the Holy Spirit that have shaped the life and work of the Church. This is an account of some of these moments of grace that have touched, directed and made fruitful the mission of the Church in its pilgrimage over history.

Before proceeding, however, it is worth exploring a little more closely the event of Pentecost and its effect on the first believers. From here we will touch on some special moments of grace in which the Spirit reveals its rich and diversified action over the last two millennia of Christian history.

The coming of the Holy Spirit

To understand Pentecost let us for a moment consider its immediate pre-history.

John the Baptist, sent as the precursor to Christ, said that he baptised with water for repentance, but Jesus would baptise "with the Holy Spirit and fire" (Lk 3:16). Christian baptism is not simply a symbolic action expressing our desire to turn to God as it was in the case of the baptism that John offered. Christian baptism would be the occasion in which God would empower us with the Holy Spirit "and with fire".

Each of us has received the Holy Spirit when we were baptised. The Holy Spirit enables us to have faith, to be able to believe – St Paul taught that we cannot say "Jesus is Lord" unless we have the Holy Spirit in us.[5] The presence of the Holy Spirit is essential for a person to come to have faith in Jesus Christ. This can explain why some people do not have even the slightest sense of faith. While human beings are destined to know and love God we cannot achieve this by ourselves. The exercise of human reason can at least lead to

---
5 See I Cor 12: 3.

some questioning about the ultimate meaning of things.[6] However, faith is a gift. It is an action of the grace of God upon the soul.

The Christian experience is that the Holy Spirit is a real and active presence in the life of a believer. But who is the Holy Spirit? What does the Holy Spirit do in us? How does the Holy Spirit work in us?

The Holy Spirit is mysterious. The Spirit is invisible, silent yet real. The Scripture speaks of the Spirit as *ruah*, the wind.[7] It is a good description. We cannot see the wind, but the wind is real. In fact the way we can tell that the wind is blowing is by seeing the effects that it has – trees move, fallen leaves or bits of paper move across the ground. The wind can be gentle or strong. The Holy Spirit is like the wind: invisible but real, and the Spirit is identified by effects. Wind is often connected with the action of God. In Psalm 18:11 it says: "He mounted a cherub and flew, borne on the wings of the wind". God appeared to Ezekiel in a storm wind. (Ez 1:4) God speaks to Job "from the midst of the storm" (Job 38:1). The classic expression of this encounter is that given in the First Book of Kings where the Lord appears to the prophet Elijah in a gentle breeze and not "in the wind ... in the earthquake ... in the fire" (I Kgs 19:12).

The Holy Scriptures reveal a great deal about the activity of the Spirit and the effects the Holy Spirit has on people's lives. The Holy Spirit was an active presence in creation and was a key agent in important moments in Israel's history but all this was a preparation for the great action of the Holy Spirit.

The defining outpouring of the Holy Spirit was at Pentecost (Acts 2:1-13). There was a sound of wind, and then there were tongues of fire. The frightened and confused apostles were wonderfully transformed. They found new courage and boldness. Peter went out on the balcony of the house where they were gathered and began to

---

6 St Paul in Romans 1:18f speaks of all humanity being in a desperate plight that requires God's special intervention if it is to be saved. Humanity can discover the reality of God and can recognise basis moral imperatives by use of natural reason, but, he says, has failed to do so. In humanity there is a basic hardness of heart.

7 In Hebrew, wind is "ruah". It also means breath, a light breeze, a puff of wind. There are two principle meanings for this word: that which is linked with natural phenomena (ruah as wind), and that which concentrates on human activity (ruah as breathing, puff of breath).

announce to the crowds that the man they crucified had risen from the dead!

The power of the Holy Spirit radically transforms lives. Christian history is full of stories of men and women who have experienced wonderful moments of grace when the Holy Spirit has come upon them. Saints were born under the influence and outpouring of the Holy Spirit.

The work of the Spirit

The Acts of the Apostles tells of the early Christians receiving various spiritual gifts. Peter and John heal a cripple at the temple (Acts 3: 1-10). St Paul describes some of the ways in which the Holy Spirit was active in the early Christian communities. He outlines some of the spiritual gifts which were manifest in the community in Corinth. He speaks of gifts of preaching and teaching, of prophesy and healing and the gift of tongues.[8] St Mark says in the final words of his Gospel – "In my name they will cast out devils, they will have the gift of tongues, they will pick up snakes in their hands, and be unharmed if they drink deadly poison; they will lay their hands on the sick who will recover". Then St Mark adds, "they, going out, preached everywhere, the Lord working with them and confirming the word by the signs that accompanied it" (Mk 16:20).

The work of the Spirit in the life of the believer takes other forms as well. In the Catholic Sacrament of Confirmation we receive the seven gifts of the Holy Spirit – wisdom, understanding, counsel, fortitude, knowledge, piety, and fear of the Lord. This list is found in Isaiah 11:1-2. These gifts expressed how the Spirit would be evident in the life of the Messiah. These same gifts are intended to be evident in the life of the Christian.

These gifts enhance the life of faith of those who receive them. The Lord taught that the Spirit is the spirit of truth (Jn 15:26; 1613). The Spirit comes to us to enlighten our minds. The Spirit thus can lead us to wisdom, knowledge, understanding and right judgement.

---

8 See 1 Cor 12:4-11.

The Spirit of God is active in the mind and in the heart. It is described as a fire that hovered over the heads of the apostles. St Peter, and then the other apostles, were filled with a new evangelical zeal. This zeal would enable them to take the gospel message "to the ends of the earth" (Acts 1:8) The Lord promised that he would bring "fire to the earth" (Lk 12:49). St Paul said to Timothy, to "fan into a flame the gift God gave you when I laid my hands on you" (2 Tim 1:6). Tongues of fire came upon the Apostles at Pentecost (Acts 2:3). This fire of the Holy Spirit is not a fire that destroys – like our bushfires – rather it is like the fire of the burning bush that attracted Moses in the desert (Ex 3:2) – this fire was alight and burning but did not consume the bush.

The spiritual tradition of the Church is testimony to the fire of the Holy Spirit igniting the hearts of individual believers to do great things for God. The significant spiritual movements which we will consider can best be described as a burst of the flame of faith and love which spread like a bushfire in hearts caught up in its path.

Making us holy

The presence of the Holy Spirit in the life of each Christian is the source of growth in personal holiness. Holiness is the goal of the Christian life. The Scriptures admonish us: "Be perfect as your heavenly Father is perfect" (Mt 5:48). St Peter teaches, "But just as he who called you is holy, so be holy in all you do for it is written: *"Be holy, because I am holy"* (1 Pet 1:16).

Catholic theology speaks of presence of "sanctifying grace" in the soul of the believer. Sanctifying grace is "a participation in the life of God."[9] This "life of God" is the life of the Holy Spirit within us. The Eastern tradition in the Church speaks of the notion of

---

9 See Catechism of Catholic Church n. 1997. The Catechism adds, "It introduces us into the intimacy of Trinitarian life: by Baptism the Christian participates in the grace of Christ, the Head of his Body. As an "adopted son" he can henceforth call God "Father," in union with the only Son. He receives the life of the Spirit who breathes charity into him and who forms the Church".

"theosis" or deification.[10] It is a rich concept highlighting that from the time of receiving baptism the Christian is in a process of being transformed and raised up in holiness.

The Catholic Catechism teaches, "The grace of Christ is the gratuitous gift that God makes to us of his own life, infused by the Holy Spirit into our soul to heal it of sin and to sanctify it. It is the sanctifying or deifying grace received in Baptism. It is in us the source of the work of sanctification".[11] The testimony of Scripture confirms this teaching: "Therefore if anyone is in Christ, he is a new creation; the old has passed away, behold, the new has come. All this is from God, who through Christ reconciled us to himself" (II Cor 5:17).

Thus each Christian lives a life in the Holy Spirit. This life is the path to holiness. The Second Vatican Council spoke of the "universal call to holiness."[12] The Holy Spirit enables a Christian to grow in holiness. The Holy Spirit helps the believer to become more like Christ. The Holy Spirit dwells within the temple of the believer's body (1 Cor. 3:16; 6:19; 2 Cor. 6:16). This indwelling presence empowers the Christian. All of the Christian's life is made holy because the Holy Spirit transforms it. The Holy Spirit does not work on us; the Spirit lives in us. Holiness is a fruit of living "in the Spirit".

Throughout the history of the Church the cry "Come, Holy Spirit" has gone up. This cry expresses the longing of the Church for the presence and transforming power of the Holy Spirit. It expresses the desire of the Christian heart for the Holy Spirit to be the agent for the growth in holiness. A prayer, which captures this desire, is attributed to St Augustine:

Breath in me, O Holy Spirit, that my thoughts may all be holy.

---

10 The Fathers of the Church used the word, *theosis* to describe the process of the Christian becoming so united with God that they are being changed already on earth towards what they will be in heaven. St Athanasius captured the concept in these words, "He became as we are that we might become as he is." (Athanasius. *On the Incarnation* 54). The Divine Word became human that humans might become divine, and the agent for this is the indwelling Holy Spirit.
11 CCC, n. 1999.
12 See *Lumen Gentium*, n. 40.

Act in me, O Holy Spirit, that my work, too, may be holy.
Draw my heart, O Holy Spirit, that I love but what is holy.
Strengthen me, O Holy Spirit, to defend all that is holy.
Guard me, then, O Holy Spirit, that I always may be holy.

The action of the Holy Spirit

The Lord knew that his disciples would need the presence and power of the Holy Spirit in their lives if they were to be capable of effectively living within the Kingdom of God and able to give convicting witness to their faith before the world. Thus in a striking piece of teaching Jesus urged his disciples to actively seek the gift of the Spirit: "Ask and you shall receive; search, and you will find; knock, and the door will be opened to you. Everyone who asks receives; everyone who searches finds; everyone who knocks will have the door opened. Is there anyone among you who would hand his son a stone when he asked for bread? Or would hand him a snake when he asked for a fish? How much more will your Father who is in heaven give the Holy Spirit to those who ask Him!" (Lk 11:9-11).

The story of the spiritual tradition of the Church is the story of the presence and activity of the Holy Spirit in the lives of believers. At times of special need the Spirit of God acted, moving "ordinary" believers into streams of Grace which transformed their lives and provided sources of spiritual renewal for the Church. Those with generous hearts enabled the power of the Holy Spirit to lead them to the heights of union with God. This book is witness to the some of the ways that the Holy Spirit has moved in the lives of believers. This simple survey of spiritual movements in the Church's history gives testimony to the wonderful ways in which God has been faithful to his Church and come to its aid especially at times of special need through diverse works of the Holy Spirit in the lives of individual Christians.

On the spiritual life

The unspiritual are interested only in what is unspiritual, but the spiritual are interested in spiritual things. It is death to limit oneself to what is unspiritual; life and peace can only come with concern for the spiritual. This is because to limit oneself to what is unspiritual is to be at enmity with God: such a limitation never could and never does submit to God's law. People who are interested only in unspiritual things can never be pleasing to God. Your interests, however, are not in the unspiritual, but in the spiritual, since the Spirit of God has made his home in you. In fact, unless you possessed the spirit of Christ you would not belong to him. Though your body may be dead it is because of sin, but if Christ is in you then your spirit is life itself because you have been justified; and if the Spirit of him who raised Jesus Christ from the dead is living in you, then he who raised Jesus from the dead will give life to your own mortal bodies through his Spirit living in you.

St Paul, Letter to the Romans

2
Two Graces given to the Early Church

As the Church began to form, movements of grace influenced its spiritual character. After the Apostolic age a number of special graces were given to the Church. There are two graces in particular that are significant spiritual influences in the early Church, and continue to be significant throughout Christian history.

The two graces are: (1) reverence for the Scriptures as the living Word of God and (2) celibacy for the sake of the Kingdom of God. These graces would be key to the future development of the spiritual life of the Church.

We will briefly consider each of these graces in turn. Firstly, let us look at how the early Church viewed the place of the Scriptures.

Reverence for the Scriptures as the Word of God

The Faith of the Fathers

After the period of the Apostles, Church history is considered to have entered into the Age of the Fathers. This era runs from the fourth to the seventh century.[13] The Fathers were leaders in the Church – scholars and bishops – who were recognised for their holiness and orthodoxy. This era marks the time when the definitive expression of the faith of the Church was clarified and consolidated after the Apostolic age. It was a time of intense debate and occasions of schism during which the Rule of Faith was defined and given

---
13 Most date the end of the age of the Fathers of the West with the death of St Isidore of Seville in 636, and the age of the Fathers of the East with the death of St John Damascene in 749.

final expression in the Nicene Creed. The Fathers of the Church engaged with the Scriptures not just as an intellectual activity but primarily as a spiritual one. Their profound love for the sacred text and their reverence before it provided the Church with a rich resource of teaching and inspiration. The Fathers understood that the Scriptures were the living Word of God. They knew that divine wisdom would be transmitted to those who approached the sacred text with humility and docility of spirit. Revelation would come to hearts that were receptive to be enlightened by the Word of God.

The Fathers, in the words of Pope Benedict XVI[14], approach the Scriptures from the "hermeneutic[15] of faith". The testimony of the Fathers reveals how the Scriptures were at the heart of the living of the faith. Origen (185-254) wrote: "The Word of God is in your heart. The Word digs in this soil so that the spring may gush out." St Jerome (342-419) similarly reveals the awareness of a personal encounter with God through the Scriptures, "You are reading? No. Your betrothed is talking to you. It is your betrothed, that is, Christ, who is united with you. He tears you away from the solitude of the desert and brings you into his home, saying to you, 'Enter into the joy of your Master.'" Both Origen and St Jerome devoted their lives to the study and exposition of the Scriptures. They wrote extensive commentaries. They had a profound knowledge of the sacred texts, yet their writings reveal the fact that it was not the intellectual grasp

---

14 Pope Benedict has addressed the question of the ways in which Catholics should approach the interpretation of Sacred Scripture. His book, "Jesus of Nazareth", is an expression of his conviction that Scripture must be approached with the "Hermeneutic of Faith". In an address to the Pontifical Biblical Commission in April 2009 he spoke of three criteria that always apply for an interpretation of Sacred Scripture to be in conformity with the Spirit that inspired it. (1) It is essential to pay attention to the content and unity of the whole of Scripture. Sacred Scripture is one by virtue of the unity of God's plan finally revealed and achieved in Jesus Christ. (2) Sacred Scripture must be interpreted in the context of the living tradition of the Church. Origen commented, "Sacred Scripture is written in the heart of the Church before being written on material instruments". (3) The importance of the "analogy of the faith", that is, to the consistence of individual truths of faith with one another and with the overall plan of God's purpose.

15 Hermeneutics is the theory of the understanding and the interpretation of written text. Aristotle, in his work, *On Interpretation*, commented: "Words spoken are symbols or signs of affections or impressions of the soul written words are the signs of words spoken". Hermeneutics has special significance in relation to the way in which the Sacred Scriptures are interpreted.

of their subject but rather their faith, inflamed by constant prayerful reflection, which inspired their writings.

The Fathers urged their Christian audience to turn to the Scriptures for spiritual nourishment. St John Chrysostom (347-407) commented, "Listen carefully to me. Procure books [of the Bible] that will be medicines for the soul. At least get a copy of the New Testament, the Apostle's epistles, the Acts, the Gospels, for your constant teachers. If you encounter grief, dive into them as into a chest of medicines; take from them comfort for your trouble, whether it be loss, or death, or bereavement over the loss of relations. Don't simply dive into them. Swim in them. Keep them constantly in your mind. The cause of all evils is the failure to know the Scriptures well." The Fathers had a profound reverence for the Scriptures. They devoted their lives to pondering the truth and wisdom revealed through them.

The Fathers built their daily lives and their preaching of the faith solidly around the Scriptures. The Fathers penetrated beyond the external words to the reality that they signified. They sought the mystery of Christ and through Christ they were led into the mystery of the divine life of God Himself. They were aware they could reach this mystery only by means of a living faith and in prayerful contemplation on the sacred texts.

The writings of the Fathers reveal a penetration of the mysteries of the faith contained in Sacred Scripture. Their approach to the sacred text was an intellectual savouring of what they knew to be divine realities communicated by the Holy Spirit. They knew that below the external covering of the words lay eternal truths. Faith was the key to this process. They understood that faith would open the mind to the revelation of the divine truth.

The Fathers were acutely aware that all the Scriptures were about Christ. St Irenaeus writes, "If one carefully reads the Scriptures, he will find there the word on the subject of Christ and the prefiguration of the new calling. He is indeed the hidden treasure in the field – the field in fact is the world – but in truth, the hidden treasure in the Scriptures is Christ. Because he is designed by types and words that humanly are not possible to understand before the accomplishment of all things, that is, Christ's second coming." St Irenaeus understood that anyone who approached the Scriptures in a spirit of faith would discover Christ. This encounter with Christ was not just gaining knowledge about him, but being drawn into a personal relationship with him. Reading the Scriptures in a spirit of faith would lead a person into a union with Christ.

St Augustine of Hippo comments: "The Scriptures are in fact, in any passage you care to choose, singing of Christ, provided we have ears that are capable of picking out the tune. The Lord opened the minds of the Apostles so that they understood the Scriptures. That he will open our minds too is our prayer."

Hermeneutic of faith

The Fathers were embedded in the "hermeneutic of faith" in their approach to the Sacred Scripture. We will examine in more detail this "hermeneutic" by considering the teaching of Origen. At little personal background can assist us in appreciating his thought.

Origen was born around year 185 in Alexandria, Egypt. He loved the Scriptures and devoted his life to studying and teaching them. He revealed how to approach the Scriptures in these words: "If anyone ponders over prophetic sayings with all the attention and reverence they deserve, it is certain that in the very act of reading and diligently studying them his mind and feelings will be touched by a divine breath and he will recognise that the words he is reading are not the utterances of men but the language of God".

For Origen, the Scriptures were the living Word of God. He understood that if they were approached with this awareness, a person would hear the voice of God. He encouraged an approach to the scriptures where one seeks out the hidden "spiritual" meaning of the text. He said, "The truth of the Word of God is hidden under the surface of the letter". What he taught was that the way to discover this truth is to read the Scriptures in the same way in which they were written: *in the Spirit*. As he described, 'The Scriptures were written under the action of the Spirit of God, and they have, beyond their apparent sense, a certain other sense which eludes most readers. For what is found in it is at one and the same time the figure of certain mysteries and the image of divine realities".

The Fathers were aware that we need to approach Scriptures in a different way than any other book we may read. We normally seek to apply our mind to understand the meaning of what we are reading. We analyse what we read – we are taught to be critical readers. But the Scriptures must be approached differently. We do use our minds to understand the text, but we listen with our hearts to what God may be saying to us. In ordinary reading we apply only our minds, in reading Scripture we listen with our minds and hearts.

Origen saw the Scriptures as having a body, soul and spirit, and explains the interrelationship between them in this way:

- Body is the immediate literal sense intended by the human author
- Soul is what the Scriptures say to us in our life. What Origen called the moral sense
- Spirit is that which conveys divine truth or wisdom which reveals God and speaks to our spirit.

When someone speaks to us, we hear their words, but we must actively listen to pick up their deeper more personal message behind the words that they speak. So it is with the Scriptures. Every time we open the Scriptures and read something, we are listening to what God wants to say to us. This is how the Fathers of the Church approached the Sacred Scriptures.

This "hermeneutic of faith" is the way in which the Church has learnt to listen to the Word of God in Sacred Scripture. However, at different times the rationalism of the age has deadened this openness to the Scriptures as the living Word of God. Our age, as Pope Benedict has warned us, can lose sight of the importance of the "hermeneutic of faith", opting for an approach to interpreting Scripture reduced to the "spirit of the age".

The history of the Church reveals that the great spiritual movements have always returned to this consciousness of the Scriptures as the living Word of God. Rediscovering this truth has been a particular source of spiritual fruitfulness in these movements. We will see many examples of this as we trace the spiritual movements in the Church's history.

Celibacy for the sake of the Kingdom

Judaism valued marriage and the bearing of children. The New Testament reveals an invitation to embrace celibacy "for the sake of the Kingdom". In contrast to the tradition of Judaism we can count the call to celibacy a particular gift or grace given to the Church. The Old Testament Scriptures give several accounts of the desperate grief of childless women.[16] Yet, contrary to this, the early Christians also lauded those who chose to remain celibate for spiritual motives. This "grace of virginity" is a particular charism of the Spirit given to the Church from the beginning. It has become established as part of the fabric of Catholic spirituality.

We cannot consider celibacy except in relation to marriage. In presenting the nature of the human person in the story of creation in the Book of Genesis, it is stated, "It is not good for man to be alone" (Gen 2:24). The story simply relates that God created human beings as male and female so that they may be united in marriage – the "two become one" (Gen 2:24). Marriage – as the invitation to an intimate communion of love and life – is the normal path for human life. This is the clear understanding of the accounts of creation in the Book of Genesis. It is the principle source for the ways the Jewish people lived their lives and it remains the prime source for the Christian understanding of the Creator's intention for human life.

Celibacy was not promoted in the Old Testament. The refrain of the account of creation – "and it was good" – emphasises the understanding that the marriage union (and family) is the natural way intended by God that human life was to be lived. The words of Genesis, "Be fruitful, multiply and fill the earth" (Gen 1:28), were seen as a divine obligation, a sacred participation in the creative work of God.

Celibacy emerges as a virtue in the Christian dispensation. We

---

16 The Scriptures make reference to a number of couples who were childless, For example there is Abraham and Sarah; there are Samson's parents; and Hannah crying out to God in the temple. In the New Testament Elisabeth and Zechariah have grown old without children. In each of these the couple does conceive. To be childless is considered a great sadness.

can call it a "grace" given to the Church. Like other things it is not an abolishment of the Law but its fulfilment (See Mt 5:17). In other words, it is not intended to replace marriage, which will always remain the usual path for Christians, but it brings in a new dimension to human living. It will be the path chosen by some. It will be chosen often because of a particular calling which invites a person to give over their entire lives to the purposes of God.

It is worth noting that the key figures associated with the birth of Jesus are celibate people: the Virgin Mary, described in Christian faith as "ever a virgin"; St Joseph, husband of Mary who accepted a non-consummated marriage relationship; and the prophetic figure of St John the Baptist who was the chosen precursor of the coming of the Messiah.

Christ's teaching

The Lord himself was celibate and acknowledged such a state as a free choice for those who would choose it "for the sake of the Kingdom" (See Mt 19:11-12). This important text is worth examining more closely. The setting for the Lord's teaching is a discussion initiated by some Pharisees who questioned him about divorce – "Is it lawful for a man to divorce his wife for any cause whatever?" (v3). The Lord gives definitive teaching about the indissolubility of marriage quoting the Book of Genesis – "So they are no longer two, but one flesh. Therefore, what God has joined together, no human being must separate" (v6). Asked why the Jewish people were permitted to divorce the Lord simply answered that it was because of their hardness of heart "but from the beginning it was not so" (v8).

Asked about the wisdom of getting married the Lord taught about the situation of those who were not married – some because they were unable to and some because they would choose such a path – "Some are incapable of marriage because they were born so; some, because they were made so by others; some, because they have renounced marriage for the sake of the kingdom of heaven. Whoever can accept this ought to accept it" (v12).

The Lord had no intention of imposing this on all his disciples. He accepted married men as his disciples – Peter had a mother in law. He did not present it as a major plank of his teaching, but he does present it as a "good". He simply presented celibacy as having a special value when done "for the sake of the Kingdom", and, as we have seen, he does speak of two types of celibacy: the involuntary celibacy where there is no choice because of defect of nature or because of the action of men but highlights a celibacy which is voluntary – in other words, a celibacy freely chosen for spiritual motives.

The word used by the Lord in this text is "eunuch". This is an English transliteration of the Greek, *eunouchos*. In ancient times eunuchs relinquished marriage in order to totally devote themselves to the service of a king or queen – an example of this can be found in the story of the eunuch of the Candace given in Acts 8:27. Jesus, it seems, had this sort of person in his mind when he spoke of some people prepared to renounce the natural call and right to marriage in order to devote themselves to the service of the Kingdom, of the King of Kings. This notion is confirmed later in the passage when Jesus says that those who forsake marriage for the sake of the Kingdom will be richly rewarded (Mt 19:29).

We note that Jesus quickly adds to his teaching: "Let anyone accept this who can" (Mt 19:12). It is an invitation, not a command. It certainly would have been a surprise for his Jewish hearers. He was proposing the embracing of celibacy for "the sake of the Kingdom". Jesus is proposing the embracing of celibacy in order to become completely available to serve the coming of the Kingdom of God. In this we can hear echoes of the parables of the Treasure and the Pearl (Mt 13:44-46), or the call of the rich young man (Mt 19:16-22) or more generally the calls to total self-renunciation (Mt 16:24-26). In these teachings the Lord urges his hearers to see possession of the life of the Kingdom something worth any price.

St Paul's teaching

For the early Christians the example and the teaching of Christ was before them. It was an invitation to devote oneself with entirety to the life of the Kingdom. It was a call to be oriented radically to spiritual things. This is certainly the view of the early Christian writers. St Paul gives us a clear picture of how being celibate for the sake of the Kingdom was to be viewed. In his first letter to the Corinthians (in chapter 7) St Paul gives his most extensive teaching on this matter. It reveals how the Church viewed this call from Christ. Indeed, we could ask: how does the Lord's teaching on celibacy for the sake of the Kingdom apply to the average Christian?

St Paul affirms the value and goodness of marriage, but then adds an interesting comment:

> For I wish that all men were even as I myself. But each one has his own gift from God, one in this manner and another in that. But I say to the unmarried and to the widows: It is good for them if they remain even as I am; but if they cannot exercise self-control, let them marry. For it is better to marry than to burn with passion (1 Cor 7:7-9).

In wishing that all men were as he is St Paul means remaining celibate. St Paul continues in his teaching to answer a question put to him in a representation made to him while a prisoner in Rome. He begins, "Now concerning virgins: I have no commandment from the Lord; yet I give judgment as one whom the Lord in His mercy *has made* trustworthy" (I Cor 7:25). Again we can note a reference to his personal situation. He urges Christians to remain in their particular state: "*it is* good for a man to remain as he is: Are you bound to a wife? Do not seek to be loosed. Are you loosed from a wife? Do not seek a wife" (I Cor 7:26-27).

This leads him to his essential position about the worth of the celibate state: "He who is unmarried cares for the things of the Lord – how he may please the Lord. But he who is married cares about the things of the world – how he may please *his* wife. There is a difference between a wife and a virgin. The unmarried woman cares about the things of the Lord, that she may be holy both in body and in spirit. But she who is married cares about the things of the world – how she may please *her* husband (I Cor 7:32-34).

We can summarise his position in this way:
- Celibacy derives from counsel and not command – "Now concerning virgins: I have no commandment from the Lord; yet I give judgment as one whom the Lord in His mercy has made trustworthy".
- Paul is celibate himself and recommends but does not impose it – "For I wish that all men were even as I myself. But each one has his own gift from God, one in this manner and another in that".
- Celibacy does enable a person to have a freedom to serve the work of the Lord – "But I want you to be without care. He who is unmarried cares for the things of the Lord – how he may please the Lord. But he who is married cares about the things of the world – how he may please his wife".

He makes one other point worth noting. This current world is transient and life is short – "But this I say, brethren, the time is short, so that from now on even those who have wives should be as though they had none". A consideration of eternity gives perspective to choices we make on earth. We can choose a path in life not in terms of the opportunities offered for this world, but in view of eternity.

Celibates in the Church

We have spent some time considering the background to this question of celibacy for the sake of the Kingdom because it has become a significant feature of Catholic spirituality and has marked the lives of many who have been caught up in various movements of the Spirit over Christian history. In Christian history many whose lives were touched by the grace of God would be drawn to embrace the celibate state. Indeed it would seem that a heart seized by the Spirit would experience a calling to a total dedication to the cause of God involving the living of a celibate life "for the sake of the Kingdom".

Thus we see that from the beginnings of the Church some experienced a call to celibacy. This call was often associated with seeking the ascetical[17] life. Over the ensuing centuries Christian communities had ascetics living in their midst. Some (particularly women) would live in their own homes with their families, while others (mainly men) chose to withdraw to more isolated locations, often in desert regions. These women chose this path as an act of personal piety, though virgins were often active in the community in carrying out good works. They were highly respected by the community and even by pagans who saw their exemplary way of life. There was no organised form to this life and virgins would rely on a simple fidelity to their chosen path. Formal rules of life would develop once the Peace of Constantine enabled the Church to be established on a more sound organisational footing.

The teaching of the Fathers

Many of the Fathers wrote treatises praising celibacy. Often writing about women embracing this gift they spoke of "virginity". Tertullian and Cyprian were early and notable examples. In the fourth century there were works by Fathers like St Athanasius, St Basil, St Gregory Nazianzen, St Gregory of Nyssa, St John Chrysostom, St Ambrose and St Augustine. The fact that so many Fathers turned their attention to the charism of virginity clearly indicates that it was a strong spiritual movement in the Christian communities.

St Gregory of Nyssa gives an eloquent presentation of the spirituality of virginity in a poem dedicated to the subject.[18] In one place he describes the spirit of the virgin: "I leave to others what makes up the reward of this life. But for me, there is only one law, one thought: that, filled with divine love, I depart from this earth towards

---

17 Asceticism – from the Greek *askesis* – literally means a polishing, a smoothing or refining. The Greeks used the word to designate the exercises used by athletes to train the body. St. Paul uses this image (see 1 Cor 9:24) to describe the Christian's pursuit of perfection. This perfection is sought because it leads the Christian towards the ultimate end, union with God. St Paul speaks of putting off of "the old man" (Eph 4:22) and then putting "on the new man" according to the image of God (Eph 4:24). Such a task involves personal disciple and self renunciation. It will include the practising the Christian virtues, and applying the means given for overcoming the obstacles found in our fallen human nature.
18 Poem I, Section II, see verses 189-562.

God who reigns in heaven, the author of light". Such sentiments express an awareness of virginity as enabling a person to enter more readily into a transcendental union with God. Virginity was seen as a sharing here on earth in the heavenly union offered to us.

St Ambrose also wrote beautifully about virginity. His focus is on virginity similarly speaks of it as being a passage towards eternal life. He developed a nuptial imagery, already explored by Origen, drawing on the Canticle of Canticles.[19] Here we see an emerging mysticism in relation to virginity. This theme will recur across the centuries as those embracing virginity see the nature of their relationship with Christ grounded in a nuptial mysticism.

Celibacy and the priesthood

In the first millennium of the Church a number of bishops, priests and deacons were married men. The practice of the Church developed whereby a precondition for married men to receive Orders was that after ordination they were required to live in sexual abstinence. With the prior agreement of their spouses they would forgo a conjugal life. From earliest times it was presumed that a married priest or bishop would refrain from sexual intercourse with his wife prior to celebrating the Eucharist.

The practice of advocating celibacy for those called to Orders grew. Various councils legislated in favour of a celibate clergy. One of the earliest known is that of the Council of Elvira (c. 306):

> Bishops, presbyters, deacons, and others with a position in the ministry are to abstain completely from sexual intercourse with their wives and from the procreation of children. If anyone disobeys, he shall be removed from the clerical office.

In 387 the Council of Carthage decreed that bishops, priests and deacons abstain from conjugal relations, in accordance with a

---

19 The Canticle of Canticles as a poetic work in the Old Testament is regarded by the Fathers as an allegory of the soul's relationship to Christ and God. The earliest attested Christian interpretation of the Canticle of Canticles is found in a work by Hippolytus. Origen interpreted the Canticle of Canticles as an allegory of the soul and Christ. The text would be taken up by St Bernard of Clairvaux as the subject of a series of homilies exploring the relationship between the soul and Christ.

tradition dating from the Apostles:

> It is fitting that the holy bishops and priests of God as well as the Levites, i.e. those who are in the service of the divine sacraments, observe perfect continence, so that they may obtain in all simplicity what they are asking from God; what the Apostles taught and what antiquity itself observed, let us also endeavour to keep... It pleases us all that bishop, priest and deacon, guardians of purity, abstain from conjugal intercourse with their wives, so that those who serve at the altar may keep a perfect chastity.

In the centuries that followed the Church teaching became more and more explicit so that celibacy for the clergy became a universal law. The Catechism of the Catholic Church summarises the Church's understanding of this obligation on clerics in these words:

> All the ordained ministers of the Latin Church, with the exception of permanent deacons, are normally chosen from among men of faith who live a celibate life and who intend to remain celibate "for the sake of the kingdom of heaven." Called to consecrate themselves with undivided heart to the Lord and to "the affairs of the Lord", they give themselves entirely to God and to men. Celibacy is a sign of this new life to the service of which the Church's minister is consecrated; accepted with a joyous heart celibacy radiantly proclaims the Reign of God.[20]

The fruit of these graces

These two graces evident in Christianity from its earliest beginnings have become key features in the outworking of the spiritual life of the Church. They immediately provided a basis

---

20 Catholic Catechism n. 1579. The Catechism goes on to mention the situation of priests in the Eastern Church, noting the practices there are not necessarily in conflict with the understanding of the Latin Rite. "In the Eastern Churches a different discipline has been in force for many centuries: while bishops are chosen solely from among celibates, married men can be ordained as deacons and priests. This practice has long been considered legitimate; these priests exercise a fruitful ministry within their communities. Moreover, priestly celibacy is held in great honor in the Eastern Churches and many priests have freely chosen it for the sake of the Kingdom of God. In the East as in the West a man who has already received the sacrament of Holy Orders can no longer marry".

for what was a surprising movement at a time when the Church was emerging from centuries of uncertainty under pagan Roman Rule. The first three centuries of the Church witnessed periods of persecution from the Roman Empire who saw the emergence of Christianity as a subversive movement threatening, in particular, loyalty to the Emperor. At the beginning of the fourth century the Edict of Constantine brought toleration of and indeed favour to Christians. At the time when it was safe to be a Christian, thousands began to flee to the deserts. There the monks would live celibate lives and devote themselves to prayer fuelled by a contemplation of the Scriptures.

Throughout the history of the Church contemplation of the texts of Sacred Scripture proved to be the wellspring for a fruitful spiritual life. Time and time again a discovery of the inner power of the Word of God led to spiritual revivals.

In a similar way, spiritual movements which many times found their origin among lay people in the Church took definitive shape through the development of religious orders of one kind or another. At the heart of these religious orders is a response to the call to "sell all you have" and embrace celibacy "for the sake of the Kingdom".

The story of the Church reveals these two elements as central to fresh impulses of the life of faith and mission.

On Virginity

But you, O happy virgins, who know not such torments, rather than ornaments, whose holy modesty, beaming in your bashful cheeks, and sweet chastity are a beauty, ye do not, intent upon the eyes of men, consider as merits what is gained by the errors of others. You, too, have indeed your own beauty, furnished by the comeliness of virtue, not of the body, to which age puts not an end, which death cannot take away, nor any sickness injure. Let God alone be sought as the judge of loveliness, Who loves even in less beautiful bodies the more beautiful souls. You know nothing of the burden and pain of childbearing, but more are the offspring of a pious soul, which esteems all as its children, which is rich in successors, barren of all bereavements, which knows no deaths, but has many heirs.

So the holy Church, ignorant of wedlock, but fertile in bearing, is in chastity a virgin, yet a mother in offspring. She, a virgin, bears us her children, not by a human father, but by the Spirit. She bears us not with pain, but with the rejoicings of the angels. She, a virgin, feeds us, not with the milk of the body, but with that of the Apostle, wherewith he fed the tender age of the people who were still children. For what bride has more children than holy Church, who is a virgin in her sacraments and a mother to her people, whose fertility even holy Scripture attests, saying, "For many more are the children of the desolate than of her that hath a husband"? She has not a husband, but she has a Bridegroom, inasmuch as she, whether as the Church amongst nations, or as the soul in individuals, without any loss of modesty, she weds the Word of God as her eternal Spouse, free from all injury, full of reason.

St Ambrose, On Virginity

3
The Call to the Desert

Since the beginnings of Christianity there were hermits, virgins and celibates. The teaching of the Lord concerning some who would embrace celibacy "for the sake of the Kingdom" was realised from the dawn of Christianity and continued to hold an attraction to those moved by the Gospel. The persecution of Christians gave rise to Christian fugitives, fleeing to desert regions for safety. The desert held an attraction to the early Christians. They were conscious of the example of John the Baptist who dwelt in desert regions beyond the Jordan. The Lord himself spent forty days in the desert prior to commencing his public ministry.

The movement that resulted in tens of thousands of Christians opting to live their life in the solitude and anonymity of the desert is what one author has called the "heresy of monasticism".[21] While Jesus himself spent a forty day period in the desert before commencing his public ministry and while he had the practice of retiring to mountain areas for solitude and prayer, he clearly engaged with people in the normal circumstances of life and did not propose a monastic life as the way of discipleship. Indeed, despite his own practices, there is no place where he particularly promotes it.

We can say that monasticism is a curiosity in the Christian tradition. Yet it has become an enduring feature of the life of the Church and has received approval and great respect. Even in our own day when there has been a downturn in vocations to apostolic religious life, the one area that has continued to hold up well has been the vocation to contemplative life.

The word, "monk", has a Syrian origin, and means single, sole,

---

21 An interesting way of seeing this extraordinary movement is to describe it as a heresy, using the term in a non pejorative sense. Here we take the word, heresy, in its full meaning, indicating a particular way, a chosen path [Greek *hairein*, to choose]. Monasticism is a particular path within Christianity. See *The heresy of monasticism; the Christian monks: types and anti-types; an historical survey*, James A. Mohler, Alba House, 1971.

alone. Monastic life is the call to solitude. In an unexpected turn of events after the persecution of Christians ended with the Peace of Constantine in 311, a spiritual movement developed whereby Christians withdrew to the desert regions of Egypt, Palestine and Syria to seek God in solitude. It was a remarkable movement fuelled by a very particular grace. It seemed to make little rational sense – why flee to the deserts?

Athanasius, Bishop of Alexandria, was the champion of orthodoxy, defending the Church's faith in the face of the Arian heresy. He was exiled five times from his diocese; on occasions forced to retreat to the Egyptian desert. There he met the monks, and in particular he came to know one named Antony. He later wrote the "Life of Antony" during the time of his third exile, 355-362. Antony had died in 356. It is a classic work that praises and to a certain extent idealises the life of a hermit. It became a "best seller" among Christians.

The story of the life of Antony captures the particular character of this extraordinary movement in the Church. He was born around 251, and experienced a call to solitude around the year 269. He withdrew to a solitary region just outside Alexandria and then later further down the Nile River. Finally he withdrew to an abandoned fort near the Red Sea, called "Inner Mountain". His ascetic life was marked by a severe spiritual struggle graphically described by Athanasius. From this struggle Antony emerged victorious and transformed.

To appreciate something of the character of this very particular grace at work in the Church it is valuable to see how St Athanasius describes the call of Antony. He describes it these words.

> After the death of his father and mother he was left alone with one little sister: his age was about eighteen or twenty, and on him the care both of home and sister rested. Now it was not six months after the death of his parents, and going according to custom into the Lord's House, he communed with himself and reflected as he walked how the Apostle Matthew (Mt 4:20) left all and followed the Saviour; and how they in the Acts (Acts 4:35) sold their possessions and brought and laid them at the Apostles' feet for distribution to the needy, and what and

how great a hope was laid up for them in heaven. Pondering over these things he entered the church, and it happened the Gospel was being read, and he heard the Lord saying to the rich man (Mt 19:21), "If you would be perfect, go and sell what you have and give to the poor; and come follow Me and you shall have treasure in heaven." Antony, as though God had put him in mind of the Saints, and the passage had been read on his account, went out immediately from the church, and gave the possessions of his forefathers to the villagers – they were three hundred acres, productive and very fair – that they should be no more a clog upon himself and his sister. And all the rest that was movable he sold, and having got together much money he gave it to the poor, reserving a little however for his sister's sake.

And again as he went into the church, hearing the Lord say in the Gospel (Mt 6:34), "be not anxious for the morrow," he could stay no longer, but went out and gave those things also to the poor. Having committed his sister to known and faithful virgins, and put her into a convent to be brought up, he henceforth devoted himself outside his house to discipline, taking heed to himself and training himself with patience.[22]

Athanasius' book was to have an extraordinary influence in presenting the ideals of monasticism to the Church and attracting many to embrace this way of life. Antony is regarded as the Father of Monasticism, though he was not the first to pursue this life. Through Athanasius he became a model to the Church of what monasticism was about.

Early Monasticism

The early monks settled in wilderness regions south of Alexandria. In 325 a monk name Ammun established himself in Nitria and it became an area that attracted other monks. About seven miles further south monks settled into a place called "The Cells". In 330 Marcarius of Egypt established the monastic settlement of Scetis. Generally Egyptian monasticism began with monks living in individual cells in close proximity to each other. These cells were

---
22 *Life of Antony*, n. 2,3.

either caves, or mud huts of two rooms. They often lived in the wadis or small valleys.

The monks gathered for the celebration of the "synaxis" or Divine Liturgy on Saturday evenings or Sundays, and the rest of the week lived in isolation. The early monks were often simple unlettered men. Later on their lack of education did give rise to some doctrinal problems, particularly on matters like the nature of the contemplative experience.

In the account of the call of Abba Arsenius we can see another example of this vocation as it was unfolding in the Church. Arsenius was born in Rome around the year 360. A well-educated man of senatorial rank, he was appointed by the Emperor Theodosius as tutor to the princes Arcadius and Honorius. He secretly left the palace in 394 and sailed to Alexandria. This is how his call came about.

> While still living in the palace, Abba Arsenius prayed to God in these words, "Lord, lead me in the way of salvation." And a voice came saying to him, "Arsenius, flee from men and you will be saved." Having withdrawn to the solitary life he made the same prayer again and he heard a voice saying to him, "Arsenius, flee, be silent, pray always, for these are the source of sinlessness."[23]

What we notice here is that as Arsenius prayed about leading a better Christian life, the Lord called him to the desert. He was called to silence and contemplation. Clearly this suggests a particular grace at work. Monasticism was a movement of God in the Church and it attracted lay people to a distinctive way of life. In our age there are other graces at work. We would not expect that the usual form of dedication to God would be a call to the desert. Why was this particular call given at this moment in the Church's history?

The historical context is important when we come to consider particular manifestation of grace. In this instance, the grace emerged at a time when the Church was able to become normalised within the Roman Empire. Indeed, forces emerged very quickly whereby it

---

[23] See *Sayings of the Desert Fathers*, translated by Benedicta Ward, Cistercian Studies 59. The quotations from the Desert Fathers that follow are taken from this work.

became advantageous to be a Christian. In earlier times persecution, or the threat of it, meant that one became a Christian from strong personal conviction and not for social advantage. The purity of faith was threatened by a new situation that favoured being baptised. Was the emergence of monastic vocations God's way of preserving, at the heart of the Church, a core of deeply committed spiritual men and women?

Secondly, the monastic movement laid the foundations not only for a tradition of consecrated life in the Church, but also was the source of much insight into the deeper dimensions of the spiritual life. The monastic movement has bequeathed to the Church a remarkable body of teaching about the psychology of the inner life and profound insight into the mystery of union with God in Christ.

The Sayings of the Desert Fathers

We have writings that have come down to us from these monks. They have come to be known as "Apophthegms", or sayings. There are about one thousand in total. These "sayings" are usually short stories, or pieces of teaching or wisdom from one of the revered monks preserved initially in an oral form and handed down. They give a taste of this particular encapsulation of the acquired spiritual wisdom born from a life singularly devoted to the spiritual life.

It was the practice for a junior monk to place himself under the direction of an older monk who was his "father" – Abba. The junior monk sought advice and asked for a word of wisdom. One such monk asked a word from Abba Arsenius and it comes down to us in these words:

> A brother questioned Abba Arsenius to hear a word of him and the old man said to him, 'Strive with all your might to bring your interior activity into accord with God, and you will overcome exterior passions.'

The monks were conscious that the interior life was built on the basis of a sound moral life. Attention to the Christian virtues was of primary importance. Abba Arsenius understood that if virtue was lacking then growth in prayer would not be possible.

> He also said, 'Going up the road again towards Scetis with some ropes, I saw the camel driver talking and he made me angry; so, leaving my goods, I took to flight.'

The monk would not allow himself to be further exposed to anger. The monks not only identified the virtues necessary as a foundation for a life of prayer, but they soon recognised the hierarchy to these virtues. Again, we draw on the wisdom of Abba Arsenius:

> He also said, 'Humility and the fear of God are above all virtues.'

Of course devotion to prayer was seen as paramount and the monks set themselves high standards of devotion to prayer:

> Abba Arsenius used to say that one-hour's sleep is enough for a monk if he is a good fighter.
>
> It was said of him that one day he was weaving rope for two baskets, but he made it into one without noticing, until it had reached the wall, because his spirit was occupied in contemplation.

Among other things the sayings reveal a depth of wisdom and of keen insight into the psychology. They are notable for their rye humour, and show the profound simplicity and humility of these men of prayer:

> One day Abba Arsenius consulted an old Egyptian monk about his own thoughts. Someone noticed this and said to him, 'Abba Arsenius, how is it that you with such a good Latin and Greek education ask this peasant about your thoughts?' He replied, 'I have indeed been taught Latin and Greek, but I do not know even the alphabet of this peasant.'

The sayings contain key concepts associated with the essential foundations for the spiritual life. They were the trailblazers for those who sought to grow in the interior life. The example and teaching of the monks provided an invaluable spiritual patrimony for the Church.

The Desert Fathers attracted pilgrims. Pilgrims from towns and villages nearby sought their prayers and spiritual advice. In due course pilgrims travelled from further afield, including Rome. Some important pilgrims were Rufinus, 394-5, who would later write "Lives of the Desert Fathers"; and John Cassian, 425-9, later established monasteries in Marseilles and wrote two classic works on the monastic life – "Institutes" and "Conferences". Basil of Caesarea also made a pilgrimage to visit and learn from the Egyptian monks and later was responsible for forming a pattern for monastic life in Cappadocia (modern Turkey). The Rule of St Basil is still the guide for monasticism in the Eastern Church. A number of noble Roman ladies came to Egypt and established a monastic community for women in Bethlehem.

Cenobitic life: Pachomius.

Pachomius was born around the year 290. He was a young conscript in the Roman army when Antony was at Inner Mountain. He was ministered to by Christians and made a vow to become a Christian if he was released from military service. He was released, baptised at Thebaid on the Nile and became a monk under the guidance of a monk named Paloman.

One day he came upon the deserted village of Tabennis and heard the words, "Stay here and make a monastery". With approval of his spiritual father he began with three disciples to establish a common life for monks. His first effort failed but realising the need for obedience and poverty he tried again. Recruits flowed in. He established a monastery and based its structure along Roman military lines with monks divided into groups of ten. By the end of his life he had founded ten monasteries populated by nine thousand monks. He also formed two monasteries of women.

In September 346 two monks from Pachomian monasteries, Zacchaeus and Theodore, met Anthony and told him of Pachomius' death. Antony commented: "Do not weep, all of you are become as Pachomius". In other words the work of Pachomius would continue through the system of common life among the monks that he established. After his death there was some disarray but eventually two leaders emerged: Horsiesi and Theodore and monastic life down the Nile valley continued.

Pachomius had written a Rule which encapsulated the way of life. His insight and genius was that he came to see the value of a communal life for monks as the way for Christian growth. Monks in a communal setting could be better guided and formed in sound spiritual principles. To avoid some of the pitfalls for individuals lacking the capacity to remain faithful, a disciplined way of life with others provided the necessary support and guidance.

The Gift of Monasticism

Monasticism pioneered by individual hermits and developed into a communal expression would become a significant feature in the Church. Thus began a phenomenon which has remained till the present day. Within the Church some would seek a separation from the world in order to devote themselves to the pursuit of God for his sake alone. Those searching after God were a barometer of the quality of the Church's spiritual life and they were key influences in strengthening the quality of the Church's faith. From the monks and the nuns the Church received many spiritual gifts. Monks and nuns have been described as the "spiritual powerhouse" of the Church. Their witness and teaching and the efficacy of their prayer and intercession are seen as vital to the spiritual health of the Church.

On the wisdom of the Desert Fathers

When the same Abba Anthony thought about the depth of the judgements of God, he asked, "Lord, how is it that some die when they are young, while others drag on to extreme old age? Why are there those who are poor and those who are rich? Why do wicked men prosper and why are the just in need?" He heard a voice answering him, "Anthony, keep your attention on yourself; these things are according to the judgement of God, and it is not to your advantage to know anything about them."

Someone asked Abba Anthony, "What must one do in order to please God?" The old man replied, "Pay attention to what I tell you: whoever you may be, always have God before your eyes; whatever you do, do it according to the testimony of the holy Scriptures; in whatever place you live, do not easily leave it. Keep these three precepts and you will be saved."

Abba Anthony said to Abba Poemen, "this is the great work of a man: always to take the blame for his own sins before God and to expect temptation to his last breath."

He also said, "Whoever has not experienced temptation cannot enter into the Kingdom of Heaven." He even added, "Without temptations no-one can be saved."

Abba Pambo asked Abba Anthony, "What ought I to do?" and the old man said to him "Do not trust in your own righteousness do not worry about the past, but control your tongue and your stomach."

Abba Antony, Sayings of the Desert Fathers

4
A School for God's Service

Monasticism as it developed in Egypt, Palestine and Syria spread East to Cappadocia and north to Europe, to Gaul and Italy. Its expression in Europe was shaped by the genius of St Benedict of Nursia. The monastic life he formulated has had an extraordinary influence on the Church and was a major force in the Church for a thousand years that continues in the Church to the present day. The spiritual history of the Church from the sixth century was dominated by the presence and contribution of monks living under the Rule of St Benedict.

It is easy to underestimate the influence of Benedictine monasticism on the spiritual and intellectual life of the Church and on its missionary endeavour. The monks significantly shaped culture of Europe. Monasteries became centres of learning. They even made significant advances in agricultural practices which assisted farm production. The advance of European civilisation owes much to the monks.

Monasticism, as a particular way of being Christian, was an extraordinary grace for the Church and in the period of the destruction of the Roman Empire provided a means of the preservation of learning and islands of stability and continuity.

St. Benedict

St Benedict lived in the first half of the 6th Century (480-547). His life began during a period of devastating war and ended during a period of war. The middle period of his life had thirty years of peace under Emperor Theodoric (493-526). He lived in Nursia, central Italy, north of Rome. Little is known of him apart from his Rule. We have to rely upon the *Dialogues* of Pope St. Gregory the Great written around 594 to provide some information about him. Gregory chooses not to provide biographical information but rather let his Rule be his testament.

St Gregory the Great writes:

> I should like to tell you much more about this venerable abbot; but I purposely pass over some of his deeds, for I hasten to get on to the lives of others. Yet I should not have you ignorant of this, that Benedict was eminent, not only for the many miracles that made him famous, but also for his teaching, In fact, he wrote a Rule for Monks, which is of conspicuous discretion and is written in a lucid style. If anyone wishes to know Benedict's character and life more precisely, he may find a complete account of his principles and practice in the ordinances of that Rule; for the Saint cannot have taught otherwise than as he lived.[24]

St Gregory the Great states that the great witness to the life of St Benedict is his Rule. The Rule he wrote became the basis of monastic life in and beyond Europe for a thousand years. It is still the inspiration for those living Benedictine monasticism today.

According to St Gregory, St Benedict was born of a distinguished Italian family in Nursia. He went to Rome for a liberal education. He abandoned Rome for the life of a hermit, first at church of St Peter Affili, then three years in a cave at Subiaco. St Benedict attracted people who sought his guidance. Then he attracted monks and established a way of life. He founded twelve monasteries of twelve monks each headed by an Abbot. His first efforts met with difficulties: some of his monks tried to poison him! He then withdrew to solitude at Monte Cassino but again attracted disciples. There he established one central monastery. He died of fever in 547. He was buried next to his sister, St Scholastica, who had founded a companion order for women.

The Rule

The Rule of St Benedict is an extraordinary work. It has lasted fourteen hundred years and still used today. It gradually supplanted existing monastic rules in western Christendom during the time of Charlemagne.

---

[24] Dialogues, St Gregory the Great, II,36.

The key quality of the rule is its common sense, or discretion, as St Gregory the Great testifies. It reveals a concern for the well-being of the individual monk. St Benedict saw the monastery as a "school in God's service". In the Prologue the Rule states, "We are about to open a school for God's service, in which we hope nothing harsh or oppressive will be directed".[25] St Benedict recognised that common life was the best instrument to foster Christian holiness. Common life was to provide encouragement through mutual example and promote the virtues of charity and humility.

The beginning of the Rule reveals St Benedict's concern for establishing a way of life for monks which can assist them in avoiding pitfalls. In Chapter One of Rule he lists different kinds of monks: coenobites, anchorites, sarabites, and the gyratory monks. He approves of the first type: "those who live in monasteries and serve under a rule and an Abbot". He sees the possibility for some mature monks to become anchorites or hermits: "those who, no longer in the first fervour of their reformation, but after long probation in a monastery, having learned by the help of many brethren how to fight against the devil, go out well armed from the ranks of the community to the solitary combat of the desert".

However it is the third kind of monk (those he called "sarabites") who is of a "detestable kind" because "these, not having been tested, as gold in the furnace (Wis. 3:6), by any rule or by the lessons of experience, are as soft as lead. In their works they still keep faith with the world, so that their tonsure marks them as liars before God". He proceeds to explain how their vocation becomes compromised: "They live in twos or threes, or even singly, without a shepherd, in their own sheepfolds and not in the Lord's. Their law is the desire for self-gratification: whatever enters their mind or appeals to them, that they call holy; what they dislike, they regard as unlawful". Monasticism had become a common vocation in the Church but not all embraced it with dedication and for the right reasons.

St Benedict also knew of a fourth kind of monk, the wandering (gyratory) monks: "These spend their whole lives tramping from

---

25 Prologue, Rule of St Benedict.

province to province, staying as guests in different monasteries for three or four days at a time. Always on the move, with no stability, they indulge their own wills and succumb to the allurements of gluttony". St Benedict established a vow of stability, requiring a monk to remain in the monastery that he entered. He knew that the way to growth in holiness was through a steady and stable way of life.

St Benedict, like his mentor Cassian[26], developed a daily pattern of work and prayer – known by the great Benedictine motto: "Ora et Labore". The day was divided into "hours" which corresponded to twelve intervals between sunrise and sunset (thus having different duration in the different seasons). The monks would do about six to eight hours manual work, pray for three and a half hours per day, and devote the same time to reading and study.

The life of the monastery was governed by an abbot who St Benedict saw as the father of the community. The abbot was pivotal to the effectiveness of the monastery. St Benedict described in detail the characteristics of an abbot in his Rule: "The Abbot who is worthy to be over a monastery, ought always to be mindful of what he is called, and make his works square with his name of Superior. For he is believed to hold the place of Christ in the monastery, when he is called by his name, according to the saying of the Apostle: 'You have received the spirit of adoption of sons, whereby we cry *Abba* (Father)'".[27] The abbot was to be first and foremost a father to his monks.

The abbot was to lead not just by authority but by example. "When, therefore, anyone takes the name of Abbot he should govern his disciples by a twofold teaching; namely, he should

---

[26] John Cassian whom we have referred to earlier has had an immeasurable effect on the spiritual thinking of Western Europe. St Benedict drew on his writings and his descriptions of the spiritual life. In particular, the *Institutes* had a direct influence on the way in which St Benedict organized his monasteries. St Benedict also recommended that ordered selections of the *Conferences* were to be read to monks living under his Rule.

[27] Chapter 2 of the Rule is dedicated to the role of the Abbot. This fact reveals that St Benedict saw the role of the Abbot as crucial to the well-being of the monastery. The Abbot, like a father, was seen as exercising the role for life. Only much later did terms of office come to be considered. Many monasteries preserving the ancient Rule have the Abbot in the role for life.

show them all that is good and holy by his deeds more than by his words" He is to exercise his role "mingling gentleness with severity, as the occasion may call for". St Benedict adds, "let him show the severity of the master and the loving affection of a father. He must sternly rebuke the undisciplined and restless; but he must exhort the obedient, meek, and patient to advance in virtue".

Based on his experience St Benedict realised that the key virtue for the monk was obedience. In the Rule[28] it is the primary virtue to which a monk should aspire: "The first degree of humility is obedience without delay. This becomes those who, on account of the holy subjection which they have promised, or of the fear of hell, or the glory of life everlasting, hold nothing dearer than Christ. As soon as anything has been commanded by the Superior they permit no delay in the execution, as if the matter had been commanded by God Himself."

However St Benedict believed the key to growing in holiness is to be found in nurturing the virtue of humility. It occupies Chapter 7 of the Rule and St Benedict's twelve steps of humility is a classic teaching for an understanding of the nature of this virtue and it foundational place in the Christian life. The chapter begins, "Brethren, the Holy Scripture cries to us saying: 'Every one that exalts himself shall be humbled; and he that humbles himself shall be exalted' (Lk 14:11; 18:14). Since, therefore, it says this, it shows us that every exaltation is a kind of pride".

The Opus Dei

At the heart of the life of the monastery was the communal celebration of the Divine Office which St Benedict called the *Opus Dei*. Detail instruction was given in the Rule as to how the Divine Office was to be celebrated. St Benedict arranged the *hora* or "hours" which punctuated the day. He organised there to be eight hora devoted to the Opus Dei. The day would begin at 2 am with Vigils. At daybreak Matins, later called Lauds, were celebrated. The day was punctuated with shorter times of prayer: Prime (6am), Tierce (9am),

---
28 See Chapter 5.

and Sext at 12 noon. In the evening there were Vespers and at dusk Compline.

This programme of prayer has influenced the Church ever since. The Divine Office required to be said by clerics and recommended to the lay faithful is based on the structure proposed by St Benedict.

Lectio Divina

St Benedict encouraged the practice of reading and study. This was called *Lectio Divina*. The Rule states in Chapter 48: "The brothers should be occupied according to schedule either in manual work or in holy reading". The monks would dedicate a significant block of time each day to the prayerful reading of holy texts, either the Scriptures, or other texts like the lives of Desert Fathers and Cassian's *Institutes* and *Conferences*. This spiritual reading was done chiefly in the earlier hours before the manual work was commenced. The practice of *Lectio* fostered the interior life of the individual monk. It was intended as a source of inspiration and nourishment to their faith and their understanding of the spiritual life.

The way in which the *Lectio* was practiced was by means of what we could call an "active reading". The monks retired to their cells and they read in a quiet vocal tone. This way of reading encouraged the memorisation process, as there was a visual memory (seeing the text), a muscular memory (the act of speaking) and an aural memory (by hearing what was being read). The reading was encouraged to be a prayerful exercise, and not simply an intellectual one. It was not study as we know it today. It opened the way to a contemplative practice. Later St Peter the Venerable wrote of this monastic practice, "Without resting, his mouth ruminated the sacred words".[29]

---

[29] Jean Leclerq, in The love of learning and the desire for God: a study of monastic culture, explains the practice of "Active Reading". See pp. 72-3.

Monastic life

Monks took a vow of stability: to remain in the same monastery all their days. Life in the monastery was calm and regulated. There were two cooked meals a day at the sixth and ninth hours.[30] A quarter litre of wine was allocated to each monk each day.[31] St Benedict legislated detail about the meals the monks were to be served: "Making allowance for the infirmities of different persons, we believe that for the daily meal, both at the sixth and the ninth hour, two kinds of cooked food are sufficient at all meals; so that he who perchance cannot eat of one, may make his meal of the other. Let two kinds of cooked food, therefore, be sufficient for all the brethren. And if there be fruit or fresh vegetables, a third may be added. Let a pound of bread be sufficient for the day, whether there be only one meal or both dinner and supper. If they are to eat supper, let a third part of the pound be reserved by the Cellarer and be given at supper".[32]

The concern of the abbot was to ensure that the monks retained a degree of discipline in their lives, but he avoided any expression of excessive demand for asceticism. Thus St Benedict decreed, "If, however, the work has been especially hard, it is left to the discretion and power of the Abbot to add something, if he think fit, barring above all things every excess, that a monk be not overtaken by indigestion".[33]

Regarding the quantity of drink, St Benedict quoting from 1 Cor 7:7[34] teaches, "It is with some hesitation, therefore, that we determine the measure of nourishment for others. However, making allowance for the weakness of the infirm, we think one hemina of wine a day is sufficient for each one. But to whom God grants the endurance of abstinence, let them know that they will have their special reward. If the circumstances of the place, or the work, or the summer's heat should require more, let that depend on the judgment

---
30 See Rule, Chapter 39.
31 See Rule Chapter 40.
32 Rule, Chapter 39.
33 ibid.
34 "Everyone has his proper gift from God".

of the Superior, who must above all things see to it, that excess or drunkenness do not creep in".[35]

In the end the Rule of St Benedict is an ascetical programme established within communal life. It was a life that was to be balanced and manageable for the ordinary monk. It did not set impossible goals and risk becoming a daily burden. It truly was a "school for God's service".

The legacy of St Benedict

We cannot underestimate the influence of Benedictine monasticism on the subsequent history of Europe – both religious and social.

At his weekly audience in April 2008, Pope Benedict XVI discussed the influence that St Benedict had on the creation of European civilization. The Pope said that "with his life and work St Benedict exercised a fundamental influence on the development of European civilization and culture" and helped Europe to emerge from the "dark night of history" that followed the fall of the Roman empire". In 1964, Pope Paul VI named St Benedict as patron saint of Europe as an acknowledgement of this fact.

Benedictine monasteries were islands of not only faith but also of learning during the difficult period that followed the collapse of Roman rule in Europe. The monasteries were stable environments at a time when society was in turmoil. The Church was able to convert barbarian tribes largely because of the presence and influence of the monks. It was monks with their dedication to learning who attracted kings and tribal chiefs to send their sons to them for education. The monks also emerged from the monasteries with a missionary intent to evangelise the barbarian tribes sweeping through Europe. St Boniface, an English Benedictine, with the approval of Pope Gregory devoted his life to preaching to the German tribes. He drew on his brethren in Britain and established monasteries of both men and women as havens of faith and learning in the area now called

---

35 Rule, Chapter 40.

Germany. He is called the "Apostle of Germany". He was a monk first, but became a missionary, then a bishop, and finally crowned his life with martyrdom. He is typical of many monks who were effective agents of evangelisation at a time when the Church, allied to the Roman Empire, lacked the personnel to engage in this task. Without the monks Europe could not have been re-evangelised in the early Middle Ages.

The monasteries preserved Christian writings and the great literature of antiquity in their libraries. They were able to preserve and hand on the tradition of western thought. The Caroline Renaissance in France in the sixth and seventh centuries established education based around the seven liberal arts and it was driven by the monks. Charlemagne looked to the Benedictines to provide the resources for his systematisation of Catholic life in his growing empire.

The monasteries, inspired by the dictum ora et labore – pray and work – became centres not only of prayer but also of agricultural development. Monks became adept at draining swamps and turning useless land into fertile pasture. The industry of the monastery led to many valuable innovations like the ability to utilise the power of water to drive mills. Many significant developments in agricultural practice were the fruit of the innovations developed by the monks. One result of this was agriculture became more efficient and productive.

The Christian monks in Europe were a major force in the development of European social and religious life. The continent was sprinkled with monasteries. They lived lives withdrawn from society but were a constant influence on that society. From the monasteries came holy men, scholars and missionaries. They shaped the character of the civilisation that we today call "Western".

On the Character of an Abbot

The Abbot who is worthy to be over a monastery, ought always to be mindful of what he is called, and make his works square with his name of Superior. For he is believed to hold the place of Christ in the monastery, when he is called by his name, according to the saying of the

Apostle: "You have received the spirit of adoption of sons, whereby we cry Abba (Father)" (Rom 8:15). Therefore, the Abbot should never teach, prescribe, or command (which God forbid) anything contrary to the laws of the Lord; but his commands and teaching should be instilled like a leaven of divine justice into the minds of his disciples.

Let the Abbot always bear in mind that he must give an account in the dread judgment of God of both his own teaching and of the obedience of his disciples. And let the Abbot know that whatever lack of profit the master of the house shall find in the sheep, will be laid to the blame of the shepherd. On the other hand he will be blameless, if he gave all a shepherd's care to his restless and unruly flock, and took all pains to correct their corrupt manners; so that their shepherd, acquitted at the Lord's judgment seat, may say to the Lord with the Prophet: "I have not hid Thy justice within my heart. I have declared Thy truth and Thy salvation" (Ps 39[40]:11). "But they contemning have despised me" (Is 1:2; Ezek 20:27). Then at length eternal death will be the crushing doom of the rebellious sheep under his charge.

When, therefore, anyone takes the name of Abbot he should govern his disciples by a twofold teaching; namely, he should show them all that is good and holy by his deeds more than by his words; explain the commandments of God to intelligent disciples by words, but show the divine precepts to the dull and simple by his works.

Rule of St Benedict

5
A Land of Saints and Scholars

When we look at the history of the Church in Europe we tend to focus on the contribution of the predominant form of monasticism in the West – Benedictine monasticism. However, there is a chapter in the religious history of Europe that deserves more recognition: the unique expression of monasticism that developed in Ireland in the sixth century.

Christianity first came to the British Isles under Roman rule in the third century. However it probably did not penetrate the population as a whole. The Council of Arles (314) mentions three British bishops (London, Lincoln, York). The Anglo Saxon invasions in the mid fifth century forced Roman withdrawal and with this withdrawal went any significant Christian presence. Some Christians retreated to the Welsh enclaves from which emerged the Arthurian legends.

Some evangelisation took place in the north of Britain by the monk, St Ninian, who had been trained under St Martin of Tours in Gaul. St Ninian established a monastery at Whithorn in south east Scotland. Likewise there was a Gallic influence in Wales where monks from Tours had established a monastery at Llanbelig. On the whole Christian presence in the British Isles was very limited by the end of the fifth century.

St Patrick

The figure who is associated with the evangelisation of Ireland is well known: St Patrick. He was born around 385 on the south west coast of Britain. As a young man he was captured by Irish pirates. Held for six years, he finally escaped to Gaul. It would seem that there he embraced monastic life at Lerins situated on the Mediterranean. Around the year 429 he was sent by the bishop Germanus of Auxierre to Ireland as a missionary. He spent next thirty years evangelising and establishing the Church in Ireland.

St Patrick was Roman in his vision and met with local opposition in later years. While a properly constituted church led by bishops was established under St Patrick the form of the Church in Ireland took a particular shape. Monasticism was central to the life of the Church.

A Monastic Church

Though St Patrick did not focus his attention on the establishing of monasteries, the church in Ireland became essentially monastic in character. Ireland did not have towns, much less cities. It was very rural, based around small hamlets. From the beginnings of the establishing of Christian life in Ireland a monastic movement began. Firstly there were hermits living in caves or in a clearing in the forest. As in Egypt communal life developed when the hermit was joined by disciples and a small monastic settlement was established. Such monastic settlements were independent.

While European monasticism was coming under the influence of the organised Benedictine system, Irish monasticism remained very simple. Each monastery lived under its own rule. The monks met normally only once a day for prayer. They tended not to become very agricultural, rather they were gatherers of berries. The abbot in the Irish system acted as spiritual guide to those in the monastery. The monastery buildings were small comprising of wood and turf huts, surrounded by a wall of stakes.

An area of importance for the monks was education. Celtic monasteries became places of learning. The monastic schools, like the one founded by St Kevin at Glendalough, became famous. They began attracting students even from Gaul and Spain. Chieftains sent their sons to these schools and they became key tools in the ongoing evangelisation of the country. At that time attending a "school" meant living in a mud hut, among the monks, helping out with the chores and receiving instruction from the learned monks in the community. The sixth century saw the extraordinary expansion of monastic life in Ireland: "the sons and daughters of kings became monks and virgins".[36]

Some of the early founders of monasteries included St Finian (d.549) who founded the monastery of Clonard.[37] He began as a recluse and later became an abbot. St Finian built a little cell and a church of clay and wattle. He lived a life of study, mortification, and prayer. The fame of his learning and sanctity became known and many came to visit his monastery. Those who came to live with him were expected to live as he did. He had little time for self-indulgence. He slept on the hard floor, resting his head on a stone He wore a girdle of iron as an act of penance. There were 3000 pupils getting instruction at one time in his school. St Finian excelled in exposition of the Sacred Scriptures, and the extraordinary popularity which his lectures enjoyed was widely attributed to his biblical scholarship. His rule of life was patterned on that of Lerins and had strict observance. He was a bishop as well as abbot. He became called the "Tutor of Saints".

In the year 555 St Comgall founded a monastery at Bangor in Ulster. Bangor became a famed seat of learning and education. There was a saying in Europe at the time that if a man knew Greek he was bound to be an Irishman, largely due to the influence of Bangor. St Comgall attracted large numbers of monks. It became a place of much missionary activity as monks like the St Columban set out to spread the Christian faith.

St Kevin of Glendalough established a famous school. Glendalough flourished for six hundred years. By the 9th century it was considered the leading monastic centre in Ireland. In its heyday, the settlement included not only churches and monastic cells but also workshops, guesthouses, an infirmary, farm buildings and houses.

---

36 It is reputed that St Patrick said, "How did it come to pass in Ireland that those who never had a knowledge of God, but until now always worshipped idols and things impure, have now been made a people of the Lord, and are called sons of God, that the sons and daughters of the kings of the Irish are seen to be monks and virgins of Christ?"
37 Clonard is situated on the river Boyne in Northern Ireland.

Missionary Activity

One of the significant features of the Irish spirituality was its missionary zeal. This appears to have become an enduring feature of the Church in Ireland. There were a number of famous missionary monks. St Columba, also called Columcille, was an Irish prince of fiery character. Born in 521 he became a monk and at 42 years old set out "wishing exile for Christ". He sailed with twelve companions and landed on the island of Iona on the west coast of Scotland. He then engaged in a thirty four year mission to evangelise the Picts. He is known as the "Apostle of Scotland". One of the features of his work was that in every Church he established he provided a copy of the Gospels, meticulously written and illustrated by his monks.

In 597, the same year as death of St Columba, Pope Gregory, himself having a monastic background, sent Augustine and forty Roman monks to Britain. They arrived in Kent where the local king, Ethelbert, had married a Christian. They undertook some evangelisation but met with set-backs and ultimately were unsuccessful.

In the year 634 Oswald, a Northumbrian king, conquered the local pagan kings after a vision of St. Columba of Iona. Then he sent for missionary monks from Iona. St Aidan responded to the king's request and established himself on the island of Lindisfarne, just off the coast of Northumbria. He began a missionary programme of building churches and schools. He laboured for seventeen years. Thus the Church became established in northern Britain and began spreading south.

Born in the year 484 in County Kerry, St Brendan founded a monastery at Clonfert in 558. He went on two extended voyages to the west of Ireland. The second, over the years 565-573 was written up in the medieval text simply called, *Navigatio*. It is claimed that he reached Nova Scotia. Along the way he founded small Christian communities on isolated islands.

One of the most extraordinary of all Irish missionary monks was St Columbanus. He was born in 546. He entered Bangor monastery and later set off as a missionary. In 580 he landed in Gaul with twelve companions. He travelled to Burgundy and founded Annegray monastery. He then founded Luxeiul monastery which became a centre of French monasticism. He travelled further into Germany, and then to Italy, founding monasteries along the way. At Bobbio in Italy he established a monastery which became one of the largest and finest monasteries in Europe. He died at Bobbio in the year 615. By the year 700 one hundred additional monasteries had been established throughout France, Germany and Switzerland.

Monasticism in Ireland had an influence well beyond its shores. It appears providential that Ireland, sufficiently isolated from barbarian incursions, was able to be a cradle of Christian life. It became a significant evangelising force in Britain, and throughout Brittany, Gaul and Germany. The monks brought the Catholic faith, learning and culture.

Monasticism was of vital importance for the Church. It was the vital source of preserving the vigour of Christian faith and a means of passing on learning. The monks became a vital evangelising force throughout Europe in the seventh and eighth centuries.

Celtic Spirituality

Monastic life and spirituality in Ireland had its own distinctive expression. Each monastery was autonomous. Each had its own rule often written by the founding saint. However in Ireland the rule was less important than the role of the abbot who had the role of being an anamchara, or "soul friend". Each monk received personal spiritual direction from the abbot.

Their acts of mortification were severe. Their way of life was hard, but they were a tough and hardy people. The monks would have just one meal a day. Meat was rarely ever eaten. Fasting was a significant part of their life. There were the three Lents: the Winter Lent (Elijah), the Spring Lent (Christ) and the Summer Lent (Moses). Stories are told of feats of self discipline revealing a tendency towards extremes in ascetical practice.

One feature of the Irish church was the development of

individual confession. Confession in the Roman Church was a public liturgical act, whereas the practice developed in Ireland of people approaching monks for absolution. To assist the monks "Penitentials" were designed. They were guide books outlining in great detail the required penance for each type of sin.

As we noted earlier the monks had a strong missionary spirit. Leaving Ireland on a missionary quest was an exile, sometimes referred to as the "Green Martyrdom". To the Irish mind there was the "White Martyrdom" of celibacy, the "Red Martyrdom" of shedding of one's blood and the "Green Martyrdom" of leaving the green isle for a lifetime exile in a foreign place.

The Irish had a wonderfully lyrical spirituality. There was a deep appreciation of nature in evidence in their prayers and hymns. The Church in Ireland has left us with a rich store of stories, sayings and poetry. One form of prayer was the "breastplate", a litany invoking the protection of God.[38] This form of prayer is called "lorica". It is a prayer of invocation for supernatural protection against the evils of life, but more particularly against pestilence and other dangers of death. Life in Ireland before the coming of Christianity was marked by violence. The Irish gods were fearsome and demanded much. Human sacrifice was common. The people lived in fear of evil. Christianity brought liberation from this dark pall that hung over life. The Christian litanies reflect the joy of being under the protection of a loving God.

One that is well known is that of the "Breastplate of St Patrick". These prayers have a strong Trinitarian dimension, invoking Father, Son and Holy Spirit. They also exhibit a focus on the saving and healing power of Christ. Irish faith was founded on solid doctrinal grounds.

---

[38] St. Paul spoke of "putting on the "amour of God" in his letter to the Ephesians (6:11). This was to provide protection in order to fight sin and evil inclinations. Prayers for protection inspired by this notion were a feature of Irish spirituality. St. Patrick's Breastplate is the best known of this genre of prayer According to tradition, St. Patrick wrote it in 433 A.D. for divine protection before successfully converting the Irish King Leoghaire and his subjects from paganism to Christianity. More recent scholarship suggests its author was anonymous.

The legacy

The development of Celtic monasticism had been in relative isolation and allowed for the emergence of a particular local character. There were Celtic traditions in liturgy, for example, the date for celebration of Easter. This would become a point of tension with the Roman view in the Church. St Augustine of Canterbury was appointed by Pope Gregory as Bishop of entire British Isles. He met with Celtic bishops to seek their submission to his authority. The Celtic bishops wanted time to consider, and a second meeting did not go well. In 664 a synod held at Whitby Abbey and Wilfred of Lindisfarne eventually held sway over the Celts and they accepted Roman authority. Celtic monasticism in Europe similarly came under Roman influence and its distinctive spirituality declined.

In the years of its flowering over the sixth and seventh centuries Irish monasticism not only made a great contribution to the Irish people, but it became a major evangelising force. The monks became missionaries and took a vibrant form of Christian spirituality to Europe. In more recent centuries the Church would again benefit from the spirit of Irish "Green Martyrdom" as missionaries travelled to the Americas, to Oceania and Africa.

As we look back to the unfolding of the spiritual history of the Church we note the continuing significance of monasticism. However we should mention that the Church did not find spiritual fruitfulness and missionary zeal from the monks and nuns alone but there is no doubt that they played a vital role in the strengthening of Christian presence in European society.

We will make one more excursion into the world of the monks as we explore a generation of reform, highlighted by the life of the extraordinary St Bernard of Clairvaux.

On "Breastplate" prayers

I bind unto myself today
The strong Name of the Trinity,
By invocation of the same,
The Three in One and One in Three.

I bind this day to me forever.
By power of faith, Christ's incarnation;
His baptism in the Jordan river;
His death on Cross for my salvation;
His bursting from the spicèd tomb;
His riding up the heavenly way;
His coming at the day of doom;
I bind unto myself today.

I bind unto myself the power
Of the great love of the cherubim;
The sweet 'well done' in judgment hour,
The service of the seraphim,
Confessors' faith, Apostles' word,
The Patriarchs' prayers, the Prophets' scrolls,
All good deeds done unto the Lord,
And purity of virgin souls.

I bind unto myself today
The virtues of the starlit heaven,
The glorious sun's life-giving ray,
The whiteness of the moon at even,
The flashing of the lightning free,
The whirling wind's tempestuous shocks,
The stable earth, the deep salt sea,
Around the old eternal rocks.

I bind unto myself today
The power of God to hold and lead,
His eye to watch, His might to stay,
His ear to hearken to my need.
The wisdom of my God to teach,
His hand to guide, His shield to ward,
The word of God to give me speech,
His heavenly host to be my guard.

Against the demon snares of sin,
The vice that gives temptation force,
The natural lusts that war within,
The hostile men that mar my course;
Or few or many, far or nigh,
In every place and in all hours,

Against their fierce hostility,
  I bind to me these holy powers.
Against all Satan's spells and wiles,
Against false words of heresy,
Against the knowledge that defiles,
Against the heart's idolatry,
Against the wizard's evil craft,
Against the death wound and the burning,
The choking wave and the poisoned shaft,
Protect me, Christ, till Thy returning.
  Christ be with me, Christ within me,
Christ behind me, Christ before me,
Christ beside me, Christ to win me,
Christ to comfort and restore me.
Christ beneath me, Christ above me,
Christ in quiet, Christ in danger,
Christ in hearts of all that love me,
Christ in mouth of friend and stranger.
  I bind unto myself the Name,
The strong Name of the Trinity;
By invocation of the same.
The Three in One, and One in Three,
Of Whom all nature hath creation,
Eternal Father, Spirit, Word:
Praise to the Lord of my salvation,
Salvation is of Christ the Lord.

St Patrick's Breastplate

6
The Cistercian Reform

From the sixth century Benedictine monasticism spread across continental Europe. There were many expressions of monasticism in Europe in the fifth and sixth centuries but gradually the Rule of St Benedict was adopted. As we have seen the monks and nuns were the dominant spiritual influence in the Church and in society. However over time the ardour waned. Monasteries became powerful and the quality of spiritual life declined. By the eighth century we see the first efforts at reform.

During the Carolingian Renaissance under Charlemagne and Louis the Pious, the monks played a key role in an intellectual and cultural revival occurring in the late eighth and ninth centuries. These Christian emperors sought to develop literature, writing, the arts, architecture, jurisprudence, and liturgical and scriptural studies. This was the period that saw the development of Medieval Latin, providing a common language and writing style that allowed for communication across most of Europe. During this period St Benedict of Aniane restored and revitalised the Benedictine spirit with his *Codex Regularum* which set the tone for the standard living of the Rule. It led the way for Benedictinism becoming more uniform in its life and practice, and helped establish the monasteries as key agents in intellectual life.

However, by the dawn of the Middle Ages Benedictinism, influenced by its role in promoting the reforms of Charlemagne, became more focused on learning and liturgy. Manual labour declined in significance and monastic life became less ascetic. Efforts were made to achieve a spiritual renewal of monastic life. One such movement of renewal in Benedictine monasticism was at the monastery of Cluny in France. It was founded in 910. The Cluniac reform established central government for a federation of monasteries. Thus limiting the autonomy of monasteries, which had been a feature of the original vision of St Benedict. For two centuries a monastic empire flourished under a series of wise and holy abbots. The Scriptorum where monks copied books and the extension of the time and liturgical quality of their common prayer dominated over manual labour. It led to the emergence of two types of monks: choir monks who worked in the Scriptorum and lay brothers who carried out basic tasks in the monastery.

There were other reforms of monasticism. St Romuald founded the Camaldolese Order in 1010. In an effort to recapture the solitude central to monastic life he introduced a form of solitary eremitical life within a communal setting. Similarly St Bruno of Cologne formed the Carthusians in 1084 in the valley of La Chartreuse. Their spirit similarly emphasised the eremitical life within the framework of the Benedictine common life.

At Citeaux in France in 1098 St Robert of Molesmes founded another expression of Benedictine monasticism. He was ordered back to his original monastery and a small community struggled on under St Alberic and an Englishman, St Stephen Harding. This new expression of monasticism sought to prune the way of life back to the original purity of St Benedict: the right balance of prayer, Lectio and manual labour. They sought to break from interdependence with feudal society – the monastery would have no serfs or labourers. It would not have large landholdings and would be established on poor and unusable land.

St Bernard of Clairvaux.

In the year 1111 an extraordinary young man who wished to embrace this purer monastic life presented himself at the monastery gate at Citeaux. He was accompanied by thirty kinsman and friends whom he had convinced to join him in this venture. His name was Bernard. Bernard of Fontaines was born in 1090 near Dijon. After three years in the monastery he was appointed abbot of a daughter house established at Clairvaux. It is there he gained the name history gave him, St Bernard of Clairvaux.

The young St Bernard embraced an austere way of life. His

health finally broke down under the impact of extreme penances and he suffered stomach pains the rest of his life. He eased back his mortifications. His magnetic personality continued to attract many to join him. The order in its early years attracted some of the most gifted men of the generation.

In a reaction to what he saw as the extravagance of Cluniac foundations and their liturgy the Cistercian renewal, under the guidance of St Bernard, kept a radical simplicity to their buildings. Their chapels had the stark simplicity of whitewashed walls. Life was to be austere. It was a "back to basics" approach. Cistercian monasteries would be found in the most inhospitable of places, often in swamps and wooded valleys. However, the industrious monks drained the swamps and use their water to drive mills and provide water features. There was a simple elegance to the Cistercian buildings. Their monasteries begun in harsh locations were transformed into beautiful and productive centres of monastic and agricultural life.

St Bernard soon experienced the cost of his success. He desired to live the life of a monk but he found himself being called more and more to work outside the cloister. First was the demand of establishing and overseeing daughter foundations. In the end he would found one hundred and sixty monasteries, from Ireland to Italy, from Portugal to Sweden. Added to this were calls to engage himself in some of the great political and religious issues of his day. He was called upon to heal schisms, to be an intermediary in political disputes, and to champion orthodoxy in the face of the new intellectualism. He became the preacher against Catharism[39], and was asked by the Pope to preach the second (and disastrous) Crusade.

Regarded as the greatest figure of his century he was a man of passionate nature alongside his considerable intellectual ability. His letters reveal a warm and affectionate heart. He was a leader and inspired men. His spiritual ideals were founded in the idea of contemplation, grounded thoroughly in Scripture. Bernard is the last of the Fathers of the Church. A new age was dawning. Scholasticism would become the intellectual approach to theology and spirituality. He stood at the end of an age.

The Spirituality of St Bernard

The finest expression of St Bernard's spirituality is a series of sermons on the Song of Songs, begun in 1135 and worked on for the last 18 years of his life. Unfinished at his death, these eighty six sermons offer a panoramic presentation of the life of the soul with God. They are monastic sermons directed to his monks who were devoted to seeking God in contemplation. The theme is simply love, the experiential love of God: the dialectic of presence and absence. St Bernard expresses the eschatological desire for God: *desiderium*. His spiritual teaching touches on what is ultimately the purpose of the monk's vocation: that of pursuing the desire of the human heart for God. The monk has the luxury, if you like, of being able to give

---

[39] The Cathars developed in Languedoc in Southern France during the 11th and 12the centuries. They were a heretical sect of Christians. One branch of the Cathars became known as the Albigenses because they took their name from the local town Albi. Cathars were fiercely anti-clerical and developed the Manichean dualism which divided the world into good and evil principles, with matter being intrinsically evil and mind or spirit being intrinsically good. They were an extreme ascetic group, cutting themselves off from others in order to retain as much purity as possible. Their theology was essentially Gnostic - they believed that there were two "gods" – one malevolent and one good. The former was in charge of all visible and material things. The benevolent god was the one the Cathars worshipped and was responsible for the message of Jesus. Accordingly, they made every effort to follow the teachings of Jesus as closely as possible. The Cathars believed that everyone should be able to read the Bible, translating into the local language. Because of this, the Synod of Toulouse in 1229 expressly condemned such translations and even forbade lay people to own a Bible.

constant attention to this goal.

There is a clear mystical dimension to the spirituality of St Bernard. It was this mystical element that lifted the spiritual level of the life of the monk. While St Benedict concentrated on the faithful recitation of the Divine Office, St Bernard fostered a more intense interior life. This interior life was contemplative in nature and built around a more directly experiential exposure to the reality of God's love. This clearly reflected the rich interior life that fuelled his call to monasticism.

The vehicle to explore this mystical relationship with God was the Old Testament text of the Song of Songs. At face value one could see it as a love song, exalting in the beauty and power of human love. St Bernard, the mystic, saw it as capturing the attraction of the soul to God, and the depth of interpersonal communion possible between the individual soul and the Divine Persons. In later centuries another mystic would take up this theme: St John of the Cross.

St Bernard also found time to advise various popes. He wrote five books entitled *De Consideratione* for Pope Eugenius III. Eugenius had been a monk at Clairvaux and St Bernard was worried about his ability to cope with the challenges of his office. Pope Eugenius had been accustomed to the contemplative life of a monastery but he was suddenly required to devote much of his time to the administrative and political affairs of the papacy. In *De Consideratione*, St Bernard advised Pope Eugenius to "set aside time for his spiritual life amidst the pressures of daily business." He believed that Eugenius, through consideration – his word for contemplation – could achieve a balance that allowed him to deal with the affairs of the church and satisfy his own spiritual needs.

St Bernard wrote a short and attractive piece *On Loving God*, and simply expressed his theme as: "You want me to tell you why God is to be loved and how much. I answer, the reason for loving God is God Himself; and the measure of love due to Him is immeasurable love". These few words capture the desire of the heart of St Bernard.

He was a beautiful writer of Latin, his work, though profound, is most simple and direct. Like the writings of St Augustine, one finds a personal style that engages easily. Bernard somehow found time write extensively. As well as his many spiritual and theological works, he has bequeathed hundreds of homilies and 530 letters.

The Contribution of St Bernard

St Bernard was a towering figure in his day. He inspired a resurgence of primitive Benedictine monasticism. Cistercian monks would continue to have a notable presence in the Church for the ensuring centuries.

One important aspect of St Bernard's spirituality which is highlighted by the moment of history in which he lived is that his spirituality was profoundly scriptural. At the dawn of scholasticism when intellectual rigour would be brought to theology and allow the "science" of theology to be developed, St Bernard lived in the Patristic tradition of spiritual contemplation of the sacred text. He was one who was nourished principally by the monastic practice of *lectio*. Each day he contemplated the Word of God. His world of thought was the biblical world. His sermons and writings reveal the monk's mind as replete with scriptural images. What drove his thought was not any intellectual analysis, but rather the pursuit of God. His goal was union, not knowledge.

St Bernard's emphasis on entering more deeply into the contemplative life and his exploration of the individual soul's search for God would be an inspiration for many in the Church. In time the Cistercian order would itself require reform, but it would continue to attract souls seeking union with God before all else. In more recent times a man like Thomas Merton emerged from the Cistercian monastic environment and inspired many with its pure spiritual ideals. With St Bernard we could say that the contemplative is a vital member of the Church, sending out spiritual waves, if you like, flowing over the Church. The monk would always remind us – and the Church – that God is worth seeking for his own sake. Monasticism was clearly a gift of the Spirit to the Church. The presence, witness and writings of the monks provided a rich spiritual resource for the Church.

But what of the rest of the Church? Immersed in the demands of pastoral service, how could the so-called "secular" clergy find sources of spiritual nourishment and inspiration?

In the next chapter we will now explore one stream of development which offers spiritual support for clerics. We will examine the emergence of Canons Regular.

On Three Kinds of Love

Christian, learn from Christ how you ought to love Christ. Learn a love that is tender, wise, strong; love with tenderness, not passion, wisdom, not foolishness, and strength, lest you become weary and turn away from the love of the Lord. Do not let the glory of the world or the pleasure of the flesh lead you astray; the wisdom of Christ should become sweeter to you than these. The light of Christ should shine so much for you that the spirit of lies and deceit will not seduce you. Finally, Christ as the strength of God should support you so that you may not be worn down by difficulties. Let love enkindle your zeal, let knowledge inform it, let constancy strengthen it. Keep it fervent, discreet, courageous. See it is not tepid, or temerarious, or timid. See for yourself if those three commands are not prescribed in the law when God says: "You shall love the Lord your God with your whole heart, your whole soul and your whole strength." It seems to me, if no more suitable meaning for this triple distinction comes to mind, that the love of the heart relates to a certain warmth of affection, the love of the soul to energy or judgment of reason, and the love of strength can refer to constancy and vigor of spirit. So love the Lord your God with the full and deep affection of your heart, love him with your mind wholly awake and discreet, love him with all your strength, so much so that you would not even fear to die for love of him. As it is written: "For love is strong as death, jealousy is bitter as hell." Your affection for your Lord Jesus should be both tender and intimate, to oppose the sweet enticements of sensual life. Sweetness conquers sweetness as one nail drives out another. No less than this keep him as a strong light for your mind and a guide for your intellect, not only to avoid the deceits of heresy and to preserve the purity of your faith from their seductions, but also that you might carefully avoid an indiscreet and excessive vehemence in your conversation. Let your love be strong and constant, neither yielding to fear nor cowering at hard work. Let us love affectionately, discreetly, intensely. We know that the love of the heart, which we have said is affectionate, is sweet indeed, but liable to be led astray if it lacks the love of the soul. And the love of the soul is wise indeed, but fragile without that love which is called the love of strength.

St Bernard of Clairvaux, Sermon 20

7
A Rule of Life for Clergy

As we have seen the Rule of St Benedict was a dominant form of monastic life in Europe in the Middle Ages. The Rule of St Benedict was designed for monks living within the ordered and calm environment of the monastery. Originally monks were lay men, as were the more ancient monks in the deserts of Egypt. Indeed there was a saying among the monks – beware of women and bishops! The two threats to the monastic life were women who could challenge their celibate life, and bishops who could call them to Orders and so cause them to abandon the solitude of the desert.

The situation of clergy working in parishes was often fraught with difficulties. Priests often were poor. They said the Mass and were not much more educated than the people they served. Their duties, as well as saying Mass, included celebrating the sacraments – baptisms, wedding and anointing the sick.

In the Middle Ages even the smallest village had a church. Everyone was expected to attend mass at 9am on Sundays. Couples were married outside the door of the Church before entering for the Nuptial Mass. Babies were baptized by immersion in a large font. The priest may but did not always preach a sermon on the Sunday at the parish Mass. The basic task of the priest was to instruct his people in the Creed, the Ten Commandments, the sacraments, the seven works of mercy, the seven virtues and the seven deadly sins. He was to care for the poor out of his own stipend or else exhort his parishioners to give alms for the poor. He also collected tithes. The priest was expected to live a life of celibacy, though records report many breaches. Ideally clerics were to live a common life, but circumstances often prevented it. They were called *canonici saeculares*, the secular clergy.

In the eighth and ninth centuries various efforts were made to offer a way for clerics to live a form of common life, while being able to continue their pastoral service in the Church. Such clerics were called Canons Regular. A Canon Regular was a cleric who lived a regular life, that is, a life under a Rule. The inspiration for this movement was a Rule of Life drawn up by St Augustine of Hippo. This Rule is found in one of his letters (Letter 211) and was actually a rule that he prepared for a community of nuns in a monastery that had been governed by his sister, and in which his cousin and niece lived.

In the letter he outlines a simple rule which emphasises the virtues and practices essential to a religious life. He dwells upon charity, poverty, obedience and detachment from the world. The Rule outlines the apportioning of labour and the mutual duties of superiors and subordinates, and covers such issues as fraternal charity, prayer in common, fasting and abstinence. It mentions the importance of spiritual practices like silence and reading during meals.

In two of his sermons (355, 356), *De vitâ et moribus clericorum suorum* St. Augustine addressed the question of the way of life that he sought to live with his clergy in Hippo. It seems that questions were being asked about his way of life. What the sermons reveal is that the bishop and his priests who lived with him observed strict poverty and held all goods in common. St Augustine desired to live a form of common life as a bishop. He embraced poverty as a foundation, but attached no less importance to fraternal charity. Although his Rule contains few precepts, it dwells at great length upon religious virtues and the importance of an ascetic life.

The approach St Augustine took to his way of life as a bishop was to have an influence many centuries later in the Medieval period. To understand the nature of the life of Canons Regular we will go back and examine the way St Augustine preferred to structure his life as a bishop in fraternity with his priests.

St Augustine and monastic life

St Augustine (354-430), like so many in his age, was drawn towards a monastic way of life. This fact stands out unmistakably in the reading of his life and works. Although a priest and bishop, he combined the practices of monastic life with the duties of his office. He viewed his house in Hippo as a monastic setting for himself and his clergy. To understand his interest in living a form of monastic life as a bishop we need to be aware of his own spiritual journey after his conversion.

In the homily to explain to the people the way of life that he sought to live as bishop, he commented on his original purposes in coming to Hippo as bishop: "I, whom you see, by God's grace, as your bishop – I came as a young man to this city, as many of you know. I was looking for a place to set up a monastery to live with my brethren".[40] Augustine came to Hippo looking to the possibility of setting up common life.

After his conversion to the Catholic faith Augustine had established a community outside Milan among a group of his philosophy companions. The monastic ideals percolated among the Christians of this period. Augustine sought a way of embracing some of the monastic ideals within the context of his own situation as a philosopher. For Augustine personally there was a strong need for fraternal companionship. He needed the stimulation and consolation of living a common life with people of like mind and intellect!

In Hippo the ageing bishop, Valerius, preached to his people about the needs of the church. Upon the death of the bishop the congregation responded by thrusting the newly arrived layman, Augustine, into priesthood and then into the episcopate. As Augustine describes in an extraordinarily frank sermon, "I was grabbed. I was made a priest...and from there I became your bishop".[41]

Augustine had established a community life in what has come to be called, the "monastery in the garden". He invited his friends to

---

40 Sermon 355,2.
41 ibid.

join him in a common life – in addition to his two close companions, Evodius and Alypius, he attracted a number of other men to join him. He referred to himself and his companions as the *servi dei*. On being ordained as bishop, Augustine did not want to live alone in his new state. With all the demands upon him as bishop a fraternal environment was of vital importance to him. He found it refreshed his spirit. After the stresses of his role as bishop, the opportunity to be able to gather with the brethren around the meal table was of the utmost importance to him.

He moved from the "monastery" into the bishop's house. Augustine invited his priests live with him in a monastic style of life: with poverty, celibacy and a rule of life. The ideal that he held before him was the description of the life of the early Church as depicted in the Acts of the Apostles, chapter 4. The life, while strict, was built around a profound spirit of brotherly love. For Augustine this love was grounded in friendship. He would call a friend, "half of my soul."[42] Table conversation was not to degenerate into gossip and he had inscribed on the table: "Whoever thinks he is able to nibble at the life of absent friends must know that he is unworthy of this table."[43]

Rule of St Augustine

The Church inherited the "Rule of St Augustine". His Rule captures the spirit of the common life he longed to live: "The main purpose for you having come together is to live harmoniously in your house, intent upon God in oneness of mind and heart".[44] St Augustine had a simple desire – to live in fraternal harmony with his brother clerics.

The Council of Lateran (1059) and another council held at Rome four years later approved a Rule for the members of the clergy based on the Rule developed the Bishop of Hippo. This gave rise to communities who became known as Canons Regular. This was

---

42 Confessions IV, vi, ii.
43 See Peter Brown, Augustine of Hippo, p. 200.
44 Rule n. 2.

more than just providing an opportunity for those clerics drawn to common life, it became a reform movement among the clergy which spread rapidly throughout the Church during the Middle Ages.

A Canon Regular is essentially a religious cleric. St Thomas Aquinas explains the distinction between a canon and a monk in these words: "The Order of Canons Regular is necessarily constituted by religious clerics, because they are essentially destined to those works which relate to the Divine mysteries, whereas it is not so with the monastic Orders". The clerical state is essential to the Order of Canons Regular, whereas it is only accidental to the Monastic Order. Erasmus, himself a Canon Regular, described Canons Regular as a middle way between monks and the secular clergy.

By the eighth century various efforts were being made to find a way in which clerics could live a common life, under a Rule. In 754 the Bishop of Metz, St Chrodegang, drew up a rule for the clergy of his diocese, an *ordo canonicus*. As well as providing guidance concerning liturgical life, the main purpose of this rule was to encourage a degree of common life among clerics. They were still to retain their own homes, but there was to be a common refectory. He did want to encourage a more complete renunciation of personal property among his priests, but it was not mandatory in the diocese, and simply served as an ideal for his clergy. Bishop Chrodegang understood that his priests needed the support of a fraternal life and saw the value of priests coming together for a common meal.

Writing for secular clergy at Metz Cathedral, Chrodegang's rule borrowed much from the Benedictine tradition, dealing with many of the same concerns as St Benedict, such as the housing, feeding, discipline of members of the community and the daily practice of the Divine Office. At a time when there was a lack of specific instruction of how clergy should live – whether they should marry or were eligible to own property – Chrodegang's rule provided clear guidance and became a source for reform for the clergy lived and their pastoral ministry.

A council held at Aachen in 817 produced a rule for clerics. The Rule of Aachen superseded the work of Bishop Chrodegang and provided an agenda for subsequent rules for canons. It drew on the teaching of the fathers: St Gregory, St Isidore, St Augustine, St Jerome, among others. Clerics, in contrast to the monks, were not required to surrender private property nor live an austere life, but they were to have some degree of common life and live in such a way to be worthy of the sacred mysteries that they celebrated. Rabanus Maurus, (c.776-856 Abbot of Fulda 822-42; archbishop of Mainz 847) wrote *De clericorum institutione*.[45] It was a detailed instruction for priests on how to conduct their life and ministry.

In the eleventh and twelfth centuries reform movements involving clerics began to find expression as congregations of canons regular. Each had its own distinctive constitutions, but the common foundation was the Rule of St. Augustine. In order to preserve uniformity and regularity among these numerous congregations Pope Benedict XII, in the year 1339, issued his Bull *Ad decorem*, which may be rather called a book of constitutions to be observed by all canons regular existing at that time.

In 1109 the famous scholar and teacher, William de Champeaux, opened a school which soon drew crowds of students from many parts. Founded by a scholar, the monastery of St. Victor for many centuries was a centre of learning and virtue. Here were formed men like Hugh, Richard, and Adam of St. Victor, all famous for their theological works and their piety. So great was the reputation of the houses they were soon established everywhere after the model of St. Victor's, which was regarded as their mother-house. The house at St Victor was a house for Canons Regular.

The Premonstratensian Congregation was founded at Prémontré, near Laon, in France, by St. Norbert, in the year 1120. It was a congregation of clerics living under a Rule. It grew large even during the lifetime of its founder. Clerics from such houses have charge of parishes and schools.

Other forms of Canon Regular developed in the Church, both as oriented around a Cathedral or as a congregation of clerics engaged in pastoral ministry.

---

45 See PL 107, 293-420.

Renewal of the Clergy

The clergy have suffered at different times with a decline in both the quality of their spiritual life and their pastoral service. Many bishops have devoted themselves to finding effective ways of supporting their clergy. As populations grew the possibility of having clergy living in common declined. With the situation of many clergy living in isolated rural villages and towns, sometimes far from the bishop's seat, the need for a support for them was important. St Augustine was committed to developing a Rule of Life for the clergy with him at Hippo. This Rule, simple and minimal in its detail, was embraced in the medieval period as the ideal Rule for clerics. The Rule was able to be implemented in larger towns where there were numbers of clergy. It was not a possibility for clergy in isolated villages and rural settings. The development of Canons Regular did provide a means of spiritual and human support for secular clergy, as well as those religious who embraced it.

Now we will turn our attention to a period where there were strong winds of change sweeping across society and the Church. They would result in a dramatically new form of consecrated life emerging. This movement was a further sign of the presence of the Holy Spirit "blowing where he will" (Jn 3:8) and providing a providential answer to the challenges of the times.

On a Rule for Clerics

Chapter I - Purpose and Basis of Common Life

Before all else, dear brothers, love God and then your neighbour, because these are the chief commandments given to us.

1. The following are the precepts we order you living in the monastery to observe.

2. The main purpose for you having come together is to live harmoniously in your house, intent upon God in oneness of mind and heart.

3. Call nothing your own, but let everything be yours in common. Food and clothing shall be distributed to each of you by your superior, not equally to all, for all do not enjoy equal health, but rather according to each one's need. For so you read in the Acts of the Apostles that they had all things in common and distribution was made to each one according to each one's need (4:32,35).

4. Those who owned something in the world should be careful in wanting to share it in common once they have entered the monastery.

5. But they who owned nothing should not look for those things in the monastery that they were unable to have in the world. Nevertheless, they are to be given all that their health requires even if, during their time in the world, poverty made it impossible for them to find the very necessities of life. And those should not consider themselves fortunate because them have found the kind of food and clothing which they were unable to find in the world.

6. And let them not hold their heads high, because they associate with people whom they did not dare to approach in the world, but let them rather lift up their hearts and not seek after what is vain and earthly. Otherwise, monasteries will come to serve a useful purpose for the rich and not the poor, if the rich are made humble there and the poor are puffed up with pride.

7. The rich, for their part, who seemed important in the world, must not look down upon their brothers who have come into this holy brotherhood from a condition of poverty. They should seek to glory in the fellowship of poor brothers rather than in the reputation of rich relatives. They should neither be elated if they have contributed a part of their wealth to the common life, nor take more pride in sharing their riches with the monastery than if they were to enjoy them in the world. Indeed, every other kind of sin has to do with the commission of evil deeds, whereas pride lurks even in good works in order to destroy them. And what good is it to scatter one's wealth abroad by giving to the poor, even to become poor oneself, when the unhappy soul is thereby more given to pride in despising riches than it had been in possessing them?

8. Let all of you then live together in oneness of mind and heart, mutually honouring God in yourselves, whose temples you have become.

Rule of St Augustine

8
An Evangelical Revival

The twelfth century was a period of political and ecclesiastical turmoil. On the political and social level the emerging merchant class was restless with older feudal structures. Town life was growing. Artisans reacted to the outdated guild system. Romance languages were replacing Latin. New forms of scholarship challenged traditional methodology. The laity were becoming more influential in the Church.

There was an evangelical spirit in the air in the twelfth century. The Church had become very clericalised and organisationally distant from the ordinary people. Monastic life by now had become formalised and it, too, lacked contact with the laity. The problem of the era was the widespread ignorance of Christian doctrine among the ordinary people and the worldliness of many clerics.

This led to a yearning for a more spiritual religion based on the Gospels. People were looking for spiritual nourishment and were attracted by the Gospel teaching of Jesus. Vernacular translations were made and the texts discussed, though sometimes in an anticlerical atmosphere. At a popular level there was increased interest in the humanity of Christ, especially in his sufferings on the cross. Art and sculpture became more graphic in presenting the sufferings of Christ. There was a desire for simplicity, and an attraction to poverty and the penitential life. In this spiritual environment a number of wandering lay preachers emerged. In reaction to perceived abuses in the Church some, like Arnold of Brescia, adopted stances of rejection of the Church and aspects of its teaching. Others, like St. Robert of Arbrissel and St. Bernard of Turon were orthodox.

People who heeded the calls of these preachers to a reformed life became known as "penitentials". They often expressed their conversion by adopting simple forms of dress, by practices of fasting and by the exercise of service to the poor and sick. Individual penitentials came together in new apostolic movements. However the situation spawned a range of heretical groups, among whom were the Albigenses, the Waldenses, the Manicheans, the Cathars, Poor Men of Lyons, the Bogomiles and others.

The Waldenses were followers of Peter Waldo, a merchant of Lyons who embraced poverty and entered upon lay preaching in 1176. He was originally loyal to the Church, but in time he rejected Church authority and his preaching incorporated a number of positions different to official Church teaching. The Catharists were another group that grew significantly at this time. They emerged particularly in the south of France. They attempted to be a new church claiming at one stage sixteen dioceses with their own bishops and priests. They proclaimed a dualistic creed, denied the validity of the sacraments and saw matter as evil. They professed beliefs similar to the Manichees of St. Augustine's day.

It is in this rather fraught atmosphere that a new form of religious life developed in the Church. It came to be called "mendicant'. A mendicant is one who lives by begging. This marks a significant departure from the pattern of religious life – monks supported themselves chiefly through agriculture, these new religious movements depended on the support from the people. They would own no tracts of land or have industries to support their life and mission. They led an itinerant life, going around from place to place proclaiming an evangelical message.

The two principal expressions of this new form of religious life were the Franciscans and the Dominicans.[46] This was a departure from the pattern of monastic life in the Church up to this time. Mendicants came to be known as friars, to distinguish them from monks.

---

46 There were five major orders of mendicants: the Franciscans (or Friars Minor); the Dominicans (called the Black Friars), the Carmelites, (sometimes called the White Friars); the Servites (Order of Servants of Mary); and the Augustinians (Hermits of St. Augustine, commonly called the Austin Friars). The Second Council of Lyons (1274) recognized these as the five "great" mendicant orders, and suppressed certain others. Among other orders that developed as mendicants were the Trinitarians (Order of the Most Blessed Trinity); the Mercedarians (Order of the Blessed Virgin Mary of Mercy); the Minims (Hermits of St. Francis of Paola);the Capuchins (Order of Friars Minor Capuchin); and the Discalced Carmelites.

The Franciscans

St Francis of Assisi is well known. He was born to a rich merchant family in 1182 in Assisi. He led a worldly life as a young man. In 1202 he was captured in a local war with Perugia and held for ransom. He was released a year later but had become sick while in prison. A conversion led him to embrace a life of radical poverty and penance. He made a pilgrimage to Rome. He lived in simplicity around Assisi caring for lepers and rebuilding dilapidated churches. He did this for three years and was joined by other young men from the town.

Twelve of them went to Rome and through miraculous circumstances a simple first Rule (now lost) was approved by Pope Innocent III (a similar request by the Waldensians in 1179 was denied). St Francis made a promise of obedience to the Pope and probably at this time he was ordained a deacon. St Francis lived by mendicancy. His rule emphasised humility and poverty. He advocated submission to the Church. There was a rapid growth in numbers in this new order. St Francis sent his friars in pairs to preach, to beg, to work on farms, and to spend time in solitude. His ideals attracted women. Chiara Offreduccio from Assisi wished to join and St Francis gave her a habit in 1212. The "Poor Ladies" established themselves at the chapel of San Damiano. St Clare became a great saint in her own right, and her order – the Poor Clares – continues to this day.

St Francis was given to preaching and was very effective. He dreamed of devoting himself to the conversion of Muslims. After three attempts he made his way to the Holy Land in 1219 and after attempting to convert the Sultan he visited the holy places.

During this time the Fourth Lateran Council was convened. At this council it was decided to forbid the formation of any religious orders adopting new rules of life – the traditional monastic rules must be adopted. Pope Innocent III informed that he had verbally approved Friars Minor (Consequently St Dominic chose the Rule of St. Augustine for his friars). The Order was spreading rapidly and required organisation. Chapters were held, with the one in 1223 approving the Rule. This Rule emphasised poverty, manual labour, preaching, missions to the heathens, and a balance of action and contemplation. Conflicts emerged as some introduced elements foreign to St Francis: study, stricter fasting and abstinence, building Churches. St Francis asked the Pope for an assistant to help govern the Order and then stepped aside as leader, handing over to Peter of Cataneo as Minister General.

Francis' health was beginning to fail. At Alverna in 17th September 1224 he received the Stigmata.[47] In April 1226 he drafted his spiritual testament. He died on 12th October 1226. Two years later he was declared a saint by the Church. His written legacy is minimal: two Rules, a last testament, a few letters and exhortations and prayers. However his spirit is captured in the works of a number of biographers, principally Thomas of Celano, Brother Leo, and St Bonaventure.

The spirituality of St Francis

In his Testament St Francis wrote,

> When God gave me some friars there was no one to tell me what I should do; but the Most High himself made it clear to me that I must live of the Gospel.[48]

This reveals that the Gospel teaching of Christ was understood by St Francis as the source point for his spirituality. But as we have seen he was not the first to do this. He reflected the spirit of his age. St Francis, though, embraced this evangelical spirit, lived it radically and inspired others to do the same. For St Francis the words of Christ found in the Gospels were taken at face value and lived

---

[47] Stigmata are the bodily marks of the wounds of Christ. They usually are accompanied by sensations of pain in locations corresponding to the crucifixion wounds of Jesus. The term originates from the line at the end of Saint Paul's Letter to the Galatians where he says, "I bear on my body the marks of Jesus." St. Francis of Assisi is the first recorded stigmatic in Christian history. Other stigmatists include Bl Lucia Brocadelli of Narn, St Catherine of Ricci, St Catherine of Siena, Bl Anne Catherine Emmerich, St Gemma Galgani, St Veronica Giuliani, St John of God, St Faustina Kowalska, St Marie of the Incarnation, Therese Neumann, St Pio of Pietrelcina, St Rita of Cascia and Myrna Nazzour.
[48] Testament, n. 68.

thoroughly.

In a discussion with Brother Leo St Francis is quoted as saying:

> Those who have cared for nothing except to know and point out the way of salvation to others, and have made no effort to follow it themselves, will stand naked and empty-handed before the judgement seat of Christ, bearing only the sheaves of confusion, shame and grief. Then shall the truth of holy Humility and Simplicity, of holy Prayer and Poverty, which is our vocation be exalted, glorified and proclaimed.[49]

In these words the four foundation stones of St Francis' spirituality are presented: Humility, Simplicity, Poverty and Prayer. For St Francis the humble knew that they were sinners – so much so that they would weep for their sins, as Francis himself did. They would daily plead for God's mercy. St Francis possessed an alarming and attractive spirit of simplicity. He took the words of Christ as face value, for instance, not possessing two tunics (see Lk 9:3) meant for St Francis just what it said. His was an innocence whereby he made no distinction between the deserving and undeserving poor and he possessed a simple trust in the Providence of God.

Bonaventure said that poverty was St Francis' profession. He embraced the ideal of total poverty. He saw the Gospel as the treasure hidden in the field (see Mt 13:44) and as the pearl of great price (see Mt 13:45-46). He called it "Lady Poverty", romanticising his relationship with evangelical poverty. For him it was the source of Christian joy. The Rule of 1221 stated:

> All the friars, no matter where they are or where they go, are forbidden to take or accept money in any way or under any form, or to have it accepted for them, for clothing or books, or as wages, or in any other necessity, except for the emergency provision of those who are ill.

Prayer was also a vital element in the spirituality of St Francis of Assisi. He said the Divine Office each day. Not possessing churches and being itinerant meant that the friars needed to pray on the road or in quiet places along the road. This is what St Francis did, eventually

---

49 SP n. 72.

discovering the beauty and peace of Mt Alverna. St Francis made all decisions after prolonged prayer, modelling himself on the example of Christ.[50] His prayer reflected his passionate longing for union with God and a desire for a complete sharing in all aspects of the life of Christ, including his suffering. Receiving the stigmata was the crowning of his desire to be completely united with his Master in all things.

After St Francis

After St Francis' death difficulties arose. St Francis left a spiritual heritage, but he was interpreted differently. Brother Leo led a group who wished to be faithful to the direct spirit of St Francis. These became known as the Observants, as distinct from the Conventuals, and were finally recognised in 1415. The Spirituals were another faction: they advocated a radical poverty as an isolated ideal. The Spirituals eventually were given status by the Church in 1294. This was a fairly turbulent group that later divided into some radical and heretical groups like the Fraticelli. The Franciscan Order was blessed by the leadership of St Bonaventure. At the age of thirty-five he was chosen General of his Order and restored calm among the internal dissensions. He did much for his Order and composed *The Life of St. Francis*.

The Franciscans made and still make a great contribution to the life and mission of the Church. Despite St Francis' own distrust of learning the Order would produce a number of outstanding thinkers and theologians like St Anthony of Padua and John Duns Scotus. St Bonaventure was its greatest thinker and among other things made a great contribution to spiritual theology especially in his work on the nature of contemplation.

The Franciscans, despite their own struggles, became a force for spiritual renewal in the Church in the centuries that followed. St

---

50 The Gospels record that Jesus often withdrew to lonely places to pray. St Mark records, "Very early in the morning, while it was still dark, Jesus got up, left the house and went off to a solitary place, where he prayed" (Mk 1:35). St Luke mentions this practice on many occasions and so comments, "But Jesus often withdrew to lonely places and prayed" (Lk 5:16).

Francis was a beacon of hope for the Church as it struggled with its own worldliness. The Franciscan movement helped the Church offer a way for living an evangelical life and helped halt the growth of heretical movements.

The spiritual legacy of St Francis

St Francis of Assisi is one of the best known and most loved of all saints. Many regard him as the saint closest in spirit to Jesus himself. He not only has provided a path for many seeking an evangelical life and has left a rich spiritual heritage. His vision for the Christian life continues to inspire thousands. Franciscanism in its many forms continues to have a significant place in the Church. Many others, inspired by his example, have sought the path of poverty and humility. In every generation he attracts men and women to an evangelical life.

We are fortunate to have many contemporary witnesses to the life and spirit of St Francis. There are various accounts of his life and collections of stories about him. Many have found their way into popular imagination. One only has to think of pictures we have of St Francis preaching to the birds or taming the wolf. St Francis, due to his poetic prayers praising God for creation, is now held up as a model for ecological sensitivity. St Francis continues to inspire the Church. His order attracts aspirants to a life of poverty, humility and evangelical service. Many are drawn to his way of following Christ. He continues to inspire people to avoid the distractions of the consumerist society and to seek simplicity of life. St Francis remains a luminous example of the attractiveness of Christian holiness.

Among the many contributions of St Francis to the Church his prayers have found a special home. Some of the best known prayers used by Catholics have St Francis as their author. One very popular prayer – called the Peace Prayer of St Francis – is not actually one of these prayers, but composed anonymously does capture the spirit of St Francis. Some of his prayers are offered below.

On the Prayers of St Francis.

Saint Francis' Prayer Before the Blessed Sacrament

We adore You,
O Lord Jesus Christ,
in this Church and all the Churches of the world,
and we bless You,
because,
by Your holy Cross You have redeemed the world. Amen.

Saint Francis' Prayer Before the Crucifix

Most High, glorious God,
enlighten the darkness of my heart and give me
true faith, certain hope, and perfect charity,
sense and knowledge, Lord, that I may carry out
Your holy and true command. Amen.

Saint Francis' Canticle of All Creatures

Most High, all-powerful, all-good Lord,
    All praise is Yours, all glory, all honour and all blessings.
    To you alone, Most High, do they belong,
and no mortal lips are worthy to pronounce Your Name.
    Praised be You my Lord with all Your creatures,
especially Sir Brother Sun,
Who is the day through whom You give us light.
And he is beautiful and radiant with great splendour,
Of You Most High, he bears the likeness.
    Praised be You, my Lord, through Sister Moon and the stars,
In the heavens you have made them bright, precious and fair
    Praised be You, my Lord, through Brothers Wind and Air,
And fair and stormy, all weather's moods,
by which You cherish all that You have made.
    Praised be You my Lord through Sister Water,
So useful, humble, precious and pure.
    Praised be You my Lord through Brother Fire,
through whom You light the night
and he is beautiful and playful and robust and strong.
    Praised be You my Lord through our Sister,

Mother Earth who sustains and governs us,
producing varied fruits with coloured flowers and herbs.
Praise be You my Lord through those who grant pardon
for love of You and bear sickness and trial.
Blessed are those who endure in peace,
By You Most High, they will be crowned.
   Praised be You, my Lord through Sister Death,
from whom no-one living can escape.
Woe to those who die in mortal sin!
Blessed are they She finds doing Your Will.
No second death can do them harm.
   Praise and bless my Lord and give Him thanks,
And serve Him with great humility.
   Heavenly Father,
You gave Your servant Francis
great love for each of Your creatures.
Teach us to see Your design in all of creation.
We ask this in Jesus' Name. Amen.

Saint Francis' Vocation Prayer

Most High, Glorious God,
enlighten the darkness of our minds.
Give us a right faith, a firm hope and a perfect charity,
so that we may always and in all things act according to Your Holy
Will. Amen.

Saint Francis' Blessing to Brother Leo

The Lord bless you and keep you;
May He show His face to you and have mercy.
May He turn His countenance to you and give you peace.
The Lord bless you, Brother Leo.

9
An Order of Preachers

Mendicant spirituality had at its heart a preaching ministry which focussed on a response to the message of Jesus himself. Another Order which rose up at the same time as the Franciscans was the Dominicans. They too were a product of the times and their charism provided a much needed resource for the spiritual renewal and the revitalisation of the Church.

St Dominic

Dominic Guzman (1170-1221) was an Augustinian Canon in Osma, Spain. With his bishop Diego of Azevedo he became involved in a mission against the Albigensian heresy in the south of France. Some Cistercian monks who were legates of the Pope tried to combat this heresy but were unsuccessful. Bishop Diego recognised that the heresy could only be effectively challenged by clerics who embraced itinerant preaching and adopted a radical poverty. Heresy could not be countered just by restatement of Catholic teaching and the teaching needed to be backed up by a holiness of life reflected by living Gospel teaching.

St Dominic took up this work. After the bishop died St Dominic continued the work alone with the approval of Pope Innocent III. Companions joined St Dominic in the mission and this led eventually to the formation of an order of preaching clerics called the Order of Preachers (OP). St Dominic left little in the way of personal writings. The Constitutions of the Order are his most significant work. Indeed, the Dominican Order produced no spiritual classics in its early years, even the sermons of early Dominicans are not available.

Knowledge about St Dominic comes from documents like "Life of St Dominic" by Jean de Mailly, a "Sermon on St Dominic" by

Thomas Agni of Lentini and the canonisation process in 1233.

The mystic St Mechtilde of Magdeburg (d 1297) in a tribute to him said of St Dominic:

> St Dominic taught the wise that they should temper their knowledge with divine simplicity; to the simple he taught true wisdom; the tempted he helped to bear their sorrows secretly. He taught the young to keep much silence that they might be outwardly modest and inwardly wise. The sick and infirm he comforted with true compassion, caring for all their needs. They rejoiced at the long years he spent among them; his gracious company made their labours light… God has specially honoured his two sons, Francis and Dominic, with four things: to welcome all, to give real help in every need, to possess the holy wisdom of Divine Truth, and cherish the power of his Holy Church.[51]

The Dominican Order has had and continues to have a strong influence in the Church. It is renown for producing preachers and its accent on study. The latter has meant that the Order has produced many great theologians. Of St Dominic's own writings we only have a short letter. Even the Rule of the Order is traced back to the Second Master of the Order, Jordan of Saxony.

One text that comes down to us from the early Dominican period is "On the Formation of Preachers" by Humbert of Romans. It is not really a spiritual work, far less a classic, but it is a witness to the importance of preaching among the Dominicans. The early part of the text offers a presentation of the spirituality of the preacher and emphasises the importance of the preaching ministry:

> Again, there are many who, spiritually, have nothing to live on. But it is the word of God which sustains man's spiritual life. "Man does not live on bread alone, but on every word which comes from the mouth of God" (Mt 4:4). Poor people who have nothing with which to keep themselves alive come running for alms; similarly people who are spiritually poor

---

51 Mechtild of Magdeburg, *The Revelations of Mechtild of Magdeburg*, sometimes called *The Flowing Light of the Godhead*.

ought to come running to sermons, to receive the word of God in their spirit, to keep themselves alive.[52]

The Dominican Order

In 1215 St Dominic moved to Toulouse in southern France where he was joined by two local men. He formed a community and got approval from the bishop of Toulouse, who declared: "We [Bishop] Faulk institute Brother Dominic and his associates as preachers in our diocese …They propose to travel on foot and to preach the word of the Gospel in evangelical poverty as religious".

In 1216 he received papal approval, though in accord with the decisions of Lateran VI adopted the Rule of St. Augustine. As we noted earlier this period in the church witnessed the rise of a number of orders of Canons Regular, like the Premonstratentians and the Canons of St Victor. It was relatively easy for St Dominic to establish this new order of preachers on the lines of canons regular because of his own background in the town of Osma, Spain. Early Dominicans were called Canons as well as Friars.

The focus of the Order was on practical apostolic work, the *vita apostolica*. For this purpose he relativised normal conventual life. Poverty and mendicancy were practiced for pragmatic reasons: to enable the credibility of the preachers. St Dominic saw poverty as a simple way of trusting in Divine Providence. He avoided rigorous austerity among his friars and did not demand all possessions to be held in common.

Study was important for those dedicated to preaching. Study replaced the monastic *lectio divina*. Each Dominican house was a house of studies. Preachers of the time needed to be able to offer sound catechesis and moral guidance. The Dominicans fostered the "new" theology of the time, scholasticism. Soon the Order became involved in universities that had begun to emerge. Later the Order was to produce great theologians like St Albert the Great and St Thomas Aquinas.

---
52 Treatise on the Formation of Preachers, Humbert of Romans, n. 59.

The celebration of the Divine Office in common was minimised to enable time to be devoted to apostolic work. The Rule said, "All the hours are to be said in church briefly and succinctly lest the brethren lose devotion and their study be in any way impeded". It goes on to add:

> The prelate shall have power to dispense the brethren of his priory when it shall seem expedient to him, especially in those things that are seen to impede study, preaching or the good of souls, since it is known that our Order was especially founded from the beginning for preaching and the salvation of souls.[53]

Obedience was the only vow members of the Order took. It was made to the Master of the Order, not to the Constitutions. The Rule was not tight and prescriptive and it provided space for initiative to be taken by the individual. Friars had freedom about their work. The "grace" of preaching was paramount. The Order became a great evangelising force in the Church by the end of the thirteenth century. They were active in Armenia, Turkestan, and then India and China. Individual prayer and piety was also left open to the individual. However one of their special areas of apostolic activity that emerged over time was that of spiritual direction.

A parallel order of women was established at Pouille in France. The friars resisted being preoccupied with ministry to the women religious, lest it divert their attention from the fundamental role of being itinerant preachers. This was later mitigated and the Dominican Sisters were approved in 1267.

Dominican Spirituality

St Dominic retained some of the basic elements of monastic life: common celebration of the Divine Office, a community celebration of the Eucharist, the cloister and silence, and fasting and

---

[53] See the Primitive Constitutions of the Order of Friars Preachers. The text of the first constitutions of the Order of Friars Preachers come to us from the time of Master Jordan, the immediate successor of Blessed Dominic. Later Brother Raymond of Penafort, Third Master of the Order, rewrote them. This revised text is the one in use today.

penance. The anonymous work, *The Nine Ways of Prayer*, provides an interesting insight into the forms of prayer of St Dominic. However it is clearly a later work. Dominican prayer, though, is largely simple, devotional and petitionary. St Dominic himself was contemplative, though not mystical. He did not have an interest in speculative or mystical theology.

It is often believed that St Dominic was responsible for developing the Rosary. The Dominicans certainly promoted devotion to the Rosary. It provided a tool to assist those won back from heresy to develop patterns of personal prayer. Dominicans wear the rosary as part of their habit. It was the writings of Alan de la Roche (d 1453) which promoted the legend that the Rosary was given to St Dominic by the Virgin Mary. We will examine the development of the Rosary in a later chapter.

The Dominican spirituality produced many great saints. One outstanding example is St Catherine of Siena (d 1380). Dominican spirituality was very significant among the Rhineland mystics of the fourteenth century, for example, Meister Eckhart, Blessed Henry Susa and John Tauler. The Dominicans became involved in spiritual direction and provided a great service to the Church in this area. This will be explored at the end of this book.

Although there is little by way of classical Dominican spiritual texts, the Order in time has made a great contribution of the spiritual tradition of the Church. The text, *The Nine Ways of Prayer*, is quoted below as it gives an insight into the ways in which St Dominic was reputed to have prayed. It is said that St Dominic seldom spoke unless it was with God (prayer) or about God (preaching). The text is interesting in that it does describe various physical postures that can be used in prayer. A consideration of posture is not a theme explored much in Catholic spiritual writings and so this text has its own interest and value.

On the Ways of Prayer of St Dominic

The First Way of Prayer

Saint Dominic's first way of prayer was to humble himself before the altar as if Christ, signified by the altar, were truly and personally present and not in symbol alone. He would say with Judith: "O Lord, God, the prayer of the humble and the meek hath always pleased Thee [Judith 9:16]. "It was through humility that the Canaanite woman and the prodigal son obtained what they desired; as for me, "I am not worthy that Thou shouldst come under my roof" [Matt. 8:8] for "I have been humbled before you exceedingly, O Lord [Ps. 118:107]."

In this way our holy father, standing erect, bowed his head and humbly considering Christ, his Head, compared his lowliness with the excellence of Christ. He then gave himself completely in showing his veneration. The brethren were taught to do this whenever they passed before the humiliation of the Crucified One in order that Christ, so greatly humbled for us, might see us humbled before his majesty. And he commanded the friars to humble themselves in this way before the entire Trinity whenever they chanted solemnly: "Glory be to the Father, and to the Son, and to the Holy Spirit." In this manner of profoundly inclining his head, as shown in the drawing, Saint Dominic began his prayer.

The Second Way of Prayer

Saint Dominic used to pray by throwing himself outstretched upon the ground, lying on his face. He would feel great remorse in his heart and call to mind those words of the Gospel, saying sometimes in a voice loud enough to be heard: "O God, be merciful to me, a sinner." [Luke 18:13] With devotion and reverence he repeated that verse of David: "I am he that has sinned, I have done wickedly." [II Kings 24:17]. Then he would weep and groan vehemently and say: "I am not worthy to see the heights of heaven because of the greatness of my iniquity, for I have aroused thy anger and done what is evil in thy sight". From the psalm: "Deus auribus nostris audivimus" he said fervently and devoutly: "For our soul is cast down to the dust, our belly is flat on the earth!" [Ps. 43:25]. To this he would add: "My soul is prostrate in the dust; quicken thou me according to thy word" [Ps. 118:25].

Wishing to teach the brethren to pray reverently, he would sometimes say to them: When those devout Magi entered the dwelling they found the child with Mary, his mother, and falling down they worshipped him. There is no doubt that we too have found the God-Man with Mary, his handmaid. "Come, let us adore and fall down in prostration before God, and let us weep before God, and let us weep before the Lord that made us" [Ps. 94:6]. He would also exhort the young men, and say to them: If you cannot weep for your own sins because you have none, remember that there are many sinners who can be disposed for mercy and charity. It was for these that the prophets lamented; and when Jesus saw them, he wept bitterly. The holy David also wept as he said: "I beheld the transgressors and began to grieve" [Ps. 118:158].

The Nine Ways of Prayer of St Dominic

10
Byzantine Traditions of Prayer

Pope John Paul II taught that the Church needs to learn once again to breathe with both lungs – the Eastern tradition and the Western tradition.[54] It is important in any consideration of the spiritual tradition of the Church to be aware of spiritual movements of the East, particularly as the Church was one – East and West – until the formal break in the eleventh century with the Great the Schism of 1054.

Over two chapters the rich vein of spirituality that enriched the Eastern tradition will be examined. It can be captured in the word *hesychasm*. The word comes from the Greek word, *hesychia*, meaning stillness, rest, quiet, silence. The tradition developed among the monks as they sought the key to interior prayer. This tradition focuses on a deep personal interiority which enables an experiential knowledge of God.

To properly understand the development of this tradition of spirituality we need to return to the Desert Fathers to discover how their teaching was expressed in the Eastern Church.

The traditions of prayer formed in the desert during the fourth to sixth centuries were preserved more in the Eastern Church than in the Western Church. The monasticism that developed in the West under St Benedict took much inspiration from the Desert Fathers. However it became more communal and structured suiting the European culture and temperament. St Benedict developed monastic prayer as formal communal worship. As we have seen it was the great *opus dei*, the work of God, combining praise of God with contemplating the Sacred Scriptures – the solemn chanting of psalms and *lectio divina* became the focus of the monks' life. Though

---

54 Pope John Paul II referred on a number of occasions to the importance of seeing the Church as both East and West. One of his earlier references was on 12 August 1993 in Denver (Colorado) when he said, "Europe has two lungs, it will never breathe easily until it uses both of them".

St Benedict never lost sight of the importance of personal silent prayer, he promoted liturgical prayer as the main form of prayer for the monk.

In the Byzantine East however the tradition of the hermit or anchorite[55] was more purely preserved and the closer cultural ties between Egypt and the Byzantine Empire encouraged a deeper fidelity to the spirit of the desert.

Prayer of the mind - Evagrius of Pontus

Born in Pontus in Asia Mino Evagrius was a friend and disciple of the great Cappadocian Fathers, St Basil and the two St Gregorys.[56] Evagrius (d 399) is regarded as the first real intellectual to adopt the life of an anchorite in the Egyptian desert. Though as an Origenist[57] he was condemned at the Fifth Ecumenical Council in 553, he wrote two books, *Praitikos* and *Chapters on Prayer* which are regarded as spiritual classics.

Evagrius was a Christian Platonist.[58] When he came to address the question of the nature of prayer he focused on the role of the mind. For Evagrius the goal of the Christian life was to purify the human soul and so be able to contemplate God in his essence.

The monks were inspired by the Scripture text, 1 Thess. 5:17 – "Pray without ceasing". Evagrius wrote in his *Chapters on Prayer*:

---

55 A person following this form of life is called an anchorite. The word anchorite (female: anchoress) comes from the Greek: ναχωρέω anachōreō, signifying to withdraw. It denotes someone who, for religious reasons, withdraws from secular society so as to be able to lead an intensely prayer-oriented ascetic life.
56 St Gregory of Nyssa and St Gregory of Naziansus.
57 Origen of Alexandria (d 254) was a Scripture scholar. In his later works he promoted the doctrine that all created beings, including Satan, will ultimately be saved.
58 Platonism is a philosophical system derived from the work of the Greek philosopher Plato. The central concept of Platonism is the distinction between that reality which is perceptible, but not intelligible, and that which is intelligible, but imperceptible. In the 3rd century AD, Plotinus added mystical elements, establishing Neoplatonism, in which the summit of existence was the One or the Good, the source of all things; in virtue and meditation the soul had the power to elevate itself to attain union with the One. Platonism had a profound effect on Western thought, and many Platonic notions were adopted by the Christian church which understood Platonic forms as God's thoughts, whilst Neoplatonism became a major influence on Christian mysticism.

"Prayer is a continuous intercourse of the mind with God."[59] In another place he says, "Do not pray by outward gestures only, but bend your mind as well to the perception of spiritual prayer with great fear."[60] Evagrius provides a definition of prayer that came to be commonly used in the Catholic tradition: "Prayer is the ascent of the mind to God."[61]

Evagrius, inspired by his Platonic philosophical vision, sought a pure form of prayer. He saw that the task of the monk was to purify the soul so that prayer would be unsullied. The monastic quest became the pursuit of *apatheia,* an eradication of all base passions, as the ground for pure prayer.

A witness to prayer of the heart - Pseudo Macarius

The teachings ascribed to St Macarius come down to us by an anonymous author of the fourth century, hence they are given the title "Pseudo Macarius". This Syrian monk wrote fifty homilies and presents a spirituality, now not of the mind, but of the heart. He teaches, "The heart directs and governs all the other organs of the body."[62] For Pseudo Macarius, the heart is the symbol of our personal unity, the centre where the physical and non-material, the created and the uncreated merge. He describes this in these words, "For there, in the heart, the mind abides as well as all the thoughts of the soul and all its hopes."[63]

This understanding that it is in the heart where prayer is fostered leads to an incarnational and affective approach to spirituality. Such an approach seeks to integrate body, soul and spirit.

Pseudo Macarius had a profound sense of the power of the indwelling Holy Spirit which transformed the heart:

"The soul that is counted worthy to participate in the light of the Holy Spirit by becoming his throne and habitation, and is covered

---
59 *Chapters on Prayer* n. 3.
60 Ibid, n. 28.
61 Ibid, n. 35.
62 Homily 15, 20.
63 Ibid.

with the ineffable glory of the Spirit, becomes all light, all face, all eye. There is no part of the soul that is not full of the spiritual eyes of light."[64]

Despite this glowing description of the transforming power of the Spirit in the human heart Pseudo Macarius knows only too well the human condition and speaks of the need to approach God with profound contrition. Thus we find in his writings the call to constant *penthos*, weeping. The prayer which he sees as best capturing this is *Kyrie Eleison*, Lord, have mercy.

The foundation of the hesychastic tradition – St John Climacus

One of the most famous and most ancient of the monasteries in the East is that of St. Catherine which is built at the foot of Mt. Sinai. In the sixth century it was an important centre of monastic life. The abbot at the time was Abba John who became abbot in 580. His teaching comes down to us in his spiritual classic, *The Ladder of Divine Ascent*. He has become known as "John of the Ladder", St John Climacus.

In keeping with the traditions of the Desert Fathers most of the book concerns spiritual teaching on the dispositions of the heart. Of the thirty steps in the ladder, only on the twenty seventh and twenty eighth does Abba John speak specifically about prayer. Step twenty seven teaches on the nature of solitude, the Greek word is *hesychia*. He describes solitude as "unceasing worship and waiting upon God."[65] Then he teaches, "Let the remembrance of Jesus be present with each breath, and then you will know the value of solitude."[66] His term "remembrance of Jesus" has a particular meaning; it refers to what has come to be known as the *Jesus Prayer*. This prayer had grown up among the Desert Fathers and is linked to the invocation of the name of Jesus combined with saying the Kyrie Eleison. Thus it became: "Lord Jesus Christ, have mercy on me a

---

64 Homily 1,2.
65 Step 27, 60.
66 Ibid, 61.

sinner". It is this prayer that St John Climacus advocated. He saw this prayer as the prayer for the solitary monk. It was to be quite literally "present with each breath."

St John Climacus is confirming a tradition of prayer that had been developing and gaining stronger adherence in the East. He had the teaching of the St Macarius behind him. Rather than seeing prayer as an exercise of the mind as proposed by Evagrius, St John Climacus confirmed what had become the preferred way of viewing the nature of interior prayer. Wishing to avoid an intellectualist view of the spiritual life, he countered this with a strong emphasis on the key place that the heart plays in prayer:

> In fact, the heart is master and king of the whole bodily organism, and when grace takes possession of the pastureland of the heart, it rules over all its members and all its thoughts; for it is in the heart that the intelligence dwells, and there dwell all the souls thoughts; it finds all its good in the heart.[67]

Prayer of the heart, from the heart, is what the great Fathers of the Eastern tradition proposed. John Climacus urges,

Let your prayer be completely simple. For both the publican and the prodigal son were reconciled to God by a simple phrase.[68]

The Jesus Prayer ideally fulfils these conditions, indeed, the very reference he makes to the publican and the prodigal show he has the Jesus Prayer in mind.[69] This prayer is the way to true hesychia, a deep quiet in which one rests in the presence of God.

Established by the monks of the desert, this tradition lies at the heart of the spiritual tradition of the Eastern Church and becomes the centre of times of spiritual flowering, first in Greece and later in Russia. In the coming chapter we will explore its great influence in these two centres of Eastern Orthodoxy.

---

67 Hom.11, 20.
68 Step 28,5.
69 The parable of Jesus given in Lk 18:9-14 teaches that the "acceptable" prayer is that of a humble recognition that one is a sinner in need of mercy, "Be merciful to me a sinner".

On prayer of the heart

When you are going to stand before the Lord, let the garment of your soul be woven throughout with the thread of wrongs suffered but forgotten. Otherwise, prayer will be of no benefit to you.

Pray in all simplicity. For both the tax collector and the prodigal son were reconciled to God by a single phrase.

The work of prayer is one and the same for all, but there are various and many different kinds of prayer. Some converse with God as with a friend and master, interceding with praise and petition, not for themselves but for others. Some strive for greater [spiritual] treasures and glory and for confidence in prayer. Others ask for complete deliverance from their adversary. Some beg to receive some kind of rank; others for complete forgiveness of debts. Some ask to be released from prison; others for remission from offences.

Before all else, let us list sincere thanksgiving first on the scroll of our prayer. On the second line, we should put confession and heartfelt contrition of soul. Then let us present our petition to the King of all. This is the best way of prayer, as it was shown to one of the monks by an angel of the Lord...

Do not be over-complicated in the words you use when praying, because the simple and unadorned lisping of the children has often won the heart of their Heavenly Father.

Try not to talk excessively when you pray, lest your mind be distracted in searching for words. One word of the tax collector appeased God, and one cry of faith saved the thief. Talkative prayer often distracts the mind and leads to phantasy, whereas brevity makes for concentration.

If during your prayer some word evokes delight or compunction within you, linger over it; for at that moment our guardian Angel is praying with us. However pure you may be, do not be forward in your dealings with God. Approach Him rather in all humility, and you will be given still more boldness. And even if you have climbed the whole ladder of the virtues, pray still for the forgiveness of sins. Heed Paul's cry regarding sinners 'of whom I am first' (1 Tim 1:15).

The Ladder of Divine Ascent; Step 28

11
The Jesus Prayer

The centre of the spirituality of the monks of the East stemmed from the prayer developed in Egypt, the Sinai Peninsula and Syria. This prayer was based simply on the continuous recitation of the simple formula: Lord Jesus Christ, be merciful to me a sinner. The prayer, faithfully said, would lead to a deep personal experience of God. This experience was not to be sought for its own sake, nor was it the seeking of God through the use of imagination.

Entry point into the mystical
– St Symeon the New Theologian

The Jesus Prayer provided an avenue for profound mystical experience. A witness to this is St Symeon, called the "New Theologian."[70] The setting for his life is Constantinople in the beginnings of the tenth century. In St Mamas Monastery in Constantinople renown for beautiful and ornate celebration of the Liturgy was a monk of the same name who endeavoured to return to a simple form of prayer where experience of the presence of God was sought and experienced. A young man aged 20 named Symeon sought guidance from this older monk. He worked in the government offices in Constantinople and was drawn to pursue the spiritual life. The old monk proposed that the young man use the Jesus Prayer. After using the prayer one evening after work he recounts his experience (using the third person):

---

[70] St Symeon is given the rare title of "Theologian" There are only three saints in the Eastern Orthodox church given the title of "Theologian" - the other two are John the Apostle and Gregory of Nazianzus. The title "Theologian" implies not so much academic ability as rather it witnesses to one who can testify to the nature of God from immediate personal experience. Theology was born of experience and St Symeon taught that it is possible to experience *theoria* - direct experience of God.

One day, as he stood and recited "God, have mercy on me a sinner" uttering it with his mind rather than his mouth, suddenly a flood of divine radiance appeared from above and filled the room...He saw nothing but light all around him and did not know whether he was standing on the ground.[71]

It was this mystical grace that fired the young Symeon to proclaim that all, monks and ordinary Christians, can have an immediate experience of the presence of God. His message was simple: enter into a serious repentance for sins and you can receive what he would describe as a "Baptism in the Holy Spirit" accompanied with the gift of tears.

Young Symeon became a monk and an abbot. He became one of the great mystics of the Eastern Church, though not without strong opposition from some in the Church which resulted in his eventual exile. His belief that all can have a direct experience of God was challenged by Church authorities. His "Discourses" and poetic writings are some of the greatest works of spiritual mysticism in the East. He linked the invocation of the name of Jesus and the sincere recognition of one's sinfulness with the outpouring of the Holy Spirit. For example in his poem, *Divine Hymns of Love* he writes of this invocation of the Holy Spirit:

> Come down, O true Light!
> Come down, Life eternal.
> Come down, hidden mystery
> Come down, ineffable treasure
> Come down, O constant rejoicing.
> Come down, Light that never fades.
> Come down, Eternal Joy.

The source of spiritual renewal – Mount Athos

The fourteenth century saw the revival of hesychism in the monastic communities on Mt Athos in Greece. The fourteenth century revival was not based on theology or mysticism as such, but rather in a return to the basic teaching of the Desert Fathers on

---

[71] St Symeon recorded in the experience in his book, *Discourses* (Disc. 22.2-4).

hesychasm.

The man associated with the early period of revival is St Nicephorus the Hesychast. He left a little treatise, "On Guarding the Heart."[72] He quotes extensively the Great Fathers, Anthony, Macarius, John Climacus, Symeon the New Theologian and others and their teaching on hesychasm. Only at the end does he give his own teaching in answer to a question: "teach us what is attention of the mind and how to become worthy to acquire it."

In his answer he describes what "attention" is and then for those who would seek it he urges them to "seek a teacher who is not himself in error". However, if no teacher is to be found he outlines his teaching. He says in part, "Having collected your mind within you, lead it unto the channel of breathing through which air reaches the heart and, together with this inhaled air, force your mind to descend into the heart and to remain there."[73] While we may consider that St Nicephorus is operating from a faulty physiology, the two keys to his teaching are firstly the need to subject the mind to the heart and secondly the important place that physical breathing plays. Both point to the clearly to an incarnational (as opposed to speculative) approach to prayer: the heart is seen as the preferred place for prayer rather than the mind, and the body is seen as providing important support to prayer.

He continues his teaching: "Moreover you should know that when your mind becomes firmly established in the heart, it must not remain there silent and idle, but it should constantly repeat the prayer, Lord, Jesus Christ, Son of God, have mercy upon me and never cease." The goal for St Nicephorus is "attention" or the guarding of the heart. The means to achieve this is through what could be described as a psycho-physiological method of prayer which establishes a ground for the movement of one's spirit

---

72 St Nicephorus lived in a hermitage near Karyes, the Athonite capital. His booklet, "On Guarding the Heart", presents the hesychast tradition. It contains a collection of quotations from earlier hesychasts. St Nicephorus recommends having a spiritual father and giving him obedience.
73 His teaching is included in the *Philokalia*. The *Philokalia* is a collection of texts on monastic prayer compiled by St Nikodimos of the Holy Mountain and St Makarios of Corinth.

through constant repetition of the Jesus Prayer.

One of the leading exponents of hesychasm of the day was St Gregory of Sinai (1255-1346) who spent some years in Athos. He directly advocated the Jesus Prayer and gives much practical advice: "When you notice thoughts arising and accosting you, do not look at them, even if they are not bad; but keeping the mind firmly in the heart, call to the Lord Jesus and you will soon sweep away the thoughts and drive out their instigators – the demons – invisibly scorching and flogging them with this Divine Name."[74] Not that the Jesus Prayer is to be the sole form of prayer, St Gregory of Sinai advocates the use of the psalms. He comments: "If he is attacked by laziness, let him psalmodise or read the writings of the Fathers."[75]

St Gregory warns the monks about the danger of visions and experiences becoming ends in themselves: "Watch with care and intelligence, you lover of God, when, while you work, you see within or without you a light or a flame, or an image – of Christ, for example, or of an angel or of some one else – do not accept it less you suffer harm. And do not yourself create fantasies; nor pay attention to those that create themselves, nor allow your mind to take their impression".[76] This teaching emphasises that God is to be sought for his own sake alone, and not for the sake of subjective experiences. St Gregory of Sinai is also notable for the fact that he took this teaching to the Slavonic lands of the Balkans, from where the teaching later penetrated Russia.

The Theology of Hesychasm – St Gregory Palamas

The hesychast tradition came under serious attack from a Calabrian Greek named Barlaam who occupied the chair of philosophy at the Imperial University at Constantinople. He

---

74 His teaching is also found in the *Philokalia*.
75 Ibid.
76 Ibid.

was heavily influenced by nominalistic humanism[77] which he had experienced in Renaissance Italy. His challenge of the very basis of hesychasm was refuted by St Gregory Palamas (b. 1296). His work, *Triads in Defence of the Holy Hesychasts*, provided a thorough-going theological presentation of hesychasm. He argued that God is truly accessible and in undertaking a life of renunciation, purification and prayer the monks are "initiated into that which transcends the human mind."[78] He comments:

> God in His overflowing goodness to us, being transcendent to all things, incomprehensible and ineffable, consents to allow our intelligence to participate in Him and becomes invisibly visible in His superessential and inseparable power.[79]

How is it possible for man to know God and at the same time affirm that God is by nature unknowable? St. Gregory answered this question by quoting St. Basil the Great who said "We know our God from His energies, but we do not claim that we can draw near to His essence. For His energies come down to us, but His essence remains unapproachable". St. Gregory added "God is not a nature, for He is above all beings... No single thing of all that is created has or ever will have even the slightest communion with the supreme nature, or nearness to it". Even though God's essence may be remote from us, He has revealed himself through his energies (or grace). These energies do not exist apart from God, but are God himself in his action and revelation to the world. It is through these energies that God enters into a direct and immediate relationship with the believer. The saints are 'deified' by the grace of God, that is, they have a direct experience of God himself through his energies (or grace), not in his essence.

This argument provided a sound theological basis for the hesychastic tradition. From the time of St Gregory Palamas the

---

77 Nominalism is a philosophical theory according to which general or abstract terms and predicates exist, while universals or abstract objects, which are sometimes thought to correspond to these terms, do not exist. It denies the existence of universals – things that can be instantiated or exemplified by many particular things. It denies the existence of abstract objects – objects that do not exist in space and time.
78 PG 150, 1225.
79 *Triads* 1,3.

hesychastic tradition of prayer had a secure place in the spiritual tradition of the Church.

A further manifestation: Russia

In the nineteenth century Russia experienced the hesychastic tradition. The source was Mt Athos, but hesychasm itself was not new to the Russian monks. For centuries they had access to the writings of the Desert Fathers. The centre of the emergence of the hesychastic tradition was the monastery of Optino re-established in 1821. The monks were disciples of Paisy Veliskovsky (1722-1794). Paisy, a Ukrainian, had been a monk at Mt Athos. He took his experience of hesychasm he learnt there firstly to Rumania and then to Russia. He was instrumental in promoting this tradition in Russia chiefly because he translated the *Philokalia* into the Russian language.

The monastery at Optino focussed its life on the use of the Jesus Prayer and the accompanying hesychast teaching. Their fidelity to the teaching of hesychasm resulted in these monks growing to remarkable heights of spiritual wisdom and insight. Years of solitude and prayer made them holy elders, *startzi* or *starets*, whom people approached for advice, wisdom and prayer.

The Way of the Pilgrim

The *Way of the Pilgrim*, published in 1860, shows that this prayer of the heart was not only the domain of monks, but that it had spread widely throughout the Russian Church. In the book an anonymous pilgrim goes in search of someone who can teach him to pray ceaselessly. Eventually he meets a starets who says, "The continuous interior Prayer of Jesus is a constant un-interrupted calling upon the divine Name of Jesus with the lips, in the spirit, in the heart."[80] The appeal is couched in these terms, "Lord, Jesus Christ, have mercy on me." Then asking how he can gain the habit of it, he is told of the *Philokalia*. The monk describes the book in

---

80 See *Way of the Pilgrim*.

these words, "it contains the full and detailed science of constant interior prayer, set forth by twenty-five holy Fathers". The pilgrim goes forth and practices the Jesus Prayer, advocating its use by all Christians.

The Jesus Prayer

As we have seen the Jesus Prayer became the vehicle by which the monks could respond to St. Paul's challenge to pray unceasingly. This form of prayer is also prayer of the heart reflecting the tradition of the East. It offers a means of concentration and can be very useful for beginners in prayer. This prayer, in its simplicity and clarity, is rooted in the Scriptures. It can be a means by which one experiences the power of the Holy Spirit – as St Symeon testifies.

The Scriptural roots of the Jesus Prayer are evident. In its brevity and simplicity, it is the fulfilment of Jesus' command that in praying we are "not to heap up empty phrases as the heathen do; for they think that they will be heard for their many words" (Mt 6:7-8). The prayer is rooted in the invocation of the name of the Lord. In the Scriptures, the power and glory of God are present in his Name. In the Old Testament to deliberately and attentively invoke God's Name was to place oneself in his Presence. Jesus is "the name which is above all other names" and as St Paul teaches, "all beings should bend the knee at the Name of Jesus" (Phil 2:9-10).

The words of the Jesus Prayer are based in three key scriptural texts: the cry of the blind man sitting at the side of the road near Jericho, "Jesus, Son of David, have mercy on me" (Lk 18:38); the ten lepers who "called to him, 'Jesus, Master, take pity on us' " (Lk 17:13); and the cry for mercy of the publican in the temple, "God, be merciful to me, a sinner" (Lk 18:14). This prayer is the recognition of our own sinfulness, our essential estrangement from God. The Jesus Prayer is a prayer in which we admit our need of a Saviour. For "if we say we have no sin in us, we are deceiving ourselves and refusing to admit the truth"(I Jn 1:8).

The monks recognised that the prayer moved the person to depths of response to God. St Theophan the Recluse, a nineteenth century Russian spiritual writer, distinguishes three levels in the saying of the Prayer. He notes that it begins as oral prayer or prayer of the lips. As we enter more deeply into prayer, we reach a level at which we begin to pray in a way that effectively engages the mind. St Theophan remarks that at this point, "the mind is focused upon the words" of the prayer, "speaking them as if they were our own." The final level occurs when the prayer becomes prayer of the heart. At this stage prayer is no longer something we do but who we are. The prayer of the heart is the prayer of adoption, when "God has sent the Spirit of his Son into our hearts, the Spirit that cries 'Abba, Father!' "(Gal 4:6).

This return to the Father through Christ in the Holy Spirit is the goal of Christian spirituality. "Growth in prayer has no end," St Theophan informs us. "If this growth ceases, it means that life ceases." This prayer is steeped in rich tradition and is made holy by its constant practice down through many centuries.

On Guarding the Heart

You, who desire to capture the wondrous Divine illumination of our Savior Jesus Christ – who seek to feel the Divine fire in your heart – who strive to sense the experience and feeling of reconciliation with God – who, in order to unearth the treasure buried in the field of your hearts and to gain possession of it, have renounced everything worldly – who desire the candles of your soul to burn brightly even now, and who, for this purpose, have renounced all this world? – who wish by conscious experience to know and to receive the kingdom of heaven existing within you – come and I will impart to you the science of eternal heavenly life or, rather, the method leading him who practices it, without labor or sweat, into the harbor of passionlessness, freeing him from the fear of prelest[81] or of defeat by the wiles of the devil. Such fear is proper only when through our transgression the circle of our life revolves far outside the life of which I intend to teach you. For then it happens to us as to Adam; associating with the serpent, he disregarded God's commandment; trusting the serpent's counsel, he tasted of the forbidden fruit and was utterly filled with prelest. Thus to our sorrow he plunged himself and all after him into the depths of death, darkness and corruption.

---

[81] The term "prelist" is a Russian word which has no precise English equivalent. It is translated as "spiritual delusion ," "spiritual deception," or "illusion".

So let us return to ourselves, brothers, and be filled with disgust and hatred for the counsel of the serpent and of all that crawls on the ground; for it is impossible for us to become reconciled and united with God, if we do not first return to ourselves, as far as it lies in our power, or if we do not enter within ourselves, tearing ourselves — what a wonder it is! — from the whirl of the world with its multitudinous vain cares and striving constantly; to keep attention on the kingdom of heaven which is within us. Monastic life is called the art of arts and the science of sciences; for it does not bring perishable blessings akin to the things of this world, which drive the mind from what is best and engulf it; but monkhood promises us wonderful and unspeakable treasures which the 'Eye hath not seen, nor ear heard, neither have entered into the heart of man' (I Cor. ii. 9). Hence, 'we wrestle not against flesh and blood, but against principalities, against powers, against the rulers of the darkness of this world' (Ephes. vi. 12). If therefore present existence is but darkness, let us flee from it, let us flee by retuning our mind and our heart. Let us have nothing in common with the enemy of God, for 'whosoever ... will be a friend of the world is the enemy of God' (James iv. 4). And who can help the enemy of God? Therefore let us imitate our fathers and, like them, let us seek the treasure existing within I our hearts and, having found it, let us hold fast to it in doing⁹ and guarding — for which task we were destined from the beginning. But if some other Nicodemus appears and begins to argue, saying: 'How can anyone enter his own heart and do and dwell therein ?' — as that one said to the Lord: ' How can a man enter the second time into his mother's womb, and be born?', let such an one also hear: 'The wind blows where it will' (John iii. 4, 8). But if, even amidst the events of active life, we display such doubts through lack of faith, how can we enter into the mysteries of contemplative life? For ascent to contemplations is active life.

But it is impossible for such unbelievers to be convinced without written proofs; so, for the service of many, let us include in this discourse features of the lives of the saints and some of the ideas they have recorded to bear out this truth, so that all may be convinced, and cast away their last doubts. Let us begin with our first father, Antony the Great, and then, taking those who followed him in order, let us collect, as best we may, their deeds and words and offer them as evidence to unbelievers.

Writings from the *Philokalia* on Prayer of the Heart

12
The Beguines

Returning to the Western Tradition the fourteenth century reveals two spiritual movements which engage lay people. Most spiritual movements to this time have invariably found an enduring expression in forms of religious life. It was lay people responded to the call to the desert but it was not long before this charism was structured into a form of consecrated life by people like Pachomius. Monastic life was a form of vowed religious life. So too in the monastic movement in Europe under St Benedict, it became highly organized and structured. Similarly, the young man, St Francis of Assisi became the catalyst of a new form of religious life. Spiritual movements often begun by charismatic individuals found enduring expression in a form of clerical or religious life.

However, there were two spiritual movements in the Low Countries which witness to the pursuit of a way of spiritual life that was neither clerical nor monastic. Both of these movements have many of the elements that we find in other spiritual movements, but these movements sought to retain a lay character. The first of these is the Beguines; the second is *Devotio Moderna*. The Beguines are not well known and their history was short but they were a significant development in ways in which a spiritual impulse could be realised.

A way of life for women outside the cloister

In the late twelfth century women began to experiment with the possibility of a way of life outside the socially endorsed alternatives of wife or cloistered nun. The independence and authority of women in the late Middle Ages were severely limited. In monastic circles some women had commanded considerable authority, but in general society there was little opportunity. Women might engage in commercial life and manage their husbands' financial affairs, but there was a general acceptance of the notion that formal authority was inconsistent with femininity.

The two options presented to women of the nobility were marriage or the cloister; women of lower social classes might enter a trade, and possibly remain single. In France, Germany, and the Low Countries there were often more marriageable women than men. This was due to local wars, feuds, crusades, and the large number of celibate secular and regular clergy. Suitable marriages could not be arranged for all the daughters of the nobility, yet it was considered disreputable for these women to earn their own livelihood through labor of any sort.

Many women found the monastic reforms and the new mendicant orders very attractive. However opportunities were limited. Furthermore, whatever their original intent, monastic communities had become the preserve of the nobility and the rich. Europe was in transition from rural feudalism to a money economy centered in towns, and monastic communities demanded high entrance fees (dowries), despite repeated protests against this practice. In short, neither marriage nor cloister was attainable for many women.

Social conditions were ripe for a new idea. It was in this situation that the Beguine movement flourished, reaching its peak in the latter half of the thirteenth century. Beguines were not bound by vows, were not subject to papal enclosure, and their piety centered on the Eucharist and the humanity of Jesus. The origin of the term "Beguine" is a little uncertain.

In the latter part of the thirteenth century there was a good degree of religious ferment. Some of the religious groups which sprang up at about the same time as the Beguines were the Waldensians, Lollards, Brothers and Sisters of the Free Spirit, Spiritual Franciscans, Apostolici, Albigensians, Joachimites, and flagellants. If anything, these were protest movements and they became more apocalyptic and extreme as the century progressed.

The common thread running through these new religious groups, also present in monastic reform and the mendicant orders, was the appeal of the "vita apostolica"– the attraction of an evangelical spirit. "liberty" and "poverty" were watchwords. The *vita apostolica* was conceived of as a return to primitive Christianity, with zeal for souls, and a simple life in common.

The rise (and fall) of the Beguines

The Beguines were a spontaneous women's movement, not an adjunct to any male figure or group. There was no founder, no Rule, no constitution. Each Beguine community was autonomous; there was no one who supervised or regulated Beguine houses scattered throughout Northern Europe. They were engaged in a number of occupations in order to support themselves and were independent of each other and of the society around them. This spirit of independence tested their relationship with the Church.

The Beguine movement began in the diocese of Liège in modern day Belgium. Lambert le Begue, who was a priest of Liège, encouraged women who wished to "live religiously" to establish a way of life. The group of women with whom he was associated were later recognized as Beguines appearing between 1170 and 1175. The first prominent woman to be identified as a Beguine was Mary of Oignies (d. 1213).

Small communities of Beguine women began to develop as complex communities. The community came to be called a Beguinage. It was a city within a city. They were developed in the midst of towns. The Beguinage comprised of a church, cemetery, hospital, public square, and streets and walks lined with houses for the Beguine women. At the beginning of the fourteen century in the Great Beguinage at Ghent with its walls and moats were two churches, eighteen convents (for the younger members in formation), over a hundred houses, a brewery, and an infirmary.

This was an end point of a process which had begun very simply. Individual women lived as *conversae* (converts to the spiritual life) in their own or their parents' homes. At this point, they were not bound by vows, nor did they renounce property or abandon their trades. Gradually associations of such women developed. A grand mistress, along with a council of other mistresses, presided over the group. In time the Beguines acquired or built infirmaries, and settled near them. This was often a natural development as community members grew older, or poorer members needed care. Gradually other buildings were added to meet the needs of the community. Large Beguine communities were designated as parishes, and sometimes given the services of clergy.

However, clerical attitudes towards the Beguines were ambivalent. The women's dedication to chastity and charity was greatly admired, but their proximity to clerics or male monastics was regarded as dangerous for both parties. The Cistercians were willing to take charge of convents but not to provide pastoral care. The Dominicans were repeatedly warned against associating with Beguines and were reminded that their mission was the intellectual battle against heresy rather than pastoral work.

The Beguines never became an approved religious order. Their status in Rome fluctuated from time to time, but the tide turned against the Beguines in the fourteenth century. The Fourth Lateran Council prohibited the establishment of any new religious orders. Some Beguines were accused of heresy and executed. At different times bishops suppressed them in their diocese. For instance, in 1318 the Bishop of Cologne called for the dissolution of all Beguine associations and their integration into Orders approved by the Pope.

The Beguines rose and fell in the period of a century but they have endured in the Church. There was something of a revival in Belgium in the seventeenth century. In 1969, there were eleven Beguinages in Belgium and two in Holland.

Beguine Spirituality

The Beguines, like many of their contemporaries, were drawn by the ideal of the *vita apostolica*. The Beguines sought to live in simplicity. The movement attracted members from the wealthier classes who were drawn to voluntary poverty as well as many women from the emerging middle class. They did not obligate their members to poverty and manual labor was valued. Beguines sought the virtues of humility, apostolic poverty, and a willingness to serve the needy.

Another component of the *vita apostolica* was zeal for souls and the defeat of heresy. Mary of Oignies wholeheartedly supported the Crusade against the Albigensians, and the Beguines in Belgium were regarded as a bulwark against heresy.

The Beguines favoured the use of the vernacular in their prayers. National languages were emerging in Europe and Latin was unintelligible to the common people. Adherents of the *vita apostolica* therefore endeavored to provide devotional literature in a language that people could understand. Ecclesiastical officials feared that this played into the hands of heretics.

Many Beguines had a strong devotion to the Eucharist. They had a desire to receive Holy Communion weekly or even more frequently. It is no accident that the feast of Corpus Christi had its origins in the diocese of Liège. Juliana of Liège had an intense devotion to the Eucharist, and from 1208 until her death in 1258 tirelessly promoted the institution of a special feast to honor the Eucharist.

Beguine spirituality found mystical expression in the writings of St Mechthild of Magdeburg (1212-1282), Beatrice of Nazareth (1200-1268), Hadewijch of Brabant, and Marguerite Porete (d. 1310). Their works focus on the union between the individual soul and God.

St Mechthild and Marguerite employ the style of autobiography: a dialogue between the soul and God. Love is feminine in both Dutch and German, and Lady Love is also Divine Love. Thus under the name of "Minne" Beguine mystics had a powerful feminine metaphor for God. These authors wrote in the vernacular, and were the first to treat of spiritual matters in these emerging languages – Middle Low German for St Mechthild, Middle Dutch for Beatrice, Flemish for Hadewijch, and Old French for Marguerite. Their works are regarded as literary masterpieces. The Beguine authors borrowed the style and imagery of courtly love and used them to describe the soul's relation to God.

The Beguines demonstrated that it was possible for a woman to be dedicated to God without necessarily retiring to a cloister. They combined manual labour, community life, works of service along with the pursuit of a life consecrated to God in the midst of the world.

On the poems of Hadewijch

To sing of Love is pleasant in every season,
Be it autumn, winter, spring, or summer,
And to plead our case against her power,
For no courageous man keeps out of her way.
But we lazy ones often say in anxiety:
„What, would she tyrannize thus over me?
I had rather share the lot of those
Who manage to secure quiet,
And remain at home! Why should I
Sally forth to meet my doom?"
    Ignoble persons of small perception
Fear the cost will be too high:
Therefore they withdraw from Love,
From whom all good would have come to them.
If they withdraw from Love's service,
They will be the conquerors, so they think.
But fidelity will show they are poor and make them known as they are,
All naked before Love's magnificence;"These are they who consumed everything they had,
But without coercion from Loce.
    He who would gladly suffer sweet exile
(The roads to the land of high Love)
Would find his beloved and his country at the end;
Of this, Fidelity gives seal and pledge,
Many a yokel, however, is such a beggar
That he takes what lies nearest his hand,
Remaining before Love unknown
With his beggar's garment;
So he has not the form or badge of honour
By which Love recognizes what is hers.
    A fine exterior, fine garments,
And fine language adorn the knight:

*To suffer everything for Love without turning hostile
Is a fine exterior for him who has such ability;
His garments then are his acts,
Performed with new ardour, not with self-complacency,
And with regard for all the needs of strangers
Rather than of his own friends:
This is the coloured apparel, best adorned with blazons of nobility, to
the honour of high Love.*

From the poem, Knight of Love

13
Devotio Moderna

The religious landscape of the medieval period was dominated by the monks of the Benedictine Order, or by one of its reform orders: the Cluniacs or the Cistercians. The devout lay person had little avenue for spiritual advancement. However as feudalism waned a new middle class emerged in the growing cities. Lay people in these urban settings sought new forms of spiritual life. A key element in this was a thirst for interior prayer. The *Devotio Moderna* movement met this need.

Geert de Groote

Geert de Groote was born in 1340 at Deventer, Gelderland (modern Holland). From the chapter school in his native town he went for higher studies first to Aachen, then to Paris, where at the Sorbonne he studied medicine, theology, and canon law. He returned home, barely eighteen years old. In 1362 he was appointed teacher at the Deventer chapter school. Later in Cologne he taught philosophy and theology.

A fellow-student at the Sorbonne and prior of the Chartreuse of Munnikhuizen, Henry Aeger of Calcar, challenged him about the vanity of his life. Geert responded and entered seriously upon the practice of a devout life. At this time he also frequently visited the famous ascetic Ruysbroek. He withdrew to the monastery of Munnikhuizen where he spent three years. From this time at the monastery he returned to urban life filled with an apostolic zeal. He was ordained a deacon and given licence to preach in the Diocese of Utrecht.

He attracted many by his preaching on Christian piety. He attacked vice fearlessly which developed considerable opposition and resulted in the withdrawal of his licence to preach. He submitted to the authority of the Bishop but applied to the Pope for redress.

While he emphasised the possibility of a strong Christian life lived in the world, at Zwolle he formed a company of the "Brethren of the Common Life". Communities inspired by his preaching spread rapidly through the Netherlands, Lower Germany, and Westphalia and he devoted his attention to them. Clerics who became associated with him formed a community of Canons Regular based at Windesheim. Before the answer to his petition to the Pope arrived Geert de Groote died from the plague which he contracted while ministering to the sick.

Devotio Moderna

Around 1430 the prior of the Augustinian house at Windesheim wrote a treatise, *On the rise of the new devotion in our Land*, seeking to describe this new spiritual movement among lay people. Hence the name given to the people associated with this movements was the "New Devout" and the movement itself became known as *Devotio Moderna*.

Despite the development of communities of consecrated members, the movement was largely among lay people continuing to live in the world. These New Devout lived a life of ordered prayer and work. They lived in their own homes, while some chose to live in common. They sought to live simply and attended their local parish churches for the sacraments. They affirmed loyalty to the Church and its teachings. Theirs was a simple spirituality of living in humility and love and seeking the pursuit of the virtues.

Collations, or sermons, were given by their own members at Sunday afternoon meetings. These meetings were opened to others. There was a practice of fraternal correction done in a spirit of brotherhood and humility. In the case of those living common life, the households of brothers or sisters were small and poor. Households of women were self-governing.

Like the Beguines the women worked to support the house principally in the textile industry. Houses of women developed first and were more numerous than those of the men. By 1460 there were thirty four houses of women in the Netherlands and another one hundred in North West Germany while only some twenty houses of men. Households tended to have around fifteen members. The Windesheim Congregation of Canons Regular grew to have some eighty four houses. A parallel movement among women led to the establishing of some thirteen houses of canonesses.

These households were houses rather than monasteries or convents. They were built in cities often close to the parish church. Thus the movement which was firstly among people living in the world, involved communities of common life and clerics living as Canons Regular. Thus all states of life were part of this movement. In a way they were a forerunner to what are now called "ecclesial movements".

The spirituality of the New Devout

Fundamentally *Devotio Moderna* was a movement of spiritual renewal. The focus was clearly directed towards Christ and promoted the notion of "living in Christ". The New Devout were encouraged to read the Gospels regularly. Emphasis was placed upon progress in the virtues. Their spirituality was moralistic rather than speculative. One important work that promoted the movement was Gerard Zerbolt's *The Spiritual Ascents*. He speaks of the three steps that will sustain and advance the spiritual ascent: reading, meditation and prayer.[82] Speaking of meditation he says,

Meditation is the means by which you studiously turn over in your heart what you have read or heard and thereby stir up your affections or illuminate your intellect. Therefore as you ascend and advance in hope, frequently reflect in your heart upon those things which aid your progress in purity, instil fear, or increase love.[83]

The book which best captures the spirit of the movement and was to become a Christian classic is *The Imitation of Christ*. Written by Thomas a Kempis from Windesheim (c. 1420) it has become

---
82 See *Spiritual Ascents*, chapter 43.
83 Ibid Chapter 45.

the most popular spiritual writing after the Bible. The *Imitation* emphasises the reform of the moral life and this can be summarised in the key terms of *Conversio*, conversion; *Resolutio*, a decision to live a new life; *Exercituum*, daily spiritual training in the practice of the virtues; *Profectus virtutem*, making progress in virtuous living; *Caritas*, the goal of Christian love; *Humilitas*, the fostering of the virtue of humility; and *Obedientia*, the conforming of the will to Christ.

The title of the book is taken from its opening words. In fact it is a composite of four separate treatises. Book 1 reflects on the separation from the world necessary to follow Christ, particularly a separation from secular learning and thinking. This is to be replaced by a humble desire to know God. The author lists those qualities necessary for spiritual advancement: "an utter disregard of the world, a fervent desire for progress in virtue, a love of discipline, the practice of penitence, readiness to obey, denial of self, and acceptance of any adversity for the love of Christ".[84] The second book concentrates upon the fostering of a closer union with Christ. Book 3 is about spiritual comfort and there is a focus upon the love of Christ for us. Book 4 deals with the reception of Holy Communion.

The *Imitation of Christ* is a handbook of practical ascetic devotion. It is a book that appeals to lay people, the religious in conventual life and the cleric striving for holiness as he goes about his pastoral ministry. It is and remains a great spiritual classic.

On Imitating Christ

Imitating Christ and despising all vanities on earth

He who follows Me, walks not in darkness," says the Lord. By these words of Christ we are advised to imitate His life and habits, if we wish to be truly enlightened and free from all blindness of heart. Let our chief effort, therefore, be to study the life of Jesus Christ.

The teaching of Christ is more excellent than all the advice of the saints, and he who has His spirit will find in it a hidden manna. Now, there are many who hear the Gospel often but care little for it because they have not the spirit of Christ. Yet whoever wishes to understand fully the

---

[84] See *Imitation of Christ*, chapter 23.

words of Christ must try to pattern his whole life on that of Christ.

What good does it do to speak learnedly about the Trinity if, lacking humility, you displease the Trinity? Indeed it is not learning that makes a man holy and just, but a virtuous life makes him pleasing to God. I would rather feel contrition than know how to define it. For what would it profit us to know the whole Bible by heart and the principles of all the philosophers if we live without grace and the love of God? Vanity of vanities and all is vanity, except to love God and serve Him alone.

This is the greatest wisdom – to seek the kingdom of heaven through contempt of the world. It is vanity, therefore, to seek and trust in riches that perish. It is vanity also to court honour and to be puffed up with pride. It is vanity to follow the lusts of the body and to desire things for which severe punishment later must come. It is vanity to wish for long life and to care little about a well-spent life. It is vanity to be concerned with the present only and not to make provision for things to come. It is vanity to love what passes quickly and not to look ahead where eternal joy abides.

Often recall the proverb: "The eye is not satisfied with seeing nor the ear filled with hearing." Try, moreover, to turn your heart from the love of things visible and bring yourself to things invisible. For they who follow their own evil passions stain their consciences and lose the grace of God.

Having a humble opinion of self
Every man naturally desires knowledge; but what good is knowledge without fear of God? Indeed a humble rustic who serves God is better than a proud intellectual who neglects his soul to study the course of the stars. He who knows himself well becomes mean in his own eyes and is not happy when praised by men.

If I knew all things in the world and had not charity, what would it profit me before God Who will judge me by my deeds?

Shun too great a desire for knowledge, for in it there is much fretting and delusion. Intellectuals like to appear learned and to be called wise. Yet there are many things the knowledge of which does little or no good to the soul, and he who concerns himself about other things than those which lead to salvation is very unwise.

Many words do not satisfy the soul; but a good life eases the mind and a clean conscience inspires great trust in God. The more you know and the better you understand, the more severely will you be judged, unless your life is also the more holy. Do not be proud, therefore, because of your learning or skill. Rather, fear because of the talent given you. If you think you know many things and understand them well enough, realize *at the same time that there is much you do not know. Hence, do not affect wisdom, but admit your ignorance. Why prefer yourself to anyone else when many are more learned, more cultured than you?*

If you wish to learn and appreciate something worthwhile, then love to be unknown and considered as nothing. Truly to know and despise self is the best and most perfect counsel. To think of oneself as nothing, and always to think well and highly of others is the best and most perfect wisdom. Wherefore, if you see another sin openly or commit a serious crime, do not consider yourself better, for you do not know how long you can remain in good estate. All men are frail, but you must admit that none is more frail than yourself.

Imitation of Christ, Book 1, Chapters 1 and 2.

14
The English Mystics

The fourteenth century was one of particular spiritual vitality. While the Beguines were finding a way of life dedicated to prayer and good works and the Devotio Moderna movement in Holland was inspiring lay people to a deeper spiritual life, there was the emergence of a number of mystics on the Continent and in England. These mystics have left us with a collection of spiritual writings of high calibre.

Mystics have been a presence within the spiritual tradition. There was a flowering of mysticism in fourteenth century in the northern part of Europe. The presence of mystics, often emerging amidst trying times, is one of the mysteries of the action of the Holy Spirit. When the spiritual landscape seems barren particular graces are given to individuals. They become beacons of light in a gray environment. Mystics walk an individual and profoundly personal path. They often appeared in the least expected places. Their lives can be quite hidden, and it is often only with the publishing of their writings that they become known. There are countless mystics in the Church who are known only to God. Those who have become known and whose writings are an inspiration to many offer a gift to the Church. They are witnesses to the mysterious actions of grace in the soul of one who is drawn to seek the depths of God. The mystics would be the first to acknowledge that they are the recipients of grace. Whether the grace is meant principally for them – searching souls – or whether their experiences are intended by God to be a light for others' paths is not always clear. Mystics and their writings are part of the spiritual heritage of the Church. They are a sign of the intense action of God in the souls of those who earnestly seek him.

For the institutional Church the thirteenth century had been something of a golden age. The mendicant orders brought a fresh impetus to the evangelical witness of the Church. The papacy under the gifted Pope Innocent III gained new levels of prestige and independence from secular rulers. It was the age of building the great cathedrals of Europe, like Chartres, Reims and Amiens in France. It was the age of the growth of universities, the rediscovery of the writings of Aristotle and the production of scholastic theology under St Thomas Aquinas. As is often the case, times of achievement can be followed by times of disintegration. This was the story for the Church in the century that followed. It saw the capture of Pope Boniface VIII and the eventual transfer of the papacy to Avignon in France.

England in the fourteenth century experienced social dislocation and much misery. There was an extended period of war against France resulting in the impoverishment of the country. It was the time of the Black Death. There was social discontent ending with the peasant uprising of 1381. There were serious attacks on Catholic beliefs and practices by people like JohnWyclife (an Oxford trained theologian who attacked doctrines like the Real Presence of Christ in the Eucharist) and the Lollard movement that continued his ideas. These were some of the forerunners to the reformation issues.

This century marked the end of the medieval period. New ways of thinking began to emerge like the philosophy of William of Ockham. There was a retreat from metaphysics and an abandoning of the attempt to unite philosophy and theology. There were the beginnings of an individualistic rather than a corporate personal self-understanding.

The religious atmosphere was influenced chiefly by the Cistercians. There were some influences that prepared the way for the mystics. St Aelred of Rievaulx wrote a treatise which was to have a considerable influence: *A Rule of Life for a Recluse*. The Carthusians enjoyed considerable expansion during this period and possibly inspired many in the pursuit of the solitary life. This was also the time when vernacular writing was developed. It was the age of William Chaucer. The mystics had recourse to the use of English rather than Latin to express their experiences. This assisted in the dissemination of their writings among the devout lay people in the Church.

There are several key figures in this rather attractive growth of the spirituality of Catholic England before the old faith would be tested and changed by the Reformation.

Richard Rolle of Hampole

After finishing studies in Oxford Richard Rolle withdrew to live a solitary life. He was established by a local landowner, John de Dalton, on his property and lived as a solitary for the next thirty years. He died in 1349 possibly of the Black Death. His major work was written in Latin, *Incendium Amoris* known in English as *Fire of Love*. He wrote other works including *The Mending of Life*, and *The Song of Love on the Blessed Virgin*, as well as various scriptural commentaries.

His was a simple faith which focussed on the desire to follow Jesus. It is captured in these words from the *Fire of Love*: "From this time forth I have sought to love Jesus and the more I have advanced in His love, the sweeter and more pleasant has the Name of Jesus tasted to me. Therefore blessed be the name of Jesus, forever and ever, Amen".

In this work he sought to educate the devout among the laity in the spiritual life. His mystical experiences were simple. The basis of his spiritual teaching was a personal mystical experience that he had after some four years living as a solitary. He describes this experience as a fire within. It occurred once while meditating in a chapel. He recognises the contemplative experience as a grace, and describes it as "fire, song and sweetness". His writing is inspired by his personal experiences. There is a warm and affective relationship with Jesus reflected in his works. He had little training himself, nor an extensive knowledge of mystical writings. His writings are more descriptive than analytical. His teaching is thoroughly sound and orthodox.

A group of disciples formed around him mainly consisting in people he directed in the spiritual life. Upon his death efforts were made to have him canonised without success. His influence continued over some two centuries after his death.

Walter Hilton

Walter Hilton was an Augustinian Canon. He died in 1396. He practiced both civil and canon law before he became a priest. He was probably educated at Cambridge. He wrote *Scale of Perfection* as a book of guidance for those seeking to grow in the spiritual life. It takes the form of a summa: a practical analysis of the devout life and an ascetical preparation for spiritual perfection. The *Scale* is considered the first major treatise on spirituality in the English language. He needed to translate a good deal of the Scriptures himself and use English equivalents for Latin and Greek technical words.

The book seems written for an anchorite living in a village or for an educated layman. He uses the traditional notion for describing the spiritual life as a ladder[85] and expounds the concepts of the purgative, illuminative and unitive states of prayer. He describes growth in prayer as moving from rational knowledge of the truth with an emphasis on the humanity of Christ to the stage of affective devotion and then to the contemplative unity of knowledge and love.

The *Scale* has two distinct parts. It is a work in ascetical and mystical theology. The first book focuses upon "reform of faith", that is, the ridding of the vices. The second book focuses on the "reform of feeling", that is, growth in mystical experience which requires recollection and self-knowledge. Hilton teaches about going beyond a reliance on experiences (a possible reference to Rolle's affectivity). He says the goal of prayer is "great rest and quietness of body and soul". In the second book he deals with the purgative "nights". His sources were Augustinian rather than the Scholastic approach of Aquinas.

He describes contemplative prayer in terms of the action of the Holy Spirit, grace and infused love. For Hilton contemplation is essentially an intensification of the life of inner devotion. His descriptions indicate that he reached the heights of contemplation, though not full union (something we will investigate in a later

---

85 As we saw this was the image used by St John Climacus.

chapter).

Like the work of Richard Rolle, a notable feature of his writing is its human warmth. It contains an evangelical piety centring upon the use of the name of Jesus: "Who will help you break down this image of sin? Truly you Lord Jesus. By virtue of him and in his name, you will break down this image of sin. Diligently pray to him and desire it, and he will help you".

The Cloud of Unknowing

This work is by an unknown author. Other works by the same author may include: *Book of Privy Counsel*, *Epistle on Prayer*, *The Epistle of Discretion*. The date of the work is also unknown, though the author knew Rolle's work and Walter Hilton knew of the *Cloud*, so it was possibly written between 1345 and 1386. The location of the author is probably East Midland. The author is most possibly a monk or a priest, because there is evidence of theological understanding; he is well read, and a solitary.

The *Cloud* is addressed to a young man of twenty four who is beginning to live a solitary life. The author reveals himself to be wise, confident and a forceful counsellor. He has a single message which is both traditional and yet profoundly his own. It is clearly based in solid personal experience. He knows of Richard and Hugh of St Victor, St Augustine and St Gregory, the Carthusian Guigo II and has the Pseudo-Dionysius[86] as a major source. He may have been influenced by the Rhineland mystics, especially the Dominican Tauler.

The distinguished English writer on mysticism, Evelyn Underhill describes his particular quality as:

What, then, were his special characteristics? Whence came

---

[86] Pseudo-Dionysius the Areopagite, also known as Pseudo-Denys, was a Christian theologian and philosopher of the late 5th to early 6th century, the author of the *Corpus Areopagiticum* . The author is identified as "Dionysos" in the corpus, which later came to be attributed to Dionysius the Areopagite, the Athenian convert of St Paul mentioned in Acts 17:34. His surviving works include *Divine Names, Mystical Theology, Celestial Hierarchy, Ecclesiastical Hierarchy*, and various epistles. His works are mystical and show strong Neoplatonic influence.

the fresh colour which he gave to the old Platonic theory of mystical experience? First, I think, from the combination of high spiritual gifts with a vivid sense of humour, keen powers of observation, a robust common-sense: a balance of qualities not indeed rare amongst the mystics, but here presented to us in an extreme form. In his eager gazing on divinity this contemplative never loses touch with humanity, never forgets the sovereign purpose of his writings; which is not a declaration of the spiritual favours he has received, but a helping of his fellow-men to share them.[87]

The author of the *Cloud* has an abiding concept – that a total abandonment to God in naked faith is required for contemplative progress. There can be nothing for the affections and nothing for the intellect. This central teaching is expressed in Chapter 4 as:

> He cannot be comprehended by our intellect or any man's - or any angel's for that matter. For both we and they are created beings. But only to our intellect is he incomprehensible: not to our love.

The way he proposes requires an asceticism of full dedication to prayer which is based in an act of love as an exercise of the will. He simply sees that there exists a "cloud of unknowing" between the believer and God:

> When you first begin, you find only darkness, and, as it were, a cloud of unknowing. You don't know what this means except that in your will you feel a simple, steadfast intention of reaching out to God. Do what you will, this darkness and this cloud remain between you and God, and stop you from seeing him in the clear light of rational understanding, and from experiencing his loving sweetness in your affection[88]

In taking this approach the author describes the transition from an "active" contemplation to a state of quiet. The reasoning and imaginative faculties are to be stilled. He considers that contemplation is the normal way to growth in perfection. He sees that all natural

---

87 The spiritual writer, Evelyn Underhill (1875-1941), produced an edition of the *Cloud* in 1912 which contains an excellent introduction from which this quote is taken.
88 See Chapter 3.

activities are suspended in order to be exposed to a pure supernatural mode of action. The way of darkness is the necessary way to come to a contemplative experience. He himself does witness to raptures and ecstatic experiences. He warns against trusting in feelings and experiences of heat, or sweetness, an obvious reference to the approach of Richard Rolle.

Julian of Norwich

In the year 1373, the Third Sunday after Easter fell on the eighth day of May. In the early morning hours of that day, a thirty-year-old woman lay on her death bed somewhere in Norwich, England. Two days before she had received the Last Rites of the Church and now it was plain that she was at the point of death. Her parish curate was sent for and he came with his acolyte carrying a crucifix. The feeling was gone from her waist down, and her sight began to fail as the room grew dark.

We do not know the baptismal name of that woman as she lay on her death bed. We do not know the name of her family or the name of her priest. What we do know that during the next eleven hours she was granted a series of fifteen visions which opened to her mystical depths of understanding about God, the Holy Trinity, the Crucified Lord, and the life of Christians. Her full recovery was almost immediate and the following evening, she was granted one final vision. She soon wrote down an account of these visions (or "showings" as she called them) and before long she had made the decision to give her whole life to meditation, prayer, and service.

She became an anchoress – hermitess – and lived the rest of her life in a small cell (or anchorhold) attached to the southeast corner of the little parish church of St Julian in Norwich. As was the custom for an anchoress of the time, she assumed the name of the patron saint of the parish church, and so became known as that great figure of late medieval mysticism: Dame Julian of Norwich.

Prior to her illness Julian had been a very devout woman, possibly living at home. She tells us in the beginning of her testament, *Revelations of Divine Love*, that she had asked for three favours from

God: "bodily sight" of the passion of Christ, that is, a desire to share in his sufferings; "of God's giving" a bodily sickness, for the sake of purification: and the three "wounds" of sorrow for sin, suffering with Christ, longing for God. It is clear her prayer was answered.

Her book presents spiritual instruction. Its title suggests its theme: *Revelations of Divine Love*. She says that she is unlettered but the book is a masterpiece of the English language. The theology of the book is sound, suggesting authentic experience. Her work is profound and sober. She describes how the revelations that she experienced in her illness were ultimately revelations of the love of God.

And from the time that [the vision] was shown, I desired often to know what our Lord's meaning was. And fifteen years and more afterward I was answered in my spiritual understanding, thus: 'Would you know your Lord's meaning in this thing? Know it well, love was his meaning. Who showed it to you? Love. What did he show you? Love. Why did he show it? For love. Keep yourself therein and you shall know and understand more in the same. But you shall never know nor understand any other thing, forever.'[89]

Revelations of Divine Love begins with a summary of the revelations, giving information about the circumstances surrounding them.

Julian can be regarded as one of the great mystics of the Middle Ages. She has a homely yet deep spirituality. One notable feature in her writings - remembering that she lived in the troubled times - is a great confidence in God. Her overriding awareness was of the love of God. A statement in the book is often quoted: "All will be well, all manner of things will be well".

---

[89] See *Revelations* Chapter 86.

To Continental Europe

These mystics reveal the vitality of the Catholic faith in England. In fact the Church was reasonably healthy during this period. However the Reformation in Continental Europe would boil over into England. This would produce a bloody period that gave rise to many martyrs for the faith. At a later time Anglicanism produced some spiritual movements coming from its post Reformation character. Later the Oxford Movement resulted in the rekindling of Catholic spirituality. The beatification of John Henry Newman in a way "canonises" the English spiritual school.

This period marks the movement from Medieval Europe to modern times. Spiritual movements take on particular characteristics associated with the national spirit of the country of origin.

On the different types of prayer

What prayer is

Prayer is profitable and speedful to be used for the getting of purity of heart by destroying of sin and bringing in virtues; not that thou shouldst thereby make our Lord know what thou desirest, for He knoweth well enough what thou needest, but to dispose thee and make thee ready and able thereby, as a clean vessel, to receive the grace which our Lord would freely give thee, which grace cannot be felt till thou be exercised and purified by the fire of desire in devout prayer. For though it be so that prayer is not the cause for which our Lord giveth grace, nevertheless it is a way or means by which grace freely given cometh into a soul.

How we should pray

But now thou wilt desire perhaps to know how thou shouldst pray and upon what thing thou shouldst set the point of thy thoughts in prayer, and also what prayer was best for thee to use. As to the first, I answer that when thou art wakened out of thy sleep, and art ready to pray, thou shalt feel thyself fleshly and heavy, tending ever downwards to vain thoughts, either of dreams or fancies, or of unnecessary things of the world or of the flesh, then behoveth it thee to quicken thy heart by prayer, and stir it up as much as thou canst to some devotion. In thy prayer set not thy heart on any bodily thing, but all thy care shall be to draw in thy thoughts from beholding any bodily thing, that thy desire may be as it were naked and bare from all earthly things, ever aspiring upward to Jesus Christ, whom yet thou canst never see bodily as He is in His Godhead,

nor frame any image or likeness of Him in thy imagination; but thou mayest, through devout and continual beholding of the humility of His precious humanity, feel the goodness and the grace of His Godhead. When thy desire and mind is gotten up, and as it were set free from all fleshly thoughts and affections, and is much lifted up by spiritual power unto spiritual favour and delight in Him and of His spiritual presence; hold thou therein much of thy time of prayer, so that thou have no great mind of earthly things, or if they come into thy mind that they do but trouble or affect thee little. If thou canst pray thus, thou prayest well, for prayer is nothing else but an ascending or getting up of the desire of the heart into God by withdrawing of it from all earthly thoughts. Therefore it is likened to a fire which, of its own nature, leaveth the lowness of the earth and always mounteth up into the air, even so desire in prayer, when it is touched and kindled of the spiritual fire, which is God, is ever aspiring up to Him that it came from.

What the fire of love in prayer is

They that speak of this fire of love know not well what it is; save this I can tell that it is neither any bodily thing nor felt by any sense of the body. A soul may feel it in prayer or in devotion, which soul is in the body, but it feeleth it not by any bodily sense; for though it is true that it works in and upon the soul, that the body itself is turned thereby into a heat and be as it were chafed through the labour and travail of the spirit, nevertheless the fire of love is not bodily, for it is only in the spiritual desire of the soul. And this is no riddle to any man or woman that have had the experience of devotion; but because some are so simple as to imagine that because it is called a fire that therefore it should be hot as bodily fire is, therefore have I set down thus much.

Walter Hilton, Scale of Perfection, Second Part, Chapter 1

15
The Rhineland Mystics

Mysticism flourished in the Rhineland region in the thirteenth and fourteenth centuries. The four significant figures, usually referred to as the Rhineland mystics, were: Meister Johann Eckhart, John Tauler, Blessed Henry Suso and Jan van Ruusbroec. They predate the emergence of mysticism in England and were influenced particularly by Dominican spirituality. Their works were subtle and became subject to serious reservation by the Church and yet they carried a profound mystical experience and insight. Their mysticism has been called a "mysticism of being", that is, a transformation of what it is to be human by a direct sharing in the life of God. It is a far more profound mysticism than that expressed in England. It marks a crowning of this mystical surge in this period of the Church, and their influence would be far more extensive than the English experience which was largely limited to the English speaking Church.

At this stage in the history of Catholic spirituality we can begin to speak of "schools" of spirituality – the Rhineland school, then later the sixteenth century Spanish and then the seventeenth century French schools. Each of these schools has its distinctive characteristics. Each in its own right has made a significant contribution to the spiritual tradition of the Church.

Mysticism has to do in the end with the experience of God. The mystic tries to express what he or she has experienced as the presence of God becoming an immediate reality to them. Their cultural and educational backgrounds will flavour the style of description.

The Rhineland mystics are described as *Wesenkystik* – a mysticism of essence. The Dominican mystics whom we will consider shortly were theologically trained in scholasticism. It was the age when the great work of St Thomas Aquinas shaped theological thought.

There was another stream of mysticism which found expression in the lives of a number of remarkable women religious. These German women mystics of the same period (St Elisabeth of Schonau, St Mechtilde von Magdeburg, St Gertrude the Great, Hadewich) had their own – particularly feminine – religious experience and it is commonly described as *Brautmystik*, or nuptial mysticism. If we could crudely differentiate we would say that the men where mystics of the mind, and the women mystics of the heart.

We will consider the four men commonly called the Rhineland mystics.

Meister Johann Eckhart

Eckhart was a Dominican preacher, recognised as a theologian and a mystic. He was born about 1260 and died in 1327 at Cologne. He was prior of the Dominican convent at Erfurt and vicar-provincial of Thuringia. He exercised a number of key roles in the administration of the Order.

As a preacher Eckhart disdained rhetorical flourish but employed a simple oratory. Using pure language and a simple style he presented short catecheses. His preaching was directed to the intellect rather than to the will and was remarkable for the depth of mystical teaching it contained. Eckhart taught on the nature of the Divine essence as a way of exploring the nature of the relationship between God and man. He explored the faculties, gifts, and operations of the human soul. Eckhart was a philosopher, a theologian, and a mystic. He is considered by many as the greatest of the German mystics and the father of German mysticism.

The very nature of Eckhart's subjects and the lack of technicality of his language led to him being misinterpreted. He was considered by some as being pantheistic.[90] He came under suspicion and was investigated. He repudiated the unorthodox sense in which some of his utterances could be interpreted, retracted all possible errors, and

---

90 Eckhart stressed the unity of God and the capacity of the individual to become one with God during life. Statements like "God is infinite in his simplicity and simple in his infinity. Therefore he is everywhere and is everywhere complete. God is in the innermost part of each and every thing" opened him to the charge that he identified God with creation. However his teaching stressed a separation of the self from God.

submitted to the Holy See. However, his writings continue to evoke suspicion.

John Tauler

Tauler was a German Dominican. He was associated with Eckhart. Tauler was not as speculative as his teacher Eckhart but he was clearer, more practical, and more adapted to the common people. The focus of Tauler's mysticism was the doctrine of the *visio essentiæ Dei*, the contemplation or knowledge of the Divine nature. He took this doctrine from Thomas Aquinas, but went further than the latter in believing that the Divine knowledge is attainable in this world. He taught that God dwells within each human being and that the way to God was through love.

Blessed Henry Suso

Blessed Henry Suso, who was also called *Amandus*, a name adopted in his writings, was born at Constance in or about 1295 and died in 1366. He was declared blessed in 1831. At thirteen years of age he entered the Dominican convent at Constance, where he made his preparatory, philosophical, and theological studies. He did further studies in theology in Cologne, where he sat at the feet of Johann Eckhart, "the Master", and probably at the side of Tauler.

Suso's life as a mystic began at the age of eighteen and he chose to make himself "the Servant of the Eternal Wisdom". This Wisdom he identified as the Divine essence. Henceforth a burning love for the Eternal Wisdom dominated his thoughts. He had frequent visions and ecstasies, practised severe austerities (which he prudently moderated in his mature years), and endured personal sufferings with patience.

He became foremost among a group called the "Friends of God" in the work of restoring religious observance in the cloisters. His influence was especially strong in many convents of women. He was esteemed as a preacher. His apostolate, however, was not with the masses, but rather with individuals who were drawn to him by his engaging personality. He became the spiritual director to many of his followers.

Suso published several books. They were practical and show that his intention was to communicate with "simple men who still have imperfections to be put off". His works have been described as the "most beautiful fruit of German mysticism". In the second half of the fourteenth and in the fifteenth century they were the most widely read spiritual books in the German language. The mutual love of God and man which is his principle theme gives warmth and colour to his style. He contributed much to the formation of German prose, especially by giving new shades of meaning to words employed to describe inner sensations.

Jan van Ruusbroec (or Ruysbroeck)

Jan Ruusbroec, surnamed the Admirable Doctor, and the Divine Doctor, was born at Ruysbroeck, near Brussels in 1293 and he died in 1381. At the age of eleven he placed himself under the guidance and tuition of his uncle, a saintly priest and a canon of St Gudule's, Brussels. This uncle provided for Ruysbroeck's education with a view to the priesthood. He was ordained in 1317. For twenty-six years Ruysbroeck led a life of extreme austerity and retirement. He wrote a pamphlet against the Brethren of the Free Spirit who were causing considerable trouble in the Netherlands. The hermitage where he lived attracted disciples and became established as a community of canons regular.

He became known widely as a man of God, a contemplative and a skilled director of souls. People came to him to seek his aid and counsel. His writings were eagerly sought. He influenced Geerte Groote and so helped mould the spirit of the Windesheim community, which in the next generation found its most famous exponent in Thomas a Kempis.

Of the various treatises preserved, the best-known and the most characteristic is that entitled *The Spiritual Espousals*. It is divided into three books, treating respectively of the active, the interior, and the contemplative life. Ruysbroeck wrote as the spirit moved him. He wandered and meditated in the solitude of the forest adjoining the cloister and would write down his thoughts as he was inspired.

The flame flickers

After Ruysbroeck the flame of mysticism in continental Europe seems to flicker. Although his spiritual legacy would find expression in the *Devotio Moderna* movement, his own influence was limited. Perhaps because he wrote in a minority language he was not readily accessible. It would be Thomas a Kempis who would become the popular spiritual writer and his work would become a spiritual classic.

With the passing of Ruysbroeck the mystical stream of spirituality quietened. Many regard him as the mystic's mystic. It is the case that after an apex is reached things rapidly taper away. However, the Church has been enriched and the legacy of the mystical flowering would lay the foundations for later spiritual movements.

After this excursion into the mystical flowerings we will now move to explore a spiritual strand which would provide a sound basis for the spiritual growth of countless thousands of devout religious and many lay people who sought a path to the interior life. It is the development of what has been variously called "mental prayer" or simply "meditation".

On going out to meet the bridegroom

The inner lover of God, who possesses God in enjoyable rest, and himself in devoted, working love, and his entire life in virtues with justice, this inner person then comes, by means of these three points and the hidden revelation of God, into a God contemplating life, at least the lover who is pious and just, whom God in His freedom wishes to choose and to elevate to a superessential contemplation in divine light and according to the way of God.

This contemplation establishes us in purity and in limpidity above all our understanding, for it is a special enrichment and a heavenly crown, and in addition, an eternal reward for all virtues and for all lives. And no one can arrive at this by means of science or subtlety, nor by any practice, but only he whom God wishes to unite with His Spirit and to illumine with Himself may contemplate God, and nobody else. The hidden divine nature is eternally active, contemplating and loving with respect to each person, and always enjoying the embrace with each person, in unity of essence.

In this embrace, in the essential unity of God, are all inner spirits one with God in loving transport, and they are the selfsame one that the essence itself is in itself. And in this sublime unity of the divine nature, the heavenly Father is the origin and the beginning of every work that is done in heaven and on earth. And He says in the immersed hiddenness of the spirit.

We are now going to explain and clarify these words with respect to the superessential contemplation which is the ground of all holiness and of all the life that one can live.

Warning

Few can arrive at this divine contemplation on account of their own incapacity and the hiddenness of the light in which one contemplates. And therefore, no one will really thoroughly understand these remarks by means of any study or subtle consideration of one's own. For all the words and everything that one can learn and understand in a creaturely fashion is alien to, and far beneath, the truth that I have in mind. But he who is united with God and enlightened in this truth can understand the truth by the truth itself. For to comprehend and to understand God, above all similitudes, as He is in Himself means to be God with God, without intermediary or any otherness which can create a hindrance or a mediation. And therefore I desire that each one who neither understands nor feels this in the enjoyable unity of his spirit not to be scandalised and to leave things as they are. For what I wish to say is true, and Christ, the eternal truth, said it Himself in His teaching in many a passage, if only we could reveal it and tell it well.

And therefore if anyone is to understand this, he must be dead to himself and live in God and turn his countenance towards the eternal light in the ground of his spirit, where the hidden truth reveals itself without intermediary.

For the heavenly Father wishes us to be seeing, for He is the Father of light. And therefore, without intermediary and without cease, He speaks eternally in the hiddenness of our spirit a single fathomless word and nothing more. And in this word, He utters Himself and all things. And this word is nothing other than « See » ; and this is the going-out and the birth of the Son of eternal light, in whom one knows and sees all blessedness.

Ruusbroec, The Spiritual Espousals, Book 3, the Third Life (the contemplative life)

16
St Ignatius Loyola – Mental Prayer

We leave the mystics now to consider another tradition of interior prayer which became the recommended approach to interior prayer for the past four hundred years. Those who desire to develop an interior life often look for appropriate practices of prayer. The emergence of practices of mental prayer reflects this searching for a form of prayer that can sustain the spiritual life on a day-to-day basis. The figure to whom the Church owes most in this area is the founder of the Jesuit Order, St Ignatius Loyola.

To appreciate how far reaching the role of mental prayer was in the life of religious, priests and many devout lay people, it is worth considering what Canon Law lays down as the requirements for the spiritual life of priests. In the section of Canon Law where the Church exhorts her priests to a life of holiness, she identifies the means to sanctity, one of which is mental prayer. It is worth quoting in full:

Can. 276 §1 Clerics have a special obligation to seek holiness in their lives, because they are consecrated to God by a new title through the reception of orders, and are stewards of the mysteries of God in the service of His people.

§2 In order that they can pursue this perfection:

1° they are in the first place faithfully and untiringly to fulfil the obligations of their pastoral ministry;

2° they are to nourish their spiritual life at the twofold table of the sacred Scripture and the Eucharist; priests are therefore earnestly invited to offer the Eucharistic Sacrifice daily, and deacons to participate daily in the offering;

3° priests, and deacons aspiring to the priesthood, are obliged to carry out the liturgy of the hours daily, in accordance with their own approved liturgical books; permanent deacons are to recite that part of it determined by the Episcopal Conference;

4° they are also obliged to make spiritual retreats, in

accordance with the provision of particular law;
5° they are exhorted to engage regularly in mental prayer, to approach the sacrament of penance frequently, to honour the Virgin Mother of God with particular veneration, and to use other general and special means to holiness.

"They are to engage regularly in mental prayer" – this statement reflects the emergence of an understanding of the key place that mental prayer came to occupy in the understanding of the nature of the interior life. The notion of "mental prayer" developed over the past four hundred years in European Catholicism. It became the defining expression of the path to interior spiritual growth. St Teresa of Avila, in her *Way of Perfection*[91] commented, "What do you mean, Christians, when you say that mental prayer is unnecessary? Do you understand what you are saying? I really do not think you can". The daily practice of mental prayer was regarded as an essential element for anyone seeking to grow in the spiritual life.

We will explore the development of this tradition in order to appreciate the extent of its influence on the spiritual life of the Church. It may be useful at the outset to outline a few distinctions with regard to terminology which will be used in this chapter and in the chapters that follow:

- Mental Prayer refers to a particular method of interior prayer
- Meditation is a more generic term to describe interior prayer of various sorts (here we can also include non-Christian forms, eg. Transcendental Meditation).
- Discursive Meditation is the use of reason in praying, normally in an ordered fashion
- Affective Prayer is prayer that involves the feelings, the emotions, that is, the affections
- Contemplative Prayer generally can be understood as prayer of stillness, or graced interior quiet
- Acquired Contemplation is the contemplative state seen as achieved by one's own efforts
- Infused Contemplation is the contemplative state seen as pure gift of the grace of God.

---

[91] Chapter 22

A history of ways of interior prayer

It may be useful by way of review to provide a brief overview of the ways of interior prayer that developed in Christian history.

From the time of the Fathers of the Church we noted the development of the tradition of the prayerful pondering of the Scriptures. Many of the early Fathers, like Origen and St Ambrose of Milan, built their interior life around prayerful reflection on the Scriptures. The Benedictine monks developed this practice under the title, *Lectio Divina*. The monastic tradition, grounded in the writings of the Fathers, encouraged this way of using the Scriptures or other holy texts as the means of spiritual nourishment.

As we shall see Mental Prayer was a development in the 16th century. It was promoted by the clerks regular, like the Jesuits, Barnabites, Theatines, Oratorians. These were apostolic clerical orders and a practical form of daily meditation was very suited to their life and apostolate. The origins of this approach, however, do lie in monastic *lectio*.

The movement towards the use of the concept of meditation is seen among the Cistercians, Aelred of Revaulx (d. 1166), for instance, proposed meditation on the Word of God. William of St Thierry (d. 1150) recommended subjects for meditation taken from the life of Jesus. From the Carthusian tradition comes the structuring of prayer as reading, meditation, prayer and contemplation proposed by Guigo II in his *Scala Claustralium*.

The Canons Regular of St Victor in Paris understood that one progressed from meditation to contemplation. Earlier St Bonaventure had understood the different forms of the soul's activities in prayer as reason, conscience, consciousness and will. The use of these essential human interior powers were to become the basis for meditation.

In the fourteenth century meditations on the life of the

Christ were developed. The Renaissance had fostered a focus on humanism.[92] Incorporating a concern for the growth of the individual but reacting to the tendency towards pagan ideals, forms of meditation were proposed that centred upon Christ as the model for Christian growth. It was in this atmosphere the *Devotio Moderna* movement emerged. Its spiritual base was daily meditation. Members of the movement prayed using an organised program of meditation topics which, as well as themes on the life of Christ, also included topics for mediation on the virtues, the Last Things, etc. It was understood that the three faculties of the soul were activated in this process, that is, memory, intellect and will.

Meditations did become quite elaborate in structure, for example, John Gansfort, a friend of Thomas a Kempis, proposed as a structure for mental prayer which included two preparatory steps, sixteen processory steps, and three concluding steps.

The preferred method of interior prayer in the Sixteenth Century

These were some of currents of thought which fostered the development of methods of meditation that provided the backdrop to its formulation in the sixteenth century.

Some Benedictines at this time were looking at ways to reform personal prayer. The *Lectio* method had become barren. Ludovic Barb, Abbot of Padua (d. 1443), developed a series of meditations. These influenced a number of monasteries, including Monte Cassino. In Spain, Garcia Ximines de Cisneros, the Abbot of Montserrat, drew up a series of systematic meditations on the subject of the life of the Lord, and he taught them to pilgrims who visited the famous monastery. One pilgrim at this time was Ignatius Loyola who visited there in 1522. Ignatius was to become the most influential advocate of mental prayer.

---

92 Renaissance humanism was an intellectual movement in the later Middle Ages, and was particularly identified with Italian culture in the period. This humanism was not an ideological programme but a body of literary and artistic works inspired by a discovery of ancient Greek and Latin writings. This humanism influenced the Christian approach to the place of the human person in spirituality.

The Mendicants were also attracted by these new approaches to personal prayer. The Dominicans of Milan sanctioned daily meditation in 1503. Louis of Granada in 1544 wrote *Book of Prayer and Meditation* which became used by the Carmelites. The Franciscans, through St Peter of Alcantara, used the work of Louis of Granada and in 1594 officially adopted mental prayer as the preferred form of interior prayer.

The use of mental prayer became a source of renewal for these older orders and it became seen as a most suitable approach to personal prayer for the newer apostolic clerical orders. It came in time to be recognised as a very useful means to promote spiritual growth among the laity. St Francis de Sales, St Alphonsus Liguori, and St Vincent de Paul all promoted mental prayer as an appropriate means for devout lay people to progress in the spiritual life.

St Ignatius Loyola

Mental prayer was particularly promoted by the Jesuits. St Ignatius of Loyola (1491-1556) perfected the method, drawing on his personal experiences during his extended period of retreat in a cave at Manresa. He recognised the importance of the use of the three faculties of the soul: memory, intellect and will. He promoted the use of daily examination of conscience which he called "particular examin". He is a master in the area of discernment and is the patron saint of retreat masters

St Ignatius wrote the *Spiritual Exercises* in the light of his personal ten month retreat at Manresa. It was designed as a manual for retreat directors and presents an ordered, deliberate programme for conversion ultimately aimed at leading the retreatant to a decision for Christ.

The *Exercises* cover a period of four weeks – they are commonly known as the Thirty Day Retreat. During the first week a focus is upon sin and repentance. In the second week a decision is called for: whom do you choose to serve? St Ignatius concentrates upon the process of making this decision and leading the retreatant to a total abandonment to Christ. The prayer that captures this is the well known prayer, "Take Lord Receive".

Take, O Lord, and receive my entire liberty,
my memory, my understanding and my whole will.
All that I am and all that I possess You have given me.
I surrender it all to You to be disposed of according to Your will.
Give me only Your love and Your grace;
with these I will be rich enough,
and will desire nothing more.

The Exercises are a series of meditations leading a person to conversion. It was St Ignatius's insistence to his flat mate in Paris that he should do the *Exercises* that led to the conversion and ultimately extraordinary missionary work of St Francis Xavier.

In the Jesuit tradition a priority is given to mental prayer over the choral office. St Ignatius received permission to release his priests from common celebration of the Office. His emphasis on prayer was that it should be realistic and immediate, and not speculative in nature. The meditation exercise is a planned activity. It is an exercise.

St Ignatius had a simple format for his meditations. There was a pre-disposing prayer, followed by "preludes" which set the scene for the meditation. Various points for meditation were offered to guide the process. Then a simple conclusion of personal prayer was offered – the colloquy.

While we focus on the mechanics of this approach to prayer it is important to recognise the special genius of St Ignatius. It was his understanding of the discerning movements of the soul. This is expressed in his "Rules for the Discernment of Spirits", found in the appendices of the *Exercises*. St Ignatius put particular emphasis upon the practice of examen – the practice of pausing during the day and assessing the movements of God and one's response to the prayer of meditation. St Ignatius had an appreciation of psychological workings of the individual and proposed ways of handling the affective experiences of consolation and desolation. He encouraged working on basis of resolutions. For St Ignatius it was decisions not feelings that were important in responding to the movements of grace.

The Practice of Mental Prayer

The practice of mental prayer was promoted in the following centuries by a number of important religious figures and became seen as a key element in the spiritual life, particularly of priests.

As we have seen St Ignatius developed a particular schema for the practice of mental prayer. The schema included steps of preparation, including preparations of "points" the evening before and the practice of putting oneself in the presence of God prior to beginning the meditation on a topic. The meditation period would conclude with a "colloquy" or talk with God. Mental prayer, thus, was divided into three parts: the preparation, the body and the conclusion. Spiritual writers further divided the preparation into the habitual, the proximate and the immediate.

For St Ignatius, responding to the dangers associated with Quietism[93], the exercise of the will was vital. St Vincent de Paul emphasised the role of the will by speaking of the importance of making resolutions: "The principal fruit of mental prayer consists in making a good resolution, and a strong one too, in grounding one's resolutions on a firm basis, in being thoroughly convinced of their necessity, in being ready to put them in practice, and in foreseeing obstacles in order to overcome them." In a similar way St France de Sales proposed what he called a "spiritual nosegay", as we like to pick a flower from a garden and take it with us to remind us of the garden, so we choose some points to take with us from the meditation.

Various spiritual writers advocated mental prayer proposing various schemas. St Francis de Sales was a renown spiritual director and encouraged an hour of meditation each day. His method followed the lines of St Ignatius Loyola though he put much emphasis on the affective aspect of prayer. In his book, *Introduction to the Devout Life*

---

93 Tendencies to Quietism – a heresy in the spiritual life - existed in the Church in various movements. St Ignatius encountered them in Lutheran writings. In Catholic circles it reached definitive form in the thought of Spaniard, **Michael de Molinos**, whose key proposition was that man must annihilate his powers in order to advance towards God. By doing nothing the soul annihilates itself and returns to its source, the essence of God, in which it is transformed and divinized, and then God abides in it. His teaching was condemned by Pope Innocent XI in 1687.

(published in 1609), he writes:

> I especially counsel you to practice mental prayer, the prayer of the heart, and particularly that which centres on the life and passion of Our Lord. By often turning your eyes on Him in meditation, your whole soul will be filled with Him. You will learn His ways, and form your actions after the pattern of His.

The meditation was to lead the person to living out the time of prayer:

> This is to take one or two thoughts which have touched us in prayer, and which before God we believe to be more useful to us, in order to think often upon them during the day, and to make use of them as ejaculatory prayers to raise ourselves to God and to unite ourselves to Him; just as we see persons of the world, who, being in a beautiful garden, carpeted with flowers, do not leave without having in their hand one or two of its flowers, whose scent they inhale now and again after leaving the garden.

St Alphonsus Ligouri (1696-1787), founder of the Redemptorists, said that there was a moral necessity for mental prayer for anyone desiring to grow in their relationship with God. He wrote, "as long as a soul gives herself to mental prayer you will behold her a model of modesty, of humility, of devotion, and of mortification; let her abandon mental prayer, and soon the modesty of her looks disappears, her pride will burst forth at the least word which offends." He emphasised the importance of prayer of petition at the end of the meditation.

The Seminary of St Sulpice in Paris was an important centre for what has become known as the "French School" of spirituality. It influenced generations of priests. The Sulpician Method of mental prayer followed the traditional form and promoted a personal relationship with Christ. Cardinal Berulle, the figurehead of the French School, taught: "Let us set our Lord in our heart".

St John Baptist de la Salle, founder of the Brothers of the Christian Schools (FSC), grounded the spiritual life of the brothers in daily mental prayer. He urged the brothers to begin with an entry into the presence of God: "The first thing that must be done in prayer is to become interiorly absorbed into the presence of God". Members of religious orders – clerical and religious – were formed on this approach to prayer. It became the basis for developing an interior life. The practice of meditation became the mainstay of the spiritual life of countless thousands up to our own time.

On Meditation on the two standards

The one of Christ, our Commander-in-chief and Lord; the other of Lucifer, mortal enemy of our human nature.
Prayer. The usual Preparatory Prayer.
First Prelude. The First Prelude is the narrative. It will be here how Christ calls and wants all under His standard; and Lucifer, on the contrary, under his.
Second Prelude. The second, a composition, seeing the place. It will be here to see a great field of all that region of Jerusalem, where the supreme Commander-in-chief of the good is Christ our Lord; another field in the region of Babylon, where the chief of the enemy is Lucifer.
Third Prelude. The third, to ask for what I want: and it will be here to ask for knowledge of the deceits of the bad chief and help to guard myself against them, and for knowledge of the true life which the supreme and true Captain shows and grace to imitate Him.
First Point. The first Point is to imagine as if the chair of fire and smoke, in shape horrible and terrifying.
Second Point. The second, to consider how he issues a summons to innumerable demons and how he scatters them, some to one city and others to another, and so through all the world, not omitting any provinces, places, states, nor any persons in particular.
Third Point. The third, to consider the discourse which he makes them, and how he tells them to cast out nets and chains; that they have first to tempt with a longing for riches – as he is accustomed to do in most – that men may more easily come to vain honour of the world, and then to vast pride. So that the first step shall be that of riches; the second, that of honour; the third, that of pride; and from these three steps he draws on to all the other vices.
So, on the contrary, one has to imagine as to the supreme and true Captain, Who is Christ our Lord.

First Point. The first Point is to consider how Christ our Lord puts Himself in a great field of that region of Jerusalem, in lowly place, beautiful and attractive.

Second Point. The second, to consider how the Lord of all the world chooses so many persons — Apostles, Disciples, etc., — and sends them through all the world spreading His sacred doctrine through all states and conditions of persons.

Third Point. The third, to consider the discourse which Christ our Lord makes to all His servants and friends whom He sends on this expedition, recommending them to want to help all, by bringing them first to the highest spiritual poverty, and — if His Divine Majesty would be served and would want to choose them — no less to actual poverty; the second is to be of contumely and contempt; because from these two things humility follows. So that there are to be three steps; the first, poverty against riches; the second, contumely or contempt against worldly honour; the third, humility against pride. And from these three steps let them induce to all the other virtues.

First Colloquy. One Colloquy to Our Lady, that she may get me grace from Her Son and Lord that I may be received under His standard; and first in the highest spiritual poverty, and — if His Divine Majesty would be served and would want to choose and receive me — not less in actual poverty; second, in suffering contumely and injuries, to imitate Him more in them, if only I can suffer them without the sin of any person, or displeasure of His Divine Majesty; and with that a Hail Mary.

Second Colloquy. I will ask the same of the Son, that He may get it for me of the Father; and with that say the Soul of Christ.

Third Colloquy. I will ask the same of the Father, that He may grant it to me; and say an Our Father.

Note. This Exercise will be made at midnight and then a second time in the morning, and two repetitions of this same will be made at the hour of Mass and at the hour of Vespers, always finishing with the three Colloquies, to Our Lady, to the Son, and to the Father; and that on The Pairs which follows, at the hour before supper.

Meditation for fourth day, Second Week, Spiritual Exercises of St Ignatius Loyola

17
St Teresa of Avila – States of Prayer

The practice of mental prayer dominated the approach to the interior life among clerics and religious in the centuries since St Ignatius Loyola. However, another tradition was quietly finding its place in the Catholic tradition. It was the contemplative practices of those who chose the withdrawn life.

Contemplatives have had an enduring place in the Church's spiritual tradition. Their experience and teaching on the nature of the spiritual life reached a climax with the teaching of St Teresa of Avila.

The Concept of the Three Ways

In the Catholic tradition growth in the spiritual life has often been presented as progress through three stages. These three stages have been variously expressed. For instance, Clement of Alexandria (150-215) spoke of the shunning of evil through *fear* (mortification of the passions), the practice of the virtues through the exercise of *hope*, and doing good inspired by *love*. Another early writer, John Cassian, used this same format and spoke of *fear* as the motivation of slaves, *hope* as the approach of mercenaries looking for reward, and *love* as becoming one who is a child of God.

St Augustine spoke of four degrees of love which he identified as incipient love, growing love, full grown love, and perfect love. St Bernard describes three degrees constituting the love that we have towards God: a love on account of his gifts, a love of God for his own sake, and a disinterested love of God. St Bonaventure speaks of knowing God *outside* oneself (through nature), knowing God *within* oneself, and finally knowing God as *above* oneself.

This tradition of thought eventually identified the Purgative way, the Illuminative Way and the Unitive way. The great modern exponent of this was Pere Reginald Garrigou-Lagrange OP expressed in his classic work, "The Three Ways of the Spiritual Life".

St Teresa of Avila

St Teresa was born in Avila, Spain, in 1515. In 1535, she entered the Carmelite Monastery of the Incarnation at Avila. The following year she received the habit and gave herself to prayer and penance. Though she would later enter a period of mediocrity in her spiritual life, she did not at any time give up praying. Eventually she had an experience of conversion in the presence of an image of "the sorely wounded Christ". At the age of 39, she began to enjoy the vivid experience of God's presence with her. She had a number of mystical experiences but was burdened by bad spiritual direction. The priests to whom she turned for advice were unable to guide her. Finally she found a young Carmelite priest just twenty five years old – later to become St John of the Cross. In August 1560 St Peter of Alcantara counselled her: "Keep on as you are doing, daughter; we all suffer such trials."

The atmosphere prevailing at the Incarnation monastery was less than favourable for the more perfect type of life to which St Teresa now aspired. A group assembled in her cell one September evening in 1560 and, taking their inspiration from the primitive tradition of Carmel, they proposed a reform of their way of life. St Teresa became the key figure in this reform of the Carmelite tradition.

This reform took the name "discalced", meaning without sandals. Initially St Teresa went barefoot. She led a penitential life, having a log for her pillow and wearing harsh clothing.

It is to her writings that we turn for insight into her experience and, more importantly, her teaching on progression in the spiritual life. The genius of St Teresa of Avila is not just that she ascended to the heights of spiritual union with God, but that she had the ability to describe it and enable others to understand the spiritual journey to deep intimacy with God. Indeed, not having formal training in the Latin language, she wrote in the vernacular.

The autobiography, or "Life", written primarily as a manifestation of her spiritual state for her spiritual director, depicts different stages of the life of prayer. She drew on the image of obtaining water to irrigate a garden. In Chapters 10 to 22 she outlines three key stages of growth in prayer. The first stage is mental prayer with a focus on prayerful reflection on the passion of Christ. She then speaks of prayer of quiet. In this development in prayer there is an evident grace at work which enables the will to surrender to God. This prayer is marked by the beginnings of an inner stillness. She goes on to explain a further step as that of ecstatic absorption into God. She speaks of a conscious rapture as she is caught up in the love of God. St Teresa speaks of a number of extraordinary experiences associated with the state of union with God.

Teresa wrote another book on the spiritual life at the request of her nuns. The "Way of Perfection" teaches them about the key virtues that lie at the basis of the spiritual life. She offers advice of the practice of prayer and uses the Our Father as a vehicle for teaching about prayer at greater depth.

Her most mature work is *The Interior Castle*. This is a book about the life of prayer, The interior castle is the soul, in the center of which dwells the Holy Trinity. Growth in prayer enables the individual to enter into deeper intimacy with God expressed as a progressive journey through the mansions of the castle from the exterior to the luminous centre. Each of the "mansions" of the castle is distinguished by a different stage in the growth of prayer.

Stages in Prayer

The contribution of Teresa to the understanding of the progress in the life of prayer was that she was able to articulate the process through various stages. This teaching is scattered over her various works. There were efforts at classifying stages in the growth in prayer prior to the sixteenth century, but the classical formulation was given by St Teresa of Avila. All other expressions since are variations on her analysis.

The following material follows the presentation of the teaching of St Teresa by Fr. Arintero (d.1928)[94] and gathers together her teaching in a more schematised form. He describes nine stages.

Stage 1. Vocal Prayer

Vocal prayer will exist until replaced by the heart's silent expression or the action of the Spirit. Such vocal prayer can lead to contemplation. St Ignatius and St Teresa both teach that saying a vocal prayer, eg. Our Father, can lead to contemplative experience. Usually, though, a person will move on to prayer of the mind or heart, to an interior conversation.

Stage 2. Meditation

Meditation is a methodical or "discursive" consideration of some religious truth. Normally a beginner uses some method, eg. Ignatian, Salesian, Sulpician, etc. With a method comes a format of acts of preparation, reading, reflection, prayer. As a person persists with a method it becomes less mechanical (cf. St Teresa, Life. Ch.13).

It moves to a loving conversation. In this approach what is important is the role of the will in making resolutions, ie. a seeking after growth in the virtues. St Teresa speaks of this as drawing water from a well with a bucket (cf. Life Ch.11-18). During this stage there can be the experience of momentary graces, of fervour, of sweetness, etc. Chiefly this is an ascetical practice, though it does tend to move towards a more passive mode. The general movement is from thinking to loving.

Stage 3. Affective Prayer (1st. Transition)

The person begins to experience a greater facility in interior prayer. There can be a growing presence of affections, ie. feelings for God; a certain disinterest in strictly discursive prayer; a growing simplicity and passivity. Generally the person recognises more fruit and less labour.

The Holy Spirit gradually leads the person away from the use of a method. The person can experience an incapacity to meditate. A dryness or difficulty may in fact be the means to set the person free

---

94 J G Arintero, Stages in Prayer (trans K Louis) 1957.

from reliance upon method. This is the beginning of the mystical life. It is a moving towards an habitual state of silence in prayer. Sometimes there can be surges of affection and interior groanings.

Stage 4. Prayer of Simplicity (2nd Transition)

This stage receives several names: prayer of loving regard, trusting surrender, etc. A dryness or darkness can be experienced. When this is the case there is a need to rest patiently and allow the heart to remain silent. Grace is now working in its own right; no longer is prayer our work under grace.

Here a purifying or "purgation" is required for the person to move on into the stage of illumination. A Dark Night of the Senses is experienced. St John of the Cross gives the best description of this aspect and his work complements that of St Teresa of Avila.

The Holy Spirit is now the director of the soul. He enlightens and purifies. It is a matter of submission to him. This is an entry into the mystical life.

There are three key signs:
- a difficulty with discursive prayer
- a pain felt at distractions
- a persistent attraction to remain silent

The evident fruit is a greater recollection and a love of virtue.

Stage 5. Infused Recollection

This represents the first stage of Union, a truly contemplative stage. The experience is of brief moments of being united with God, a lively sense of the presence of God. There can be a focus on a single maxim, or a line of Scripture. The person has a sense of the majesty, beauty, and love of God and leads to a deep spiritual silence. The person also receives an enlightenment of the mind in the area of spiritual wisdom and understanding beyond the result of study.

Stage 6. Prayer of Quiet

A spiritual joy overflows all the faculties, a peace and sweetness is experienced. There is a great increase in spiritual health and a facility for doing good. It is an inebriation of love. There can be cries, groans, songs of praise, and leaps of joy accompanying this experience. Teresa speaks of "follies of love" (cf. Life Ch. 16). There can be the experience of mystical sleep combined with touches of love.

Stage 7. Prayer of Union

This represents entry into the highest levels of prayer. All interior faculties are captivated. The external senses are free though helpless and inoperative. There is great intensity of experience, though for brief moments. The soul solely desires to serve God; there is a willingness to suffer any trials and a desire for penance and solitude. The phenomena associated with this stage are mystical touches, flights of the spirit, fiery darts of love and wounds of love. The soul melts, sometimes the exterior faculties fail. There can be mysterious wounds of love and pain (stigmata). And levitation and bi-location can be present.

Stage 8. Ecstatic Union

Here there is the suspension of the external senses and the experience of ecstasy, a gentle and progressive swooning. Sometimes it can be violent (rapture), though no harm is done to the person. In this state of ecstasy the soul receives a spiritual espousal, ie a promise of full union.

Stage 9. Transforming Union

The soul at this level seems more God than soul. It is a prelude to the Beatific Vision – seeing God "face to face" (see Ex 33:11). There is a mutual surrender and acceptance as in marriage (see Canticle of Canticles). St Teresa experienced a vision of Christ and the bestowal of a ring. A permanent union is established. The effects of this are: a desire to suffer for God, a detachment from everything created, an absence of ecstasy. Sometimes the person is able to live on little sleep and no food except the Eucharist. Such people are known to give off a celestial fragrance.

The Classic formulation

St Teresa of Avila provided the classic formulation of the stages of the spiritual life. She herself progressed to the highest levels of personal intimacy with God. The depiction of the ecstasy of St Teresa sculptured by Bernini (Chapel of Santa Maria della Vittoria, Rome) shows the figure of the swooning nun and the angel with the spear directed at her heart. It was inspired by the description given by Teresa, "I saw in his hand a long spear of gold, and at the iron's point there seemed to be a little fire. He appeared to me to be thrusting it at times into my heart". She adds that "the pain was so great, that it made me moan; and yet so surpassing was the sweetness of this excessive pain, that I could not wish to be rid of it. The soul is satisfied now with nothing less than God. The pain is not bodily, but spiritual; though the body has its share in it. It is a caressing of love so sweet which now takes place between the soul and God, that I pray God of His goodness to make him experience it who may think that I am lying".[95]

St Teresa of Avila is a witness to the transforming grace of God in the life of one who opens to Him in surrender. St Teresa teaches us the path from effort to grace, from activity to passivity. It is the classical formulation of the path to the fullest possible spiritual union outside the Beatific Vision.

Spread of the Reform

The history of the Carmelites helps put the Teresian reform into context. The first Carmelites were hermits living on Mount Carmel in Israel. In the thirteenth century St Albert, Patriarch of Jerusalem, brought the hermits on Mount Carmel together, at their request, into community. He wrote a rule of life. The Carmelites moved from Israel to Europe and became widespread. As with spiritual movements over time laxity set in. This was the case of the Carmelite Convent of the Incarnation in Avila which St Teresa joined in 1535.

St Teresa's reform included among things establishing smaller

---

95 Autobiography, chapter 29.

communities of around twenty sisters to ensure a more intense shared life among the sisters. These communities were completely enclosed so that they would be free from the distractions of the world. The community's way of life was simple and austere but truly joyous and humane. The sisters were called to be friends with one another and with Christ. For St Teresa the holier the nuns were the more joyful and sociable they would be. The celebration of the liturgy was to be simple so as to ensure a focus on contemplative prayer.

It was when she was making her second foundation in 1567 that St Teresa met a young, newly ordained Carmelite friar, John of the Cross. He was dissatisfied with his vocation and wanted to leave the Carmelites. St Teresa recruited him for her reform. Eventually St John of the Cross began a male branch of the reform at Duruelo. They lived an intense life of prayer and poverty, and took responsibility for the pastoral care of the people of the area. The male Discalced Carmelites combine contemplative life and apostolic work.

The Carmelite reform has made a major contribution to the Church. It continues to be one of the principal forms of contemplative life in the Church today and continues to attract men and women to a life devoted to prayer. The writings of St Teresa of Ávila and St John of the Cross are a vibrant source of inspiration of many. The Order has produced some of the great saints of the Church – St Thérèse of the Child Jesus and of the Holy Face, Blessed Elizabeth of the Trinity, St. Teresa of the Andes, and martyrs like Edith Stein (St Teresa Benedicta of the Cross), Père Jacques and the sixteen Martyrs of Compiegne.

It is the grace of the Holy Spirit that nurtures the contemplative aspect of the Church. In every era there are those who are drawn to seek God in silence and anonymity. To those without faith it seems such lives are wasted. A society which prizes productivity can see little benefit in the contemplative life. Yet the Church highly regards the contemplative dimension to its life. Contemplatives are often described as the "spiritual powerhouse" of the Church. It is for this reason that St Thérèse of the Child Jesus was made the Patroness of Missions.⁹⁶

On visions and graces received

For two years and a half God granted me this grace very frequently; but it is now more than three years since He has taken away from me its continual presence, through another of a higher nature, as I shall perhaps explain hereafter. And though I saw Him speaking to me, and though I was contemplating His great beauty, and the sweetness with which those words of His came forth from His divine mouth, – they were sometimes uttered with severity, – and though I was extremely desirous to behold the colour of His eyes, or the form of them, so that I might be able to describe them, yet I never attained to the sight of them, and I could do nothing for that end; on the contrary, I lost the vision altogether. And though I see that He looks upon me at times with great tenderness, yet so strong is His gaze, that my soul cannot endure it; I fall into a trance so deep, that I lose the beautiful vision, in order to have a greater fruition of it all.

Accordingly, willing or not willing, the vision has nothing to do with it. Our Lord clearly regards nothing but humility and confusion of face, the acceptance of what He wishes to give, and the praise of Himself, the Giver. This is true of all visions without exception: we can contribute nothing towards them – we cannot add to them, nor can we take from them; our own efforts can neither make nor unmake them. Our Lord would have us see most clearly that it is no work of ours, but of His Divine Majesty; we are therefore the less able to be proud of it: on the contrary, it makes us humble and afraid; for we see that, as our Lord can take from us the power of seeing what we would see, so also can He take from us these mercies and His grace, and we may be lost forever. We must therefore walk in His fear while we are living in this our exile.

Our Lord showed Himself to me almost always as He is after His resurrection. It was the same in the Host; only at those times when I was in trouble, and when it was His will to strengthen me, did He show His wounds. Sometimes I saw Him on the cross, in the Garden, crowned with thorns, – but that was rarely; sometimes also carrying His cross because of my necessities, – I may say so, – or those of others; but always in His glorified body. Many reproaches and many vexations have I borne while

---

96 In 1927 Pope Pius XI declared her patron Saint of all Catholic Missions. She had spent nine years in the convent at Lisieux yet she prayed constantly for the mission of the Church. The choice of this contemplative confirms the Church's awareness that the mission of the Church is spiritual and prayer is the hidden source of the fruitfulness of evangelisation.

telling this – many suspicions and much persecution also. So certain were they to whom I spoke that I had an evil spirit, that some would have me exorcised. I did not care much for this; but I felt it bitterly when I saw that my confessors were afraid to hear me, or when I knew that they were told of anything about me.

St Teresa of Avila, Life, Chapter 29

18
Devotion to the Sacred Heart

The Church encouraged clerics to develop the practice of meditation as a daily practice for the nourishment of their spiritual life. As we have seen meditation was also being recommended to lay people. However ordinary Catholics found forms of popular piety as the mainstay of their faith. In particular there were two currents of devotion that sustained the spiritual life of ordinary Catholics: devotion to the Sacred Heart and to the Blessed Virgin Mary. These devotions provided avenues for popular prayer and devotion for Catholics over the centuries.

One feature of the fostering of these devotions is that they have been accompanied by apparitions. While the Church's spiritual history records many examples of people testifying to apparitions, it appears that a number of apparitions of the Lord and the Blessed Virgin have not just been localised phenomena, but have become major influences upon the whole Church.

The first devotion with its accompanying apparitions that we will consider is that of devotion to the Sacred Heart and the apparitions of the Lord to St Margaret Mary Alacoque.

The French School

In what we could regard as the modern period, which is from the sixteenth century onwards, spirituality is best understood under national titles. This was the time of the emergence of the European nations as we know them today. We now speak of the Italian School, the French School and the English School of spirituality.

In the seventeenth century the richest area of spiritual activity was to be found in the French School. The century and beyond produced a host of saints, many well known to the Catholic world: St Francis de Sales, St Vincent de Paul, St John Baptist de la Salle, St. John Vianney, St Jeanne de Chantelle, St Margaret Mary Alacoque, St Claude la Columbiere, St John Eudes and many others. A key figure who drew out the best in this School is St Francis de Sales (1567-1622). In him the French spiritual renaissance is baptised as a devout humanism. The French School would ultimately suffer from two heresies: Quietism[97] and Jansenism.[98]

In this chapter we will consider one aspect of the spirituality to come out of the French Church at this time: devotion to the Sacred Heart.

Sources of the Devotion in the Fathers of the Church

The appearances of Our Lord to St Margaret Mary climaxed a tradition in the church which focussed on the passion and sufferings of Christ. The period of the Fathers of the Church evidences an awareness of these themes: the Fathers referred to the piercing of the heart of Jesus especially in relation to the outpouring of sacramental grace; and there are periodic references to the Five Wounds, something that would grow into an important medieval devotion.

St John Chrysostom (d. 407) says, "We are all one, for we issue together from the side of Christ", referring to sacramental baptism. Again on this theme he writes, "Access to the Sacraments is through Christ's wounded side."[99] St Anslem (1033-1109) wrote, "Jesus, dear as he inclines his head in death; death, in the extending of his arms; dear in the opening of his side. Opened so that there is revealed to us the riches of his goodness, the charity, that is, of his heart towards

---

97 Quietism, from the Latin *quies*, meaning passivity, is the belief that the state of perfection is achieved by a sort of personal self-annihilation and a consequent absorption of the soul into the Divine Essence. The mind becomes wholly inactive and no longer thinks or wills on its own account. It remains passive while God acts within it. The notion of Quietism is foreign to the tradition of Catholic spirituality because it disengages the person from the spiritual search for God. It is dangerous in that this passivity can become a licence for immorality.
98 Jansenism is a theology and a spiritual movement. It was condemned as a heresy by Pope Innocent X in 1655. It emphasized the effects of original sin which led to human depravity. Man could do nothing to save himself and had to depend entirely on of divine grace. It proposed the notion of predestination (similar to what was proposed by Calvin). Originating in the writings of the Dutch theologian Cornelius Otto Jansen, Jansenism formed a distinct movement within the Catholic Church from the 16th to 18th centuries, and found its most important stronghold in the convent of Port-Royal in Paris. It had many influential supporters including Blaise Pascal. The Jesuits were active opponents. Despite being condemned it continued as a spiritual cancer well into the nineteenth century.
99 See *Catecheses* 3:13 19 SC 50, 174-177.

us."[100] The Benedictine monk, John of Fecamp (990 - 1078), wrote of desiring to be wounded in his heart as Jesus allowed himself to be wounded – "so that my soul may be able to say to thee: I am wounded by thy love."

St Bernard of Clarvaux (d. 1153) dwelling upon the love of God, wrote: "Utterly generous, for not a mere drop, but a wave of blood flowed unchecked from the five Wounds of his body", and "The secret of his heart is laid open through the clefts of his body; that mighty mystery of love is laid open, laid open too the tender mercies of our God".[101]

The Medieval Mystics

The late medieval period witnessed an emphasis upon the passion of Christ and received special expression in the visions of various mystics. Such mystics as Angela of Foligno (d. 1309), Bridget of Sweden (d. 1373), and Julian of Norwich (b.1342) reveal concentration on the sufferings of Christ in their visions. One particular location of mystical activity where this theme was expressed was the Cistercian convent at Helfta in Saxony.

Mechthild of Hackborn (d.1299), a nun of Helfta, received many visions and wrote *The Book of Special Grace*. Her focus was upon the love of Christ: Christ's heart was full of reverence and love towards his Father; it was full of pity and mercy towards all men; and it was full of humility and self-abasement with regard to himself. She wrote, "In my great sufferings God revealed himself to my soul, showed me the wounds of his Heart and said, 'See how they have made me suffer.'"[102] In another place she writes, "Remember the sharp spear's wound which pierced even to the depths of the Heart and weep over that which you have done."[103]

Other mystics in this time like St Gertrude the Great (d.1301) had visions in a similar vein: "With both hands turned towards her,

---

100 See *Liber Meditationum et Oratium 10*, PL Vol 158 p. 761.
101 St Bernard of Clarvaux is credited as a major promoter of devotion to the heart of Christ due to his constant reference to the wounds of Christ. He himself had a mystical love for Christ which focussed on his birth and passion. Along with St Francis he is considered the main source of fostering popular devotion to the wounded heart of Christ.
102 *The Flowing Light*, 6, 26.
103 ibid.

pointing to his Heart, which is full of every sweetness". She goes on to pray:

By thy wounded Heart, dearest Lord, pierce my heart with the arrows of thy love so deeply that it can no longer understand anything earthly, but must be controlled by the operations of thy Godhead alone.[104]

The spirit of the devotion to the Sacred Heart of Jesus was thus emerging and was carried into the following centuries by the Carthusians, especially at Cologne.

St Margaret Mary Alacoque

St Margaret Mary Alacoque (1647-1690) was a nun of the Visitation Order. The order was founded by St Jeanne de Chantelle and St Francis de Sales. She was a member of the community at Paray-le-Monial in central France. In the chapel of the convent she experienced a series of apparitions beginning on December 27th, 1673 (Feast of St John the Beloved). In the first vision the Lord said:

> My divine heart is so impassioned with love for men, and for you in particular, that being unable any longer to contain within itself the flames of its burning charity, it must spread them abroad by your means and manifest itself to others in order to enrich them with the precious treasures that I reveal to you, and that contain graces of sanctification and salvation necessary to withdraw them from the abyss of perdition.[105]

St Margaret Mary was being chosen. She received a vision of the Sacred Heart and was being called upon to promote devotion to the Sacred Heart. In a second vision some time later the picture of the Sacred Heart was presented to her:

The divine heart was represented to me as on a throne of fire and flames, shedding rays on every side, brighter than the sun and transparent as crystal. The Wound which he received upon the Cross appeared there visibly; a crown of thorns encircled the divine heart, and it was surmounted by a cross.

---

104 *Prayers* (Burns and Lambert, 1861) p 111.
105 The references are taken from the *Autobiography of St Margaret Mary*, available in a number of translations.

It was the Lord's desire that his heart be venerated in its physical form – a picture should be made and worn. There was a third vision, the emphasis being on reparation for others by means of frequent communion, especially on First Friday, and the practice of the Holy Hour. In the third vision St Margaret Mary was before the Blessed Sacrament and saw Jesus revealed in glory with five wounds shining like five suns. He opened his breast which was like a furnace and showed his Heart the source of the flames. This vision left St Margaret Mary huddled in a corner of the convent: she had fainted! From then on each Thursday St Margaret Mary would share in the agony of Gethsemane – from eleven in the evening to twelve midnight she would lie prostrate on the ground, pleading for sinners.

In the fourth vision Jesus asked for a special feast in honour of the Sacred Heart. Showing her his heart, he said,

Behold this heart which has loved men so much that it has spared nothing but has utterly consumed and exhausted itself in order to show them its love and for reward I receive from most of them nothing but ingratitude, through irreverence and blasphemy, the coldness and contempt, which they show towards me in this Sacrament of love. But it hurts me still more that hearts consecrated to me should treat me so.

Jesus then called for reparation on the feast of Sacred Heart on Friday after the Octave of Corpus Christi. St Margaret Mary received two more visions. One was a message for the King of France, Louis XVI, to consecrate himself and country to Sacred Heart. Secondly, the Lord spoke about the role of the Order of the Visitation and the Jesuits in promoting the devotion.

St Margaret Mary was to become a victim soul. She experienced much physical and spiritual trial during the rest of her life. Still the message spread. Confraternities promoting devotion to the Sacred Heart were formed. The official Church resisted establishing a feast but finally in 1765 Polish Bishops received permission and this was extended to whole Church in 1865. St Margaret Mary was canonised in 1920. In 1928, the encyclical, *Miserentissimus Redemptor* was written and in 1956, the definitive encyclical on devotion to the Sacred Heart, *Haurietis Aquas*, was promulgated.

Devotion to the Sacred Heart

In the centuries that followed Devotion to the Sacred Heart became one of the principal forms of devotion among Catholics. Churches built in the eighteen to twentieth centuries often had two main side altars – one devoted to the Blessed Virgin Mary and the other to the Sacred Heart. There were innumerable new apostolic religious orders that were founded during this time that took their names and spirituality from devotion to the Sacred Heart. One would find images of the Sacred Heart in Catholic homes as the main devotional image after that of the Blessed Virgin Mary. The practice of the "Nine First Fridays" was very common among Catholics.

Devotion to the Sacred Heart encouraged the use of the image of the pierced heart of Jesus exposed, surrounded with the crown of thorns and topped with flames of fire and the silhouette of the cross. The devotion encouraged prayers of reparation for the sins against the love of God. The practice of going to Mass and receiving Holy Communion on nine consecutive first Fridays of the month was to be preceded by going to Confession. This practice encouraged regular (monthly) confession, attending a weekday Mass and, initially at a time when people did not approach the altar for Holy Communion regularly it encouraged more frequent Holy Communion.

The devotion which has become so prominent in Catholic spirituality is the fruit of a divine intervention – the apparitions of the Lord to St Margaret Mary. The devotion, focussed as it was on the human heart was a means by which a person could consider the state of their own heart – was it warm with love of God and neighbour, or cold and uncaring. It was just as Jansenism was causing a "coldness" to enter into Catholic life in France, that the revelations to St Margaret Mary Alacoque, concerning devotion to the Sacred Heart of Jesus, were made. The revelation of the depth and power of the love of God revealed in the Sacred Heart of Jesus led many to conversion and renewed faith. The devotion to the Sacred Heart was a significant source for Catholic spirituality till the middle of the twentieth century. The significance of the devotion in moulding the Catholic spirit should not be underestimated, nor should its importance in counteracting various pessimistic and puritanical views of the human condition be ignored.

A Postscript – The apparitions of the Lord to St Faustina.

From the diary of a young Polish nun, a special devotion began spreading throughout the world in the 1930s. The message is nothing new, but is a reminder of what the Church has always taught through scripture and tradition: that God is merciful and forgiving and that we, too, must show mercy and forgiveness. St Faustina Kowalska, an uneducated Polish nun who, in obedience to her spiritual director, wrote a diary of about 600 pages recording the revelations she received about God's mercy. The apparitions to St Faustina bear extraordinary similarity to those to St Margaret Mary, three centuries before. The image that she described is remarkably similar to that of the Sacred Heart given to St Margaret Mary. The message of mercy is very closely allied to that of the love in the heart of God revealed at Paray-le-Monial.

The devotional practices – saying the Chaplet of Mercy – echo the call to intercessory prayer that was at the core of devotion to the Sacred Heart.

This message which had as its theme – "Jesus I trust in you" – was received in Poland in the mid 1930s. Europe was to be trust into a period of war. Nazism would rise and fall, Communism would threaten freedom and religion. Poland, caught in the middle, suffered terribly. As devotion to the Divine Mercy sought to support the faith of Catholics during a scorching ordeal, so devotion to the Sacred Heart helped Catholics avoid the dangers of Jansenism and brought a touch of human love to many who had to endure many difficulties caused by the early manifestations of industrialism. It would appear that devotion to Divine Mercy is a refreshed expression of the devotion to the Sacred Heart which would wane in the latter part of the twentieth century.

We can see in the apparitions of the Lord to St Margaret Mary and later to St Faustina signs of the desire of God to sustain his people as they were to endure difficult times that could smother Christian love and hope. They are streams of divine grace that have nourished ordinary Catholics through difficult times.

Revelations of the Sacred Heart of Jesus

Once being before the Blessed Sacrament having a little more leisure than usual, I felt wholly filled with this Divine Presence, and so powerfully moved by it that I forgot myself and the place in which I was. I abandoned myself to this Divine Spirit, and yielded my heart to the power of His love. He made me rest for a long time on His Divine Breast, where He revealed to me the wonders of His love and the inexplicable secrets of His Sacred Heart, which He had hitherto kept hidden from me. Now He opened it to me for the first time, but in a way so real, so sensible, that it left me no room to doubt, though I am always in dread of deceiving myself"

This as it seems to me, is what passed: The Lord said to me, My Divine Heart is so passionately in love with men that it can no longer contain within Itself the flames of Its ardent charity. It must pour them out by thy means, and manifest itself to them to enrich them with its precious treasures, which contain all the graces of which they have need to be saved from perdition. I have chosen you as an abyss of unworthiness and ignorance to accomplish so great a design, so that all may be done by Me

He demanded my heart, and I supplicated Him to take it. He did so, and put it into His own Adorable Heart, in which He allowed me to see it as a little atom being consumed in that fiery furnace. Then drawing it out like a burning flame in the form of a heart, He put it into the place whence He had taken it, saying: Behold, My beloved, a precious proof of My love. I enclose in thy heart a little spark of the most ardent flame of My love., to serve thee as a heart and to consume thee till thy last moment. Until now, you have taken only the name of My slave; henceforth you shalt be called the well-beloved disciple of My Sacred Heart.

From the writings of St Margaret Mary

19
Devotion to the Blessed Virgin Mary

Devotion to the Blessed Virgin Mary has always been a hallmark of Catholic spiritual life. The Virgin Mary has been honoured since apostolic times. She has been the constant subject of Catholic religious art. We cannot begin to canvas the entire history of devotion to the Mother of God, so will focus on recent aspects to this devotion. We will examine the phenomenon of apparitions of the Blessed Virgin in recent centuries. It seems that devotion to the Blessed Virgin has been fuelled in a particular way by various apparitions. Certainly Catholics are very aware of the two key apparitions: Lourdes (1858) and Fatima (1917).

Devotion to the Blessed Virgin has been the subject of criticism of Catholics by some other Churches, especially those whose roots can be traced back to the Reformation in the sixteenth century. The Second Vatican Council sought to address this question and lay the theological understanding of the role of the Blessed Virgin the Catholic life. We will begin by considering how the Church views the place and role of devotion to the Blessed Virgin Mary in Catholic life.

Lumen Gentium, Vatican II

In Dogmatic Constitution on the Church, *Lumen Gentium*, the Fathers of the Second Vatican Council spoke of the place of the Blessed Virgin Mary within Catholic theology and devotion. This definitive teaching developed the Church's understanding, presenting her as mother (a theme subsequently promoted by Pope Paul VI):

The Catholic Church taught by the Holy Spirit honours her with filial affection and devotion as most beloved mother.[106]

---

106 Lumen Gentium n. 53.

The Dogmatic Constitution explored the rich scriptural theology surrounding Mary in numbers 55 -59. The Council Fathers addressed the question of the place of Mary in the Church.[107] We can note the sensitivity to ecumenical issues in the opening statement which goes on to emphasise the maternal role of the Virgin Mary both in the Church and in the life of every Christian:

There is but one Mediator as we know from the words of the apostle, "for there is one God and one mediator of God and men, the man Christ Jesus, who gave himself a redemption for all". The maternal duty of Mary toward men in no wise obscures or diminishes this unique mediation of Christ, but rather shows His power. For all the salvific influence of the Blessed Virgin on men originates, not from some inner necessity, but from the divine pleasure. It flows forth from the superabundance of the merits of Christ, rests on His mediation, depends entirely on it and draws all its power from it. In no way does it impede, but rather does it foster the immediate union of the faithful with Christ.[108]

Catholic devotion to the Virgin Mary has been a point of controversy with Protestant and evangelical churches. Catholics are often accused that we worship of the Virgin Mary. The Council sought to ensure that Catholic devotion was properly moderated by Church authority to ensure that there was no imbalance in popular devotion. The Council taught: "Highlighting her maternal role, the Council acknowledges the continual cult of Mary through the ages and refers to the need for a correct development of the cult."[109] A simple distinction between the notion of *adoration* and that of *veneration* can diffuse misunderstanding. Adoration and worship belongs to God alone,[110] while veneration is the act of honouring someone because of their relationship with God. Catholic tradition has always venerated the saints, and the Virgin Mary is pre-eminent among them.

---

107 Ibid., n. 60.
108 Ibid.
109 Lumen Gentium n. 67.
110 See Deut 6:13.

Marialis Cultus

In 1974, Pope Paul VI wrote *Marialis Cultus*, describing it as a document on the "right ordering of Devotion to the Blessed Virgin Mary". The document, written in the light of the teaching found in Vatican II, is concerned to relate devotion to the Blessed Virgin Mary to the liturgical life of the Church:

> Therefore, venerable Brothers, as we consider the piety that the liturgical tradition of the universal Church and the renewed Roman Rite expresses towards the holy Mother of God, and as we remember that the liturgy through its pre-eminent value as worship constitutes the golden norm for Christian piety, and finally as we observe how the Church when she celebrates the sacred mysteries assumes an attitude of faith and love similar to that of the Virgin, we realize the rightness of the exhortation that the Second Vatican Council addresses to all the children of the Church, namely "that the cult, especially the liturgical cult, of the Blessed Virgin be generously fostered." This is an exhortation that we would like to see accepted everywhere without reservation and put into zealous practice.[111]

It is evident from these opening remarks that Pope Paul VI sought to expand on the approach taken by the Council. He later referred to the historical elements in the tradition of Marian devotion and sought to ensure that contemporary cultural expressions of the devotion were rightly ordered to the Church's theological and liturgical understanding:

> The piety of the faithful and their veneration of the Mother of God has taken on many forms according to circumstances of time and place the different sensibilities of peoples and their different cultural traditions. Hence it is that the forms in which this devotion is expressed, being subject to the ravages of time, show the need for a renewal that will permit them to substitute elements that are transient, to emphasize the elements that are ever new and to incorporate the doctrinal data obtained from theological reflection and the proposals of the Church's magisterium.[112]

---

111 *Marialis Cultus* n. 23.
112 Ibid., n.24.

In the final section of the document the Pope spoke specifically on the value of two key expressions of devotion to the Virgin Mary, the Angelus and the Rosary. He gives particular attention to the practice of saying the Rosary. In speaking about the Rosary the Pope called it "the compendium of the entire Gospel' and emphasised the encouragement of its frequent recitation.[113]

He highlighted the contemplative dimension to saying the Rosary. Without this dimension he said it is a "a body without a soul".[114] He goes on to state, "By its nature the recitation of the Rosary calls for a quiet rhythm and a lingering pace, helping the individual to meditate on the mysteries of the Lord's life as seen through the eyes of her who was closest to the Lord. In this way the unfathomable riches of these mysteries are unfolded".[115]

Finally the Pope adds a cautionary note: "we desire at the same time to recommend that this very worthy devotion should not be propagated in a way that is too one-sided or exclusive" and recommends the devotion to all hoping that Catholics will "be drawn to its calm recitation by its intrinsic appeal".

Some Comments on the Rosary as Devotion

For Catholics the Rosary is seen as the key element to Marian devotion. It is worth reflecting on the emergence in history of the use of the rosary in order to understand the relationship of devotional practices to the official prayer of the Church, the Liturgy. St Dominic Guzman (1170-1221), founder of the Order of Preachers, or Dominicans, is generally regarded as the creator of the rosary. However that attribution is not historically accurate. The Rosary predated the Spanish saint, though he and the Dominicans became its strong promoters.

The rosary developed as a form of prayer from the twelfth century. At the start of that century the praying of the Hail Mary spread in the West. Until the seventh century the angel's annunciation to Mary, described in the Gospel, was the antiphon of the Offertory of the fourth Sunday of Advent. This was a Sunday with a particularly

---
113 Ibid., n. 42.
114 Ibid., 47.
115 ibid.

Marian significance. However only the first part of the Hail Mary as we know it today was recited. The name of Jesus and the second part – "Holy Mary..." – were introduced around 1483 and formally recognised by the Catechism of the Council of Trent in 1556. Between 1410 and 1439 Dominic of Prussia, a Cologne Carthusian, proposed to the faithful a form of the Marian Psalter in which there were fifty Hail Marys, each followed by a verbal reference to a Gospel passage. The Carthusian's idea was a great success and psalters of this type multiplied in the fifteenth century. The final references to the Gospel were extremely numerous, at one point reaching some three hundred, according to the regions and favourite devotions.

Dominican Alain de la Roche (1428-1478) did great work in promoting the Marian Psalter, which at this time began to be called "Rosary of the Blessed Virgin Mary," thanks to his preaching and to the Marian confraternities he founded. The rosary was simplified in 1521 by Dominican Alberto da Castello, who chose fifteen evangelical passages for meditation, which included the short prayer at the end of the Hail Marys. Pope St Pius V (1566-1572) instituted the essence of the rosary's present configuration with the document *Consueverunt Romani Pontifices*.

This prayer which is the most used of all Catholic prayers has its base in the Scriptures and has emerged from the faith and devotion of the Church. The Hail Mary expresses our desire to honour the Blessed Virgin Mary and then to seek her intercession for us. The Rosary developed as an alternative to the Psalter of 150 psalms which were the basis of the Divine Office. The Rosary is, if you like, a lay person's psalter, encouraging quiet reflection of the key mysteries of the faith.

Modern Apparitions of the Blessed Virgin Mary: Lourdes

The story of the apparitions to fourteen year old Bernadette Soubirous at Lourdes in 1858 is well known by Catholics. On Thursday 11 February that year Bernadette saw a beautiful young girl in a niche at a rocky outcrop called Massabielle, about a half mile outside her town. She was near a wild rose bush and surrounded by a brilliant light and a golden cloud, smiling, with her arms extended towards Bernadette, who took out her rosary beads.

When she had finished praying the rosary the apparition beckoned to her, but Bernadette did not move and the girl smiled at her before disappearing. She later described that she had seen a young girl of about her own age and height, clothed in a brilliant and unearthly white robe, with a blue girdle around her waist and a white veil on her head.

This was the beginning of a whole sequence of apparitions, eighteen in all, which occurred during the spring and early summer of 1858. The Virgin Mary first spoke to Bernadette on 18 February when she asked her if she would come to the grotto each day for a fortnight. Thursday, 25 February, a crowd of about three hundred gathered with Bernadette, and the discovery that was to make Lourdes famous, that of the miraculous spring in the grotto.

The local bishop set up a Canonical Commission into the apparitions and in 1862 delivered his verdict: "We adjudge that the Immaculate Mary, Mother of God, really appeared to Bernadette Soubirous on February 11th, 1858, and subsequent days, eighteen times in all, in the Grotto of Massabielle, near the town of Lourdes: that this apparition possesses all the marks of truth, and that the faithful are justified in believing it certain. We humbly submit our judgement to the judgement of the Supreme Pontiff to whom is committed the Government of the whole Church."

One of the messages of Our Lady at Lourdes was to pray the rosary. The apparitions and the message were embraced by Catholics and became a major inspiration to the devotion of saying the Rosary.

Fatima

World War I has been referred to as the "war to end all wars". The conduct of war took on a form that produced immense suffering and futile loss of life. It was against this backdrop that the Virgin Mary appeared to three children - Lucia dos Santos, aged ten, and her cousins Francisco and Jacinta Marto, brother and sister, aged eight and seven respectively. The apparitions took place in a small village of Fatima, north of Lisbon.

In the spring of the previous year, 1916, that the children had an apparition of an angel. The angel appeared again in the autumn and gave the children Holy Communion.

On the 13 May 1917 after the children who were minding their flocks had said a Rosary, the Virgin Mary appeared to them. Lucia described it in these words, "A lady, clothed in white, brighter than the sun, radiating a light more clear and intense than a crystal cup filled with sparkling water, lit by burning sunlight."[116] She asked them to meet her on the 13th of the month for the next six months. The request she put to the children was: "Say the Rosary every day, to bring peace to the world and the end of the war."

During the apparition in July Our Lady requested. "When you pray the Rosary, say after each mystery: O my Jesus, forgive us, save us from the fire of hell. Lead all souls to heaven, especially those who are most in need." This request has been heeded and is now part of Catholic devotion.

News spread about these apparitions and large crowds gathered with the children on the 13th of the month. At the apparition in September 1917 Our Lady promised, "In October I will perform a miracle so that all may believe". Thus it was that the well known "miracle of the son" occurred the following month. Believers and sceptics alike experienced the phenomenon.

As well as promoting the saying of the Rosary the Virgin Mary spoke of sufferings coming upon the world and the Church and in particular made reference to Russia, which at that time was experiencing the beginnings of the Bolshevik Revolution. On July 13, 1917, Our Lady told Sister Lucy that "God is about to punish the world for its crimes, by means of war, famine, and persecutions of the Church, and of the Holy Father. To prevent this, I shall come to ask for the Communions of reparation and for the consecration of Russia to My Immaculate Heart ... In the end, My Immaculate Heart will triumph. The Holy Father will consecrate Russia to Me, which will be converted, and a period of peace will be granted to the world." Our Lady's request is very simple: Russia – the fount of so much evil in the 20th Century – must be set apart and made

In 1930 Pope Pius XI decreed that "Prayers for the conversion of Russia" were to be said at the end of every Mass. It was not until

---

116 Accounts of the Apparitions to the children are found in many books. A key resource is Lucia Santos, *Fatima in Lucia's Own Words*. Lucia's first four memoirs were written for the investigation for her cousins' canonization.

March 25, 1984 that Pope John Paul II made the consecration to Mary's Immaculate Heart.

Some Concluding Remarks

Devotion to the Blessed Virgin has always been attractive to Catholics and remains so. The first place for devotion is to be found in the liturgical feasts of the Blessed Virgin Mary of dogmatic standing, for example, the Feasts of the Immaculate Conception and the Assumption, the Feast of the Mother of God (January 1). Other Marian feasts follow in significance. At the personal level Catholics make use of the traditional Marian prayers like the Hail Mary, or the Hail Holy Queen (11th century), or the Memorare attributed to St Bernard of Clarvaux. Devotional practices like saying the Rosary, or reciting the Angelus (coming from 16th century) and other devotions provide a rich source of expression to devotion to the Blessed Virgin Mary.

Devotion to the Blessed Virgin Mary has been a hallmark of Catholic spirituality. In more recent times the various apparitions have called Catholics to such devotion. The Lord has desired that the Mother of God would speak more directly to her children. Her message has been consistently the same – prayer (particularly the Rosary), repentance and living a faithful way of life as a Catholic.

On apparitions of the Blessed Virgin Mary to St Bernadette Soubirous

The first time I went to the Grotto, was Thursday, 11th February, 1858. I went to gather firewood with two other little girls (Toinette, her sister, and Jeanne Abadie, nicknamed Balourn). When we got to the mill (of Savy), I asked the other two if they would like to see where the water of the mill joins the Gave. They said 'Yes.' From there we followed the canal. When we arrived there (at the foot of the rock of Massabielle) we found ourselves before a grotto. As they could go no further, my two companions prepared to cross the water lying before their path; so I found myself alone on the other side.

They crossed the water; they started to cry. I asked them why and they told me that the water was cold. I begged them to help me throw a few rocks into the water so that I could cross without taking my stockings off. They replied that I could do as they had done. Then I went a bit further to see if I could cross without taking my stockings off, but without success.

I came back towards the grotto and started taking off my stockings. I had hardly taken off the first stocking when I heard a sound like a gust of wind. Then I turned my head towards the meadow. I saw the trees quite still: I went on taking off my stockings. I heard the same sound again. As I raised my head to look at the grotto, I saw a Lady dressed in white, wearing a white dress, a blue girdle and a yellow rose on each foot, the same color as the chain of her rosary; the beads of the rosary were white.

The Lady made a sign for me to approach; but I was seized with fear, and I did not dare, thinking that I was faced with an illusion. I rubbed my eyes, but in vain. I looked again, and I could still see the same Lady. Then I put my hand into my pocket, and took my rosary. I wanted to make the sign of the cross, but in vain; I could not raise my hand to my forehead, it kept on dropping. Then a violent impression took hold of me more strongly, but I did not go.

The Lady took the rosary that she held in her hands and she made the sign of the cross. Then I commenced not to be afraid. I took my rosary again; I was able to make the sign of the cross; from that moment I felt perfectly undisturbed in mind. I knelt down and said my rosary, seeing this Lady always before my eyes. The Vision slipped the beads of her rosary between her fingers, but she did not move her lips. When I had said my rosary the Lady made a sign for me to approach, but I did not dare. I stayed in the same place. Then, all of a sudden, she disappeared.

I started to remove the other stocking to cross the shallow water near the grotto so as to join my companions. And we went away. As we returned, I asked my companions if they had seen anything. 'No,'; they replied. 'And what about you? Did you see anything?'

'Oh, no, if you have seen nothing, neither have I.'

I thought I had been mistaken. But as we went, all the way, they kept asking me what I had seen. I did not want to tell them. Seeing that they kept on asking I decided to tell them, on condition that they would tell nobody. They promised not to tell. They said that I must never go there again, nor would they, thinking that it was someone who would harm us. I said no. As soon as they arrived home they hastened to say that I had seen a Lady dressed in white. That was the first time.

From Writings of Saint Bernadette

20
Streams of Grace Today

This survey of the Catholic spiritual tradition began with reference to the outpouring of the Holy Spirit upon the apostles as Pentecost. The Church's true story – the story of its engagement with God – is the story of the presence and activity of the Holy Spirit in the lives of Catholics over the centuries. It is the story of those who opened their lives and hearts to God in such a way that they enabled the power of the Holy Spirit to lead them in ways of responding to streams of Grace.

An account of the various spiritual movements in the Church reveals how the Spirit of God has moved in ways that were necessary at particular moments in history. We saw how the call to the desert came about as the Church moved from a time of being a persecuted minority to receiving official sanction. We followed the growth of monasticism and noted how monasteries were islands of faith and culture able to resist the destructive forces of the so called "Dark Ages". The mendicants offered an evangelical pattern of life at a time when the Church risked becoming distanced from the ordinary people. The thirteenth century witnessed a new evangelical zeal being released in the Church in the face of the rise of various heretical sects. Similarly the spiritual impetus of the Catholic Counter Reformation expressed through such great saints as St Ignatius of Loyola and St Teresa of Avila ensured that the Church would be able to be regenerated from within.

Such spiritual movements often were incardinated in new forms of consecrated life and they also provided a significant impetus to the spiritual life of ordinary members of the Church. The spiritual movements were, in the end, for the Church as a whole and they became rich sources of spiritual renewal and a path for many believers in entering into the mystery of God. The rich tapestry of forms of devotion and expressions of prayer that have come to nourish the inner life of Catholics have been built up through the experience and witness of men and women caught up in these streams of Grace. Catholics have a rich storehouse from which to take forms of prayer and spiritual teaching to enable them to walk paths of personal holiness.

Like the wise steward referred to in the Gospel parable (Mt 13:52), Catholics today are able to draw on the past and receive from the fresh movements of the Spirit at this time in history. Indeed, a survey of the ways in which the action of God stimulated spiritual movements in the past invites the question: what is God doing today?

We will conclude this excursion through the spiritual tradition by considering this question: How is God active in the Church today? To answer this question we will restrict ourselves to spiritual movements that have been evident in the Church in the past fifty years – in other words, in the period after the Second Vatican Council and are still operative today.

Blessed Pope John Paul the Great

One figure has dominated the Catholic Church in the period after the Council until the beginning of the third millennium, the figure of Pope John Paul II, who is given the title, "the Great" by many in the Church. Among the enormous range of his influence, he was singularly instrumental in providing a renewed identity and focus for the Church and this had had significant influence on its spiritual vitality. He provided a foundation for Catholic identity within the Church and across the world. He clarified and reaffirmed Catholic teaching in a range of areas which has given Catholics a new confidence in the distinctiveness of the Catholic view of reality. From this clarified identity has come a resurgence of Catholic life and spirituality.

Pope John Paul II exercised his pontificate during a critical period when the Church was struggling to come to terms with a number of new realities: in particular, the ravages of the sexual revolution of the 1960s and the rise of a subtle yet cancerous secularism which was eroding faith in First World countries. Such challenges required teaching and spiritual renewal to provide the impetus for a renewal in faith. Of the many initiatives that he brought to this task – including a constant programme of travel to visit countries and Catholic communities across the globe – he promoted international gatherings of young people, called World Youth Days. These have proved singularly fruitful in mobilising young people to embrace Catholic life and more importantly to become effective witnesses of that faith to the world. The World Youth Days are essentially spiritual pilgrimages that have resulted in the conversion and re-energising of the faith of countless young people over a twenty five year period.

The contribution of Pope John Paul II to the spiritual life of the Church is captured in his apostolic exhortation marking the entry into a new millennium: *Novo millennio inente*. In this letter he explores the question of how the Church can effectively "start afresh from Christ"[117]. He mentions that the Church does not have to invent a "new programme" because it already exists. He says the programme for the Church exists in the Gospel and in the Tradition – "it is the same as ever", he says. This is an important point for consideration. The Church is "ever old, ever new". This means that while the Church must bring a fresh impetus to each age and situation, it does not mean that the Church must reinvent itself. It must be effectively what it is and always has been.

The Pope mentions what he considers are the "pastoral priorities" needed at this time. The first of these priorities is personal holiness. The Pope refers back to the Vatican Council and its teaching on the "universal call to holiness". The first need for the Church is saints! Many times he spoke of this. He said, "The time has come to re-propose wholeheartedly to everyone this *high standard of ordinary Christian living*: the whole life of the Christian community and of Christian families must lead in this direction".[118]

In pursuing a path of holiness the Pope proposes the importance of prayer. He mentions the "primacy of Grace" and speaks about the importance of listening to and proclaiming the Word of God. The Pope calls Catholics back to the fount of faith – a personal relationship with God in Christ through the power of the Holy

---

117 See Chapter 3.
118 *Novo millennio ineunte* n 31.

Spirit. This call has not gone unheeded. There is a noticeable recovery of traditional Catholic spirituality – from adoration of the Blessed Sacrament to the cult of saints, from Marian devotion to the practice of pilgrimage, from prayerful reflection on Sacred Scripture to the desire for contemplative prayer. This reinvigoration of traditional forms of Catholic piety has led to a fresh spiritual impetus in the life of the Church.

Most of the renewal of the Church has been "from below", that is, from among the ordinary people of the Church. We have seen this evidenced in many of the spiritual movements we have investigated. Fruitful movements of renewal "from above" have been the work of some of the greatest of the Popes, like Pope St Gregory the Great and Pope St Leo the Great. The influence of Pope John Paul II has been of that calibre.

The reinvigoration of Catholic life in our time owes much to the leadership of Blessed Pope John Paul the Great.

Role of Marian Devotion

We noted earlier that apparitions of the Blessed Virgin Mary have been a feature of Catholic spirituality in recent centuries. While there have been reports of apparitions over the centuries, it seems that there is a growing frequency of apparitions in recent centuries. There have been a number of reported apparitions in the past half century. The one that has attracted most attention has been that at Medjugorje, in Bosnia-Hercegovina.

On June 24, 1981, six teenagers from the Parish of Medjugorje reported the apparition of the Blessed Virgin Mary on a hill close to the town. These apparitions continued daily and, after a time, the visionaries gathered each evening in a side room of the parish Church. In the decade that followed thousands of pilgrims began to visit Medjugorje and there were reports of many conversions and personal miraculous experiences. Since 1981 over one million pilgrims visit Medjugorje each year.

The Blessed Virgin Mary has become known through Medjugorje as the Queen of Peace. The core message given by the visionaries is that the Blessed Virgin is saying that interior peace will be achieved through a spiritual life built on faith, prayer, penance, fasting and conversion. The messages encouraged the saying of the Rosary, fasting twice a week on bread and water, monthly confession and a deeper conversion to God.

Through the continuing influence of devotion to the Blessed Virgin Mary inspired by the apparitions at Lourdes and Fatima, and now Medjugorje, the spiritual lives of many Catholics has been strengthened. The Grace of God has touched the lives of many the intercession of the Blessed Virgin Mary. For many Catholics across the world devotion to the Blessed Virgin Mary is a conduit to a deeper spiritual life and a closer relationship with God. This has been the case over the history of the Church and continues to be an important source of spiritual fruitfulness in our time.

It seems that in our time the presence of the Virgin Mary is an important figure. She is rallying her children and, like a good mother, trying to guide them through the vicissitudes of life. And her voice is being heard and her message heeded.

The Charismatic Renewal

The impact on the Church of the Charismatic Renewal, which came into the Church from the later 1960s, should not be underestimated. The Renewal has touched the lives of tens of millions of Catholics right across the world, and still continues to be a potent spiritual force. The movement – which had origins in Protestantism – is identified as coming into the Catholic Church through a group of young university students at Duquesne University in Pittsburg in 1967. It spread rapidly throughout North America. Within a few years, Charismatic prayer groups were springing up in every continent.

The Charismatic Renewal focuses on the active role of the Holy Spirit in the Christian life, especially through the exercise of the spiritual charisms. The Renewal initially expressed itself through the formation of prayer meetings. The "Life in the Spirit Seminar" a seven-week course of teaching, discussion and scripture study, proved a key instrument for personal conversion and openness to receiving the charisms of the Spirit. The Charismatic Renewal had no founder or organisation, but was simply and clearly an action of Grace. While the exercise of the charisms is a distinguishing feature of the Charismatic Renewal, it is the personal experience of the presence of the Holy Spirit that results in a revitalised faith which is the most important aspect of its spiritual significance.

The Charismatic Renewal has reawakened a consciousness of the life of the early Church which was described as growing "under the consolation of the Holy Spirit" (Acts 9:31). The charisms were in clear evidence in the early apostolic communities (cf. 1 Cor. 12:4, Eph 4:11-12), and were a significant influence in the first Christian communities. The exercise of the charisms – not without difficulties at times[119] – not only built up the faith of the first Christian communities but was a significant tool in evangelisation as the Acts of the Apostles testifies[120]. The Lord promised that the Holy Spirit would always be with the Church (cf. Jn 14:16). Christian history reveals that there have been moments of particular outpourings of grace – the Spirit blows where he wills (Jn 3:8), and the Charismatic Renewal witnesses to a particular outpouring of the Holy Spirit in our time. As Pope Paul VI noted, "we are living in a privileged moment of the Holy Spirit."[121]

What is the significance of the Renewal for the Church in our time? In the Holy Year of 1975 the third International Congress of the Charismatic Renewal met in Rome. After a Mass celebrated by Cardinal Suenens, Pope Paul VI addressed the delegates in these

---

119 See the teaching of St Paul given in I Cor 14.
120 Acts 2:43 says, "Many wonders and signs were done through the apostles". Later in Acts 5:12ff St Luke comments, "Now many signs and wonders were done among the people by the hands of the apostles... so that they even carried out the sick into the streets, and laid them on beds and on pallets, that as Peter came by at least his shadow might fall on some of them!" Again Acts 6:8 records, "And Stephen, full of grace and power, did great wonders and signs among the people". Another reference is found in Acts 8:6 , "And the multitudes with one accord gave heed to what was said by Philip, when they heard him and saw the signs which he did". Finally one more text – Acts 8:13, "Even Simon (the magician) believed, and after being baptised he continued with Philip. And seeing signs and great miracles performed, he was amazed". Acts of the Apostles speaks about what happened at the Council of Jerusalem, "all the assembly kept silence; and they listened to Barnabas and Paul as they related what signs and wonders God had done through them among the Gentiles" (15:12). St Paul experienced signs and wonders accompanying his preaching as Acts 19:11 records, "And God did extraordinary miracles by the hands of Paul, so that handkerchiefs or aprons were carried away from his body to the sick, and diseases left them..." Acts ends its story by remembering that after Paul had laid hands on and healed a man, "the rest of the people on the island who had diseases also came and were cured" (28:9).
121 *Evangelii Nuntiandi*, n. 75.

words, "In such a world, more and more secularized, nothing is more necessary that the witness of this spiritual renewal which we see the Holy Spirit stirring today, in such diverse regions and circles". Pope Paul VI spoke many times and in a most eloquent way about the gift of the Spirit, reflecting his consciousness that the Church was receiving a special grace from God of a particular outpouring of the Holy Spirit.

In November 1972 Pope Paul VI commented:

> On several occasions, we have asked about the greatest needs of the Church. What do we feel is the first and last need of this blessed and beloved Church of ours. We must say it, almost trembling and praying, because as you know well, this is the Church's mystery and life: the Spirit, the Holy Spirit. He it is who animates and sanctifies the Church. He is her divine breath, the wind in her sails, the principle of her unity, the inner source of her light and strength. He is her support and consoler, her source of charisms and songs, her peace and joy, her pledge and prelude to blessed and eternal life.

This passage expresses most eloquently the role of the Holy Spirit in the Church. The Spirit has always been with the Church and active in its midst as we have seen through this excursion on the spiritual history of the Church. Yet it appears that this is a special moment of the Spirit, poured out in an explicit way upon believers.

At a meeting in Rome in May 1998 Pope John Paul II spoke of the activity of the Holy Spirit in the Church in these words:

> Whenever the Spirit intervenes, he leaves people astonished. He brings about events of amazing newness; he radically changes persons and history. This was the unforgettable experience of the Second Vatican Ecumenical Council during which, under the guidance of the same Spirit, the Church rediscovered the charismatic dimension as one of her constitutive elements: "It is not only through the sacraments and the ministrations of the Church that the Holy Spirit makes holy the people, leads them and enriches them with his virtues. Allotting his gifts according as he wills (cf. 1 *Cor* 12:11), he also distributes special graces among the faithful of every rank.... He makes them fit and ready to undertake various tasks and offices for the renewal and building up of the Church" (*Lumen gentium*, n. 12).

The Pope here identifies the emergence of charisms of the Spirit as "co-essential" for the Church. The charisms exist for the "renewal and building up of the Church". In so many ways the Charismatic Renewal has enriched the Church and contributed much to the life and mission of the Church.

We could summarise the contribution of the Charismatic Renewal to the Church in the following ways. The grace of the Renewal leads people into a deeper interior life of prayer and, particularly, an appreciation of worship of the Lord. The Renewal has revealed the spiritual charisms – like the gift of tongues, prophesy and healing. The exercise of the charisms teaches believers that the Spirit is an active presence in their lives and wants to work through them. The grace of the Renewal is <u>for</u> the Church, and so those in the Renewal are led deeper into the mystery and inner life of the Church. It results in a deeper consciousness of Catholic identity and encourages people to seek a further knowledge of the riches of the Catholic theological, liturgical and spiritual tradition. The grace of the Renewal has engendered a fresh desire to proclaim the Gospel and has helped develop the work of the New Evangelisation proposed by Pope John Paul II.

Ecclesial Movements

As we have looked over the history of the Church from a spiritual perspective we have seen various spiritual movements that have resulted in new forms of common life in the Church. This has been particularly noticeable in relation to the emergence of monasticism, in both its eremitical and communal forms; we saw it in the mendicant movement of the thirteenth century. Often fresh impetuses in the spiritual realm have led to the creation of new forms of religious life.

There is a phenomenon particular to our own time which marks a significant departure from this usual process. In the period after the Second Vatican Council we have witnessed the emergence of what has come to be known as "new ecclesial movements". These Ecclesial Movements[122] are movements that include all vocations

---

[122] The emergence of new movements in the Church in our time is the subject of a book I wrote entitled *New Wine and Fresh Skins*, published in 2010., (Connor Court).

in the Church – the laity, the religious and the clergy. They cannot be characterised as lay movements, nor religious movements, nor clerical movements. They embrace all these vocations, and in this regard they are something new in the Church. They are "ecclesial" movements. Examples of such movements are Focolare, Opus Dei, Neo Catechumenal Way, Emmanuel Community, Communion and Liberation, San Egidio Community, and many others.[123]

In St Peter's Square at the Vigil of Pentecost, 2006, at a gathering of these movements called by Pope Benedict shortly after he became pope, the Pope addressed them in these words,

Time and again in history the advent of the Holy Spirit has brought the experience of the beauty of being a Christian to those swept up in the moments of Grace – the monks in deserts, the monks living under the Rule of St Benedict, those inspired by the ideals of St Francis of Assisi, those seeking to live the Imitation of Christ, the students of Paris reaching out to the poor, and now those called to a new way of holiness in the movements in the Church.[124]

With these words the Pope was linking this new phenomenon in the Church with the great movements of the past.

How are we to define what an ecclesial movement is? It is not an easy matter. Pope John Paul attempted a definition of ecclesial movements in these words, "The term is often used to refer to realities that differ among themselves, sometimes by reason of their canonical structure. Though the term certainly cannot exhaust or capture the wealth of forms aroused by the life-giving creativity of the Spirit of Christ, it does indicate a concrete ecclesial reality with predominantly lay membership, a journey of faith and a Christian witness which bases its own pedagogical method on a precise charism given to the person of the founder in specific circumstances and ways."[125]

Thus the pope identifies four elements. An ecclesial movement is, to his mind, (a) a concrete ecclesial reality; (b) composed mainly of lay people; (c) which proposes a way of living the faith; and (d) is

---

[123] The Pontifical Council for the Laity has been engaged in establishing formal links between the movements and the Church. It currently has approved the Statutes of one hundred and twenty movements and has ongoing relationships with many more.
[124] Address to new movements, 2006.
[125] Message, 27 May 1998 n.4.

based in the charism of the founder.

This is a broad definition. While many of the new movements identify with this definition, some groups resist the description. Opus Dei, for instance, prefers not to be considered as one of the ecclesial movements. The Neocatechumenal Way, likewise, prefers not to use the description. The Charismatic Renewal similarly sees itself as not so much a movement as a grace for the Church. It nominates the fact that there is no founder to the Charismatic Renewal and it has no formal structure or membership. These are all valid comments, however, the Pope's attempt to identify something of the nature of the movements stands as a useful point of departure. The term is an elastic term which defies tight definition. However, one can use the term to capture the experience of the Church at this time where many groups are emerging which incorporate an inner renewal of Christian life, unite in some form of common life and have an apostolic orientation.

Ecclesial movements flourished in the Church after the Second Vatican Council. We should not underestimate how significant the Council was in laying the framework for the emergence and, importantly, the acceptance of the new movements. It goes without saying that many of the new movements in the Church's history have not always been easily received by the institution of the Church. The ecclesiology of the Second Vatican Council, one could say, prepared the ground for the movements to be embraced by the Church.

The Dogmatic Constitution, *Lumen Gentium*, in its second chapter, taught that the Church is "the People of God". On the basis of this understanding of the nature of the Church, the right of association among members of the Church does not depend on the hierarchy, and is a right of every baptised member. The Council Fathers built on this ecclesiology of the People of God, and recognized the common priesthood shared by all. This laid the foundation for an appreciation of the role of lay people in contributing directly to the evangelising mission of the Church. Furthermore, the Dogmatic Constitution on the Church, in the fifth chapter, proposed "The Universal Call to Holiness". In this statement the older notion of various "levels" of holiness was not used. Particularly any distinction between the clerical and religious life and that of the laity in terms of the pursuit of holiness was avoided. Finally, *Lumen Gentium* proposed the notion of charism. Thus the Dogmatic Constitution stated: 'It is not only through the sacraments and the ministrations of the Church that the Holy Spirit makes holy the people, leads them and enriches them with his virtues. Allotting his gifts according as he wills, he also distributes special graces among the faithful of every rank…He makes them fit and ready to undertake various tasks and offices for the renewal and building up of the Church." [126]

Pope John Paul II saw the significance of the ecclesial movements and spoke in more general terms of them in 1981. By 1987 he recognised the apostolic dynamism of the movements and saw them as a significant presence in the Church, commenting, "The great blossoming of these movements and the manifestations of energy and ecclesial vitality which characterise them are certainly to be considered one of the most precious fruits of the vast and profound spiritual renewal promoted by the last Council."[127] In 1998 he said that the movements "represent one of the most significant fruits of that springtime in the Church which was foretold by the Second Vatican Council"[128]. He spoke of the movements as "a new Pentecost for the Church".

The ground upon which people from all states of life in the Church can become involved in an ecclesial movement is their common baptism. Indeed, we can say that the movements are simply the actualisation of baptismal grace. Pope John Paul II commented on this when he said, "Even in the diversity of their forms, these movements are marked by a common awareness of the 'newness' which baptismal grace brings to life, through a remarkable longing to reflect on the mystery of communion with Christ and with their brethren."[129]

Members of movements in effect live out the full reality of their Christian identity and calling. Again we refer to the words of the Pope, "members of the Church who find themselves in associations and movements seek to live, under the impulse of the Spirit, the Word of God in their concrete lives. They do so by stimulating, with their witness, constantly renewed spiritual progress, by evangelically

---

126 *Lumen Gentium* n.12.
127 Address, 2 March 1987 n.1.
128 Message, 27 May 19988 n.2.
129 Message, 27 May 1998 n.2.

vivifying temporal realities and human values, and enriching the Church through an infinite and inexhaustible variety of initiatives in the realm of charity and holiness".[130] He commented that the movements "have helped you all to rediscover your baptismal vocation."[131]

What is significant about participation in the movements is that the Christian life of the members is not just partially involved; their whole Christian life is engaged. Movements are more than associations where individuals contribute to a work or cause in the Church, they are rather a completely involving experience.

The gathering of the new movements and communities in 2006 came together under the theme of the "Beauty of being a Christian". This theme reveals an aspect of what the new movements have brought to the Church. They have helped their members to rediscover the beauty of being a Christian and the members of the new movements can give a witness to the world of the beauty of the Christian life.

The new movements through their work of evangelisation and formation can help people be truly recreated according to the truth of who they are in God – what God intends them to be by virtue of their Baptism. This is another vital service that the new movements can bring to the Church.

On Starting afresh from Christ

30. First of all, I have no hesitation in saying that all pastoral initiatives must be set in relation to holiness. Was this not the ultimate meaning of the Jubilee indulgence, as a special grace offered by Christ so that the life of every baptized person could be purified and deeply renewed?

It is my hope that, among those who have taken part in the Jubilee, many will have benefited from this grace, in full awareness of its demands. Once the Jubilee is over, we resume our normal path, but knowing that stressing holiness remains more than ever

---

130 Address, 2 March 1987, n.3.
131 Address, 30 May 1998, n.7.

an urgent pastoral task.

It is necessary therefore to rediscover the full practical significance of Chapter 5 of the Dogmatic Constitution on the Church Lumen Gentium, dedicated to the "universal call to holiness". The Council Fathers laid such stress on this point, not just to embellish ecclesiology with a kind of spiritual veneer, but to make the call to holiness an intrinsic and essential aspect of their teaching on the Church. The rediscovery of the Church as "mystery", or as a people "gathered together by the unity of the Father, the Son and the Holy Spirit",[15] was bound to bring with it a rediscovery of the Church's "holiness", understood in the basic sense of belonging to him who is in essence the Holy One, the "thrice Holy" (cf. Is 6:3). To profess the Church as holy means to point to her as the Bride of Christ, for whom he gave himself precisely in order to make her holy (cf. Eph 5:25-26). This as it were objective gift of holiness is offered to all the baptized.

But the gift in turn becomes a task, which must shape the whole of Christian life: "This is the will of God, your sanctification" (1 Th 4:3). It is a duty which concerns not only certain Christians: "All the Christian faithful, of whatever state or rank, are called to the fullness of the Christian life and to the perfection of charity".[16]

31. At first glance, it might seem almost impractical to recall this elementary truth as the foundation of the pastoral planning in which we are involved at the start of the new millennium. Can holiness ever be "planned"? What might the word "holiness" mean in the context of a pastoral plan?

In fact, to place pastoral planning under the heading of holiness is a choice filled with consequences. It implies the conviction that, since Baptism is a true entry into the holiness of God through incorporation into Christ and the indwelling of his Spirit, it would be a contradiction to settle for a life of mediocrity, marked by a minimalist ethic and a shallow religiosity. To ask catechumens: "Do you wish to receive Baptism?" means at the same time to ask them: "Do you wish to become holy?" It means to set before them the radical nature of the Sermon on the Mount: "Be perfect as your heavenly Father is perfect" (Mt 5:48).

As the Council itself explained, this ideal of perfection must not be misunderstood as if it involved some kind of extraordinary existence, possible only for a few "uncommon heroes" of holiness. The ways of holiness are many, according to the vocation of each individual. I thank the Lord that in these years he has enabled me to beatify and canonize a large number of Christians, and among them many lay people who attained holiness in the most ordinary circumstances of life. The time has come to re-propose wholeheartedly to everyone this high standard of ordinary Christian living: the whole life of the Christian community and of Christian families must lead in this direction. It is also clear however that the paths to holiness are personal and call for a genuine "training in holiness", adapted to people's needs. This training must integrate the resources offered to everyone with both the traditional forms of individual and group assistance, as well as the more recent forms of support offered in associations and movements recognized by the Church.

Pope John Paul II, *Tertio millennio ineunte*

21
Epilogue

The Prophet Ezekiel was a priest. He prophesied while the Jewish people were in exile. The temple in Jerusalem had been destroyed. Yet his words spoke of life-giving waters flowing from the sanctuary of the temple in Jerusalem: "and I saw water flowing out from beneath the threshold of the temple toward the east" (Ez 47:1).

The image of the stream of life-giving water is found in other biblical passages. For example, in the Book of Joel, we read, "In that day the mountains shall drip sweet wine, the hills shall flow with milk, and all the stream beds of Judah shall flow with water; a fountain shall come forth from the house of the Lord and water the Wadi Shittim (Joel 3:18). In the Book of Zechariah, we read, "On that day living waters shall flow out from Jerusalem, half of them to the eastern sea and half of them to the western sea; it shall continue in summer as in winter. And the Lord will become king over all the earth; on that day the Lord will be one and His name one." (Zech. 14:8-9). In the Book of Revelation we read, "Then the angel showed me the river of the water of life, bright as crystal, flowing from the throne of God and of the Lamb" (Rev. 22:1).

The angel said to Ezekiel, "This water flows toward the eastern region and goes down into the Arabah; and when it enters the sea, the sea of stagnant waters, the water will become fresh. Wherever the river goes, every living creature that swarms will live, and there will be very many fish, once these waters reach there. It will become fresh; and everything will live where the river goes." The Arabah is the deep rift valley that forms the Dead Sea and continues southward. The life-giving effect of the waters is apparent from the freshening of the salt waters and the abundance of fish. This water flowing from the sanctuary transforms the environment which it enters.

The image of water is understood as a description of the action of the Holy Spirit. The evangelist John records (7:53), "On the last and greatest day of the Feast, Jesus stood and said in a loud voice,

'If anyone is thirsty, let him come to me! Let the man come and drink who believes in me.'" The evangelist then refers to Scriptural sources that refer to fountains of living water. The reference, for instance, evokes the story of Moses tapping the rock in the desert to release water for the people of Israel (Ex17:1-7) and evokes the prophetic image of Ezekiel. St John then comments, "He was speaking of the Spirit which those who believed in him were to receive." (Jn 7:39)

This image of streams of water is a rich scriptural theme which can be seen as being fulfilled definitively at Pentecost. It continues to be experienced in the Church throughout its history. The book, in recalling some moments in Catholic history, gives testimony that the prophesy of Ezekiel continues to be fulfilled right up to our own day.

The Holy Spirit is present and active in the Church. Streams of Grace have flowed out upon the Church, coming from the heavenly sanctuary, and bringing life and fruitfulness to the Church.

Appendix

An overview of the Catholic Spiritual Tradition

There are many excellent works outlining the history of the Catholic Spiritual Tradition. This material is offered as a background to the topics presented in this book. It presents a broader context to the spiritual movements which we explored. It also can help in situating certain movements in relationship to one another.

1. BEGINNINGS.

We can describe New Testament spirituality as having three principle sources: the Synoptic Gospels, St Paul and St John. The spirituality of the Synoptic Gospels (Matthew, Mark and Luke) focussed on the preaching of Jesus about the Kingdom of God and about the meaning of the death and Resurrection of the Lord. St Paul emphasises that the salvation achieved by Christ cannot be earned but is a gift of God's mercy. St John's writings, which have a certain mystical aspect, focused on the gift of life given by God who is love.

The early Apostolic Fathers like St Ignatius of Antioch wrote on subjects like the spirituality of martyrdom. Alongside this spirituality came an emphasis on the spirituality of virginity, and they both came together in the cult of the virgin martyrs (St Agnes). They began linking the Christian teaching with Greek thought patterns. In the beginning Neo-Platonic thought provided a philosophical basis for the attempt of the Fathers to communicate with the intellectual world of the time. One problem the Fathers, like St Irenaeus of Lyons, had to contend with was the problem of Gnosticism.

There were two "schools of thought" in early Christianity. One, the Alexandrian School, was influenced by Greek thought which flourished in Alexandia at that time. St Clement of Alexandria c.195 founded a famous Catechetical School which produced the great Scripture scholar, Origen. He emphasised the spiritual meaning of Sacred Scripture, and this school developed the allegorical[132] method of interpreting Sacred Scripture. The other "school" was the Antiochian School, influenced more by Syrian culture. This school as exemplified by the preaching of St John Chrysostom (d.407) focussed on the ethical implications of the Gospel.

Monasticism was a defining spiritual movement in the early centuries of Christianity. The life of the hermit was captured in St Athanasius' *Life of Antony*. The Church has benefited by collections of the *Apothegmata*, or "Sayings of the Desert Fathers."

Two steams of thought emerged among the spiritual theologians inspired by monastic experience. Evagrius Ponticus emphasised the role of the intellect in the life of prayer. He also made a significant contribution in teaching on the eight basic sins. The other stream of thought finds expression in the writings of Pseudo-Macarius who developed a spirituality of the heart. It would be this spirituality that found expression in the Eastern Christian spiritual tradition. A key exponent was St John Climacus and his concept of the ladder of perfection.

Western monasticism owes much to John Cassian (d.435) whose *Conferences* brought the spirituality of Egyptian monasticism to the West.

In what is modern Turkey the Cappadocian Fathers marked a particular highpoint of spiritual theology. St Basil the Great (330-379) produced many important writings, among them were liturgical prayers still used today and a monastic Rule providing for a form of monasticism in an urban setting. His work *On the Holy Spirit* was foundational for the Church's eventual teaching on the role of the

---

132 Allegorical method is an approach to the interpretation of Sacred Scripture which seeks to present the symbolic meaning of the biblical text. The method continued to be used until late medieval times.

Holy Spirit in the Christian life. St Gregory Nazianzus, his friend, was called "The Theologian", while St Gregory of Nyssa is regarded as the Father of Christian Mysticism. He wrote the very influential book describing the mystical ascent: *Life of Moses*. He described the interaction of God and the human person as a theosis[133] – a key theological understanding of the Christian spiritual life that influenced the Christian East.

Teaching on Christian mysticism was found in the influential work of Dionysius the Pseudo-Aeropagite. His writings were of a speculative nature and he spoke of the mystery of God in terms of cloud and darkness. He taught what was to become known as the Via Negativa or Apophatic spirituality.

A reaction to this speculative mysticism took the form of an affective ascetical moralism which characterised the work of the Antioch School.

In the ancient West a number of important Fathers emerged. St Ambrose of Milan wrote many treatises among them *De Viginitate*: a spirituality of virginity. He also wrote hymns which continue to be used in the Church today. St Jerome who spent much of his life Bethlehem as an ascetic advocated the historical study of Sacred Scripture. He is best known for his Latin translation of the Bible – the Vulgate.

A towering figure in the Western Church was St Augustine of Hippo (d.430). In distinction to the deification concept popular among the Greek Fathers he saw the Christian life as a battle against concupiscence. Opposing the ideas of the priest Pelagius (d 420), he taught that salvation cannot be achieved by human effort alone. St Augustine became known as the "Doctor of Grace".

St Leo the Great was pope from 400-461. Part of the legacy of his papacy were his sermons which reveal a piety based in liturgy.

St Benedict of Nursia (d.550) was the father of Western monasticism. His monastic *Rule* is a model of moderation, emphasising stability, obedience and humility. The Church today

---

133 Theosis, or deification is the transforming effect of divine grace on the human person.

bases the Divine Office on the *Opus Dei* that he developed for his monks. Similarly we are indebted to his emphasis on *Lectio Divina* as the prayerful reading of the Sacred texts.

2. MIDDLE AGES.

In the early Middle Ages Western spiritual teaching is marked by Benedictine spirituality. Pope St Gregory the Great (540-604) was a monk and the first Benedictine to become pope. His *Pastoral Rule* is regarded as a classic work. His thesis focuses on the notion of "Servitude"- service marked by humility and penance.

St Bede the Venerable (625-735), an English monk, wrote on the patterns of prayer flowing from Lectio Divina – lectio, meditatio, oratio, intentio.

This period was the time when the Church in Ireland flourished and Celtic spirituality made its distinctive contribution to the Church. Irish Catholicism was strongly influenced by monasticism which remained close to the people. This monasticism was marked by a penitential spirit. The "green martyrdom" saw a missionary spirit take the monks on great voyages of evangelisation. Sts Aidan, Columba and Columban were responsible for remarkable evangelising missions.

The Carolingian Renaissance provided a period of intellectual and cultural revival in Europe occurring from the late eighth century. The Carolingian rulers Charlemagne and Louis the Pious provided a newly stabilized society which helped introduce the notion of Christendom. St Anselm (1033-1109) a Benedictine theologian and Archbishop of Canterbury contributed *Meditations and Prayers*. Rabanus Maurus (784-856) gave us the hymn *Veni Sante Spiritus*

It was the monastic influence though that dominated the spirituality of medieval society. The monk was the ideal Christian. Among the laity faith was often rudimentary and with verbal prayers – *Pater, Confiteor, Credo* – the heart of their lived faith.

The High Middle Ages (from the year 1000) witnessed various reforms of Benedictinism. Reforms occurred at Cluny in France.

Individual autonomous monasteries were replaced by a system of monasteries as daughter houses of the founding monastery. The Cluniac reform promoted a "high" liturgical celebration of the Divine Office. Guigo II (d.1193) continued to encourage the practice of reading, meditation and prayer. The Carthusian reform by St Bruno (d. 1084) gave greater emphasis to solitude.

The great reform movement was that of St Bernard of Clairvaux (1090-1153). His teaching was steeped in Scripture. He is regarded as the last of the Fathers. He was not given to visions. He saw love of God as the all encompassing Christian virtue. The key quality in the spiritual life was *devotio*.

Other contributors to spiritual thought at the time included the Benedictine William of St Thierry (1085-1148) who combined Origin and St Gregory of Nyssa and emphasised affective love. The Cistercian John of Fecamp similarly highlighted affective piety and emphasised the humanity of Jesus. Finally mention should be made of Aelred of Revaulx (1109-1167) an English Cistercian who also wrote about affective piety.

This period witnessed the rise of a number of outstanding women mystics. St Gertrude the Great (1250-1311) from the Monastery of Helfta in Saxony was a forerunner of a spirituality of the heart of Jesus. St Mechtilde of Helfta (d.1298) recounted her mystical visions. St Bridget (1302-1373) of Sweden experienced revelations centering on the passion of Christ.

The emergence of Scholasticism as the preferred theological method produced the School of St Victor in Paris. These Augustinian canons were theologians with a strong spiritual bent. Hugh of St Victor (1096-1141) was a synthesiser and his *On the Mysteries of Christian Faith* emphasised a link between *lectio*, theology, morality and contemplation. Richard of St Victor (d.1173) was mystical and wrote on the four degrees of love.

Popular piety of the time focussed upon the humanity of Jesus. It was in this period that many expressions of popular devotions associated with the Virgin Mary also developed. Christian life as marked by the popularity of pilgrimages and a fascination with demons, angels and saints.

The development of Friars with their emphasis on poverty and mendicancy marks a new chapter in forms of religious life. The great figure is St Francis of Assisi (1181-1226) who promoted evangelical preaching, penance and prayer. His piety was concrete, particular, human and moral. His affective devotion to the humanity of Jesus gave rise to the crib and the stigmata.

St Bonaventure (1217-1274) was the great Franciscan theologian who systematised Franciscan spirituality. Raymond Lull (1235-1316), a Franciscan, wrote on contemplation being achieved through the methodical application of memory, understanding and will. Bl Angela of Foligno (1248-1309) was a Franciscan mystic.

The other great figure of the time was St Dominic (1173-1221) who set out to combat heresy and came to realise that preaching can only be fruitful when a radical Christian life is lived by the preacher. He advocated radical poverty. He placed importance on learning as the basis for good preaching and set the scene for the Dominican contribution to spiritual direction.

The great intellectual St Thomas Aquinas (1224-1274), the "Angelic Doctor", was a pupil of Albert the Great. His contribution to spirituality was his distinctions between meditation (discursive) and contemplation (vision). St Catherine of Siena (1347-1380) was a Dominican tertiary and one of the great lights of the Church. Though illiterate her *Divine Dialogue* earned her the title of Doctor of the Church. Her life was at the same time active and ecstatic.

As we move to the Late Middle Ages (the period 1300-1500) we enter a dark period of European history. The thirteenth and fourteenth centuries were times of the division of the papacy, the One Hundred Years War, the plague and a time of intellectual sterility. However there were isolated heroic witnesses to the faith.

Rhineland mystics emerged inspired by Dominican spirituality. Meister Eckhart (1260-1327) was speculative and dwelt on the idea of the darkness of unknowing. He was accused of heresy mainly in relation to pantheism and was condemned 1329. After his death he was exonerated. John Tauler (1300-1361) was a Dominican pupil of Eckhart. He was a pastor and preacher, more practical in his teaching than his master.

Under Nicholas of Basle the "Friends of God", a lay movement focussed on personal prayer. Henry Suso (1295-1366) was a recluse and ascetic. John Ruysbroek (1293-1381) was a Flemish Augustinian and provided a balanced approach to contemplative prayer.

At this time spiritual associations among laity led to the development of the Beguines who experienced a troubled history.

The "Ancren Riwle" gives testimony to an anchorite movement in England and the fourteenth century witnessed a number of significant spiritual writers. Richard Rolle of Hampole, (1295-1349) wrote of his spiritual experiences in a simple and practical way. The "Cloud of Unknowing", possibly written by a Midland priest around 1370, is a spiritual classic in the tradition of the Via Negativa. It speaks of the darkness of unknowing. Julian of Norwich recorded her visions as she lay dying in 1373. She focussed on the passion. The Augustinian Canon Walter Hilton (c1396) produced the most scholarly work, *Scale of Perfection*.

The Fifteenth century saw the demise of spiritual writings. The century was marked by pietism which declined into subjective sentimentality. It was a time where there was a preoccupation with witches.

Devotio Moderna movement promoted by Gerard Groote (1340-1384) offered a way to grow in the practical practice of virtue. There is a reaction in these writings to speculative mysticism. It produced the great classic by Thomas a Kempis (1380-1471) *Imitation of Christ*.

3. BYZANTINE SPRITUALITY.

The Church was one until the Great Schism of 1453. While East and West grew along different lines over the centuries they reflected a common heritage of spiritual experience and thought. The Church today rightly draws on the teachings of the great saints of both East and West.

Eastern Christian spirituality was strongly monastic. There were two streams – one centred in Mt Sinai of which St John Climacus is the defining figure. This steam tends to ascetical austerity. The second stream centred on Constantinople. Here the Studite tradition was dominant. St Maximus the Confessor (580-662) is the defining figure here. His mysticism emphasised the divine operation and presented the notion of the spiritual life being one of deification. The other great figure in this tradition is St Simeon the New Theologian whose mystical writings presented the notion of deification achieved through the transforming influence of the Holy Spirit.

The Byzantine tradition gave particular importance to the Divine Liturgy and to iconography. The liturgy was seen as a participation in heavenly worship, while icons were understood as windows into mystery of God.

A major monastic revival occurred in the tenth century at Mt. Athos. It was a revival of hesychasm and the use of the Jesus Prayer. It emphasised prayer of the heart. St Gregory Palamas (1296-1359) in his theological controversy with Balaam provided a critical defence of the hesychastic tradition.

In the eighteenth a further revival of hesychasm occurred in Russia. A key early figure was Paissy Velichkovshy (1722-1794). The *Philokalia*, a collection of various writings, was an important instrument in promoting this spiritual revival. Prominent figures in popularising the movement were St Theophane the Recluse (1815–1894) and St Seraphim of Sarov (1759-1833) who is called the "St Francis of Russia". The book which promoted the spiritual movement among the people was the anonymously written *Way of the Pilgrim*.

4. MODERN PERIOD.

In the modern period we speak of "schools" of spirituality associated with particular countries.

The Spanish School was very influential and produced saints who have had a lasting influence on spirituality in the modern era.

Their work was preceded by the Benedictine abbot of Monserrat, Garcia Ximenes (1475-1510). He sought to produce an ordered form of meditation which he called the "Spiritual Exercises." Another significant figure was St Peter of Alcantara (1499-1562), a Franciscan, who served as an early adviser to St Teresa of Avila.

It was the work of St Ignatius Loyola (1491-1556) and his manual for spiritual directors, the *Spiritual Exercises* that was to be a standard format for cultivating the spiritual life. His teaching on the use of memory, understanding and will in meditation became the standard practice for the next four hundred years. His teaching on the recognition of consolation and desolation has guided the practice of spiritual direction.

In the Ignatian tradition a number of spiritual works deserve mention. Louis Lallemant (d.1638) wrote *Spiritual Doctrine*. Jean Pierre de Caussade (1693-1751) wrote the classic text *Self-abandonment to Divine Providence*.

The other great Spanish stream of spiritual teaching comes from St Teresa of Avila (1515-1582). She founded the Discalced Carmelites. Her writing on the stages of spiritual growth was very influential. She was a contemplative and mystic who was able to articulate the unfolding of spiritual growth. Her work was complemented by St John of Cross (1542-1591). He was a poet, a psychologist, a theologian and a mystic. He emphasised the purifications required for spiritual growth. He is known for his teachings about the dark night of senses and spirit. He understood the need for complete detachment.

The Carmelite tradition has produced a number of great saints. St Teresa of the Child Jesus (1873-1897) became a very popular saint and her teaching on the "Little way" of spiritual childhood was attractive to many. Other saints in this tradition include St Elizabeth of the Trinity and the Jewish convert Bl Edith Stein who was killed in a Nazi concentration camp.

The Italian School was influenced by the effects of Renaissance which threatened to promote a new paganism. The school is marked by Christian humanism. Some key figures were the Dominican

Jerome Savanarola (1452-1498), the Jesuit St Robert Bellermine (1542-1621) and the Theatine Lawrence Scupoli (1530-1610) whose *Spiritual Combat* is a classic work.

The French School produced a great array of saints well known to the Catholic world. The holy bishop of Geneva, St Francis de Sales (1567-1622) was a spiritual director who combined the teaching of St Ignatius and St Teresa. His spirituality, captured in the classic, *Introduction to the Devout Life*, proposed a devout humanism. St Jeanne de Chantal, inspired by St Francis de Sales founded the Congregation of Visitation and from that congregation St Margaret Mary Alacoque (1647-1693) experienced revelations of the Sacred Heart which fostered a devotion that spread across the Catholic world.

In Paris a group of pious laypeople met with Mme Acarie (1566-1618) and developed contemplation according to the teaching of St Teresa. Cardinal de Beruille (1575-1629) founded the French Oratory whose spirituality came to be known as "The French School". Priestly spirituality found expression in the example and teaching of St Vincent de Paul (1576-1660). Jean-Jacque Olier (1608-1657) from the Oratory of St Sulpice promoted a spirituality centred on the Sacred Heart. He promoted the practices of Benediction and saying the Rosary. St John Eudes (1601-1680), also from the Oratory promoted devotion to the heart of Jesus and the heart of Mary. Marian devotion was promoted by St Louis Grignion de Montfort (1673-1716).

St Jean Baptiste de la Salle (1651-1719), founder of the Brothers of the Christian Schools, developed a meditation method which he saw as the basis for the daily spiritual life of the brothers.

This period however gave rise to two spiritual heresies which were to severely damage the Church. The first was Quietism connected initially with Miguel de Molinos (1640-1697). Other figures caught up in this heresy were Mme de Guyon (1648-1717) and Bishop Francis Fenelon (1651-1715) who defended Quietism with his teaching on "holy indifference". The other great heresy was Jansenism. Initially associated with the teachings of the Dutch priest Cornelius Jansen (1585-1638) it adopted a pessimism about human nature. It was the Cistercian convent of Port Royal which became the centre of this teaching during the period 1622-1709. The Jansenists adopted a moral rigorism and embraced Predestination. They attracted some significant followers including Blaise Pascal (1623-1662), a mathematician and philosopher, His work *Pensees* was influenced by Port Royal. The heresy had an influence in Ireland and hence Australia.

If we are to speak of an English School, then we receive examples of Anglican piety which had its roots in the fourteenth century. Dom Augustine Baker (1575-1641) was Catholic priest and his book *Holy Wisdom* expresses an English individualism. Anglican piety is found in the works of the metaphysical poet John Donne (1573-1631). The mystic Lancelot Andrews and the poet George Herbert offer further examples of an affective piety.

The Oxford movement led to a renewed interest in the Catholic tradition. Bl John Henry Cardinal Newman (1801-1890) whose *Meditations and Devotions* and many sermons is the best known advocate of this movement.

The Classical Protestantism of people like Martin Luther, John Calvin and Jacob Boehme did in time underscore a pietism in the Lutheran tradition. This in turn fostered an evangelical movement that touched England and America. Men like Phillip Spener (1635-1705) and Johann Arndt (1555-1621) influenced Ludwig Graf van Zinzindorf (1700-1760) who founded the Moravian Brethren who in turn inspired the young Anglican John Wesley (1703–1791). This led to the development of Methodism and a wave of evangelical preachers like George Whitfield (1714-1770) preached on both sides of the Atlantic. The Welsh revivals and the "Great Awakening" in the American colonies opened the doors to modern evangelicalism.

An offshoot of this movement was Pentecostalism, a twentieth century phenomenon, which began in Topeka, Kansas, 1901, and saw a revival in the 1960s.

When we turn our attention to Catholicism in the twentieth century, we note a number of movements. At the ecclesial level the

Biblical and Liturgical Movements had significant impact through the teaching of the Second Vatican Council. The "universal call to holiness" promoted by Vatican II found expression in the emergence of lay movements in the Church.

Two spiritual streams of importance are, firstly, the influence of apparitions of the Blessed Virgin Mary at Lourdes, Fatima, Medjugorje, and other places. The second stream is the Charismatic Renewal.

The Church was guided by to find a new sense of identity and mission by the twenty five year papacy of the now Blessed Pope John Paul II, called by many "the Great". The Church, as it enters the third millennium, is experiencing the eroding of the faith through secularism, but is witnessing many movements of renewal particularly among the lay people. Grace is still active in the Church!

Bibliography

General works on the history of Christian Spirituality

Aumann, J., *Christian Spirituality in the Catholic Tradition*. London: Sheed & Ward, 1985.
Bouyer, L., *Introduction to Spirituality*, London: Darton, Longman & Todd, 1961.
Bouyer, L, Leclercq J., Vandenbroucke, F. and Cognet, L., *A History of Christian Spirituality, Vol I: The Spirituality of the New Testament and the Fathers*. New York: The Seabury Press, 1982.
Bouyer, L, Leclercq J., Vandenbroucke, F. and Cognet, L., *A History of Christian Spirituality, Vol II: The Spirituality of the Middle Ages*. New York: The Seabury Press, 1982.
Bouyer, L, Leclercq J., Vandenbroucke, F. and Cognet, L., *A History of Christian Spirituality, Vol III: Orthodox Spirituality and Protestant and Anglican Spirituality*. New York: The Seabury Press, 1982.
Holmes, U. T., *A History of Christian Spirituality: An Analytical Introduction*. Minneapolis: The Seabury Press, 1980.
Knox, R. A., *Enthusiasm: A Chapter in the History of Religion with Special Reference to the XVII and XVIII Centuries*. Westminster, Maryland: Christian Classics, 1983.
McGinn, B., Meyendorff, J. and Leclercq, L. eds., *Christian Spirituality: Origins to the Twelfth Century*. New York: Crossroad, 1985.
Raitt, J., McGinn, B., and Meyendorff, J. eds., *Christian Spirituality: High Middle Ages and Reformation*. New York: Crossroad, 1987.

Works on the Spiritual Life

Aumann, J., *Spiritual Theology*. London: Sheed & Ward, 1980.
Barker, K., *Becoming Fire: A Spiritual Journey of Faith*. Melbourne: Freedom Publishing Co., 2001.
Barker, K., *A Radical Way of Love*. Garran: Missionaries of God's Love, 2007.
Colin, L., *The Interior Life*. England: Fowler Wright Books, 1962.
Cuskelly, E. J., *A Summa of the Spiritual Life*. New York: St Paul, 1963.
De Chantal, St. J. F. F., *The Spiritual Life: A Summary of the Instruction on the Virtues and on Prayer given by Saint Jane Frances Frémyot De Chantal*. London: Sands & Co., 1929.
De Guibert, J., *The Theology of the Spiritual Life*. London: Sheed & Ward, 1956.
de Stoop, M., *Spiritual Direction: Who is it for & What are its benefits*. Sydney: Catholic Communications, 2005.

Faricy, R., *Seeking Jesus in Contemplation and Discernment.* Wilmington, Delaware: Michael Glazier, 1983.
Fleming, D. A., ed. *The Fire and the Cloud: An Anthology of Catholic Spirituality.* London: Geoffrey Chapman, 1978.
Groeschel, B. J., *Spiritual Passages: The Psychology of Spiritual Development.* New York: Crossroad, 2002.
Hickey, B. J., *Living Biblically: How to find answers to life's deepest questions in God's Word.* Leederville, WA: Record Books, 2008.
James, W., *The Varieties of Religious Experience: A Study in Human Nature.* London: Fontana Library, 1971.
Malatesta, E., ed., *Jesus in Christian Devotion and Contemplation.* Hertfordshire: Anthony Clarke Books, 1974.
Massam, K., *Sacred Threads: Catholic Spirituality in Australia 1922-1962.* Sydney: UNSW Press, 1996.
Newton, P. A., *Making Sense of Private Revelations.* Camberwell: Divine Mercy Publications, 2004.
Ouspensky, L., *Theology of the Icon.* Crestwood, New York: St. Vladimir's Seminary Press, 1978.
Pasquini, J. J., *Light, Happiness & Peace: Journeying Through Traditional Catholic Spirituality.* China, Indiana: Shepherds of Christ Publications, 2007.
Parente, P. P., *The Ascetical Life.* St Louis: B. Herder Book Co., 1944.
Raguin, Y., *Attention to the Mystery: Entry into the Spiritual Life.* New York: Paulist Press, 1982.
Ranson, D.,*Living in the Holy Spirit: Elements of Catholic Spirituality.* Australian Catholic Bishops' Conference, 2008.
Ryan, N. J., ed. *Christian Spiritual Theology: An Ecumenical Reflection.* Melbourne: Dove Communications, 1976.
Smart, N., *The Religious Experience of Mankind.* London: Fontana Library, 1971.
Špidlík, T., *The Spirituality of the Christian East: A Systematic Handbook.* Kalamazoo, Michigan: Cistercian Publications, 1986.
Tanquerey, A., *The Spiritual Life: A Treatise on Ascetical and Mystical Theology.* Tournai, Belgium: Desclee & Co., 1930.
Underhill, E., *The Spiritual Life.* Hodder & Stoughton, 1937.
Walker, D., *God is a Sea: The Dynamics of Christian Living.* Homebush: St Pauls, 1977.

Works on Prayer

Borst, J., *A Method of Contemplative Prayer.* Homebush: St Pauls, 1973.
Congregation for the Doctrine of the Faith, *Letter to the Bishops of the Catholic Church on Some Aspects of Christian Mediation (Vatican Translation).* Boston: St

Pauls, 1989.
de Jaegher, P., *An Anthology of Mysticism*. London: Burns Oates & Washbourne, 1935.
Doctrinal Commission of the International Catholic Charismatic Renewal Services, *Guidelines on Prayers for Healing*. Melbourne: ICCRS, 2007.
Freeman, L., *Christian Meditation: Your Daily Practice*. London: Medio Media, 2003.
Freeman, L., *A Pearl of Great Price: Sharing the Gift of Mediation by Starting a Group*. Tucson, Arizona: Medio Media, 2002.
Lehodey, V., *The Ways of Mental Prayer*. Dublin: M. H. Gill & Son, 1944.
Leonard, J., *St Vincent de Paul and Mental Prayer*. London: Burns Oates & Washbourne, 1925.
Lercaro, Archbp. G. Cardinal, *Methods of Mental Prayer*.London: Burns & Oates, 1957.
Gibbard, M., *Prayer and Contemplation: An Invitation to Discover*. London: Mowbray, 1985.
Hamman, A., *Prayer: The New Testament*. Chicago: Franciscan Herald Press, 1971.
Jungmann, J. A., *Christian Prayer Through the Centuries*. New York: Paulist Press, 1978.
Martin, R., *The Fulfillment of All Desire: A Guidebook for the Journey to God Based on the Wisdom of the Saints*. Steubenville, Ohio: Emmaus Road Publishing, 1997.
Merton, T., *Contemplative Prayer*. London: Darton, Longman & Todd, 1973.
Nigro, A. M., *Mainly About Prayer*. Richmond, Victoria: Messenger of the Sacred Heart.
Poulain, R. P. A., *The Graces of Interior Prayer: A Treatise on Mystical Theology*. London: Kegan Paul, Trench, Trübner & Co., 1910.
Poulain, A.., *Revelations and Visions: Discerning the True and the Certain from the False or the Doubtful*. New York: Alba House, 1998.
Rosage, D. E., *Speak, Lord, Your Servant is Listening: A Daily Guide to Scriptural Prayer*. Ann Arbor, Michigan, Servant Books, 1970.
Underhill, E., *Mysticism: A Study in the Nature and Development of Man's Spiritual Consciousness*. New York: E. P. Dutton & Co., 1961.
Underhill, E., *Worship*. London: Fontana Library, 1968.
Voillaume, R., *The Need for Contemplation*. London: Darton, Longman & Todd, 1972.
von Balthasar, H. U., *Prayer*. New York: Sheed & Ward, 1961.

The Desert Fathers

The Life and Teaching of Pachomius. Translated by Sr Mary Dominique OC and D. Mary Groves OSB. Herefordshire: Gracewing, 1998.
Allen, P., Canning, R., Cross, L. and Caiger, B. J., eds. *Prayer and Spirituality in the Early Church*. Everton Park, Queensland: Australian Catholic University,

1998.

Athanasius, Bishop of Alexandria, *Life of Saint Anthony* (c. 350 AD). Red Sea, St. Anthony Monastery. Reprinted 1992.

Basil the Great, *Gateway to Paradise*. Edited by Oliver Davies. Translated by Tim Witherow. New York: New City Press, 1991.

Chitty, D. J., *The Desert a City: An Introduction to the Study of Egyptian and Palestinian Monasticism under the Christian Empire*. Oxford: Mowbray, 1966.

Chitty, D., (trans). *The Letters of St Antony the Great*. Oxford: SLG Press, 1975.

de Dreuille, M., *Seeking the Absolute Love: The Founders of Christian Monasticism*. Herefordshire: Gracewing, 1999.

Gregory of Nyssa: The Life of Moses. Translation, introduction and notes by Abraham J. Malherbe and Everett Ferguson. New York: Paulist Press, 1978.

Hill, R. C., *St. John Chrysostom: Spiritual Gems from the Book of Psalms*. Boston: Holy Cross Orthodox Press, 2004.

Kamil, J., *Coptic Egypt: History and Guide* (Revised Edition). Cairo, Egypt: The American University in Cairo Press, 1990.

Maximus Confessor, *Selected Writings*. Translation and notes by George C. Berthold. New Jersey: Paulist Press, 1985.

Meinardus, O. F. A., *Monks and Monasteries of the Egyptian Deserts* (Revised Edition). Cairo, Egypt: The American University in Cairo Press, 1992.

Merton, T., (trans) *The Wisdom of the Desert: Sayings of the Desert Fathers of the Fourth Century*. London: Sheldon Press, 1960.

Molloy, M. E., *Champion of Truth: The Life of Saint Athanasius*. New York: Alba House, 2003.

Russell, N., (trans) *The Lives of the Desert Fathers: The Historia Monachorum in Aegypto*. Oxford: Mowbray, 1980.

St Basil the Great, *On the Holy Spirit*. Translated by David Anderson. New York: St. Vladimir's Seminary Press, 1980.

St Maximus the Confessor, *The Church, the Liturgy and the Soul of Man*. Translated, with Historical Note and Commentaries by Dom Julian Stead, O.S.B. Massachusetts: St. Bede's Publications, 1982.

Waddell, H., (trans) *The Desert Fathers*. London: Fontana Library, 1962.

Ward, B, . S.L.G.,(trans) *The Sayings of the Desert Fathers*. Oxford: Mowbray, 1975.

Eastern Christian Spiritual Tradition

Antioch & Alexandria: Discovering the Heritage of Oriental Christianity. Edited by Fr. Peter A.L. Hill and Dr. Youhanna Nessim Youssef. Ballan: Victorian Council of Churches, 2003.

St John Climacus, *The Ladder of Divine Ascent*. Translation by Archimandrite Lazarus Moore. California: Eastern Orthodox Books, 1959.

John Climacus, *The Ladder of Divine Ascent*. Translation by Colm Luibheid and Norman Russell. New York: Paulist Press, 1982.
Pseudo-Macarius, *The Fifty Spiritual Homilies and the Great Letter*. Translated and edited by George A. Maloney, S.J. New York: Paulist Press, 1992.
Evagrius Ponticus, *The Praktikos & Chapters on Prayer*. Translated by John Eudes Bamberger, O.C.S.O. Kalamazoo, Michigan: Cistercian Publications, 1981.
St John Chrysostom, *Six Books on the Priesthood*. Translated by Graham Neville. New York: St Vladimir's Seminary Press, 1996.
Symeon the New Theologian, *The Discourses*. Translation by C. J. deCatanzaro. New York: Paulist Press, 1980.
Krivocheine, Archbishop Basil, *In the Light of Christ: Saint Symeon the New Theologian 949-1022) Life – Spirituality – Doctrine*. Translated by Anthony P. Gythiel. New York: St. Vladimir's Seminary Press, 1986.
Meyendorff, J., *St. Gregory Palamas and Orthodox Spirituality*. New York: St. Vladimir's Seminary Press, 1974.
St. Theodore the Studite, *On the Holy Icons*. Translated by Catharine P. Roth. New York: St. Vladimir's Seminary Press, 1981.
Writings from the Philokalia on Prayer of the Heart. Translated by E. Kadloubovsky and G. E. H. Palmer. London: Faber & Faber, 1979.
Zander, V., *St Seraphim of Sarov*. New York: St. Vladimir's Seminary Press, 1975.
Jones, F. ed., *The Spiritual Instructions of Saint Seraphim of Sarov*. Los Angles: Dawn Horse Press, 1973.
Fedotov, G. P., ed. *A Treasury of Russian Spirituality*. Massachusetts: Nordland Publishing Co., 1975.
Maloney, G. A., *Prayer of the Heart*. Notre Dame, Indiana: Ave Maria Press, 1981.
Sjögren, P., *The Jesus Prayer*. Translated by Sydney Linton. London: SPCK, 1975.
The Way of the Pilgrim and The Pilgrim Continues His Way. Translated by R. M. French. New York: Seabury Press, 1965.
Macarius, Starets of Optino, *Russian Letters of Direction 1834-1860*. Selection and Translation by Iulia de Beausobre. New York: St. Vladimir's Seminary Press, 1975.
Reflections on the Jesus Prayer: A phrase-by-phrase analysis of "The Prayer of the Heart" by A Priest of the Byzantine Church. New Jersey: Dimension Books, 1978.
Sophrony, Archimandrite, *The Monk of Mount Athos: Staretz Silouan 1866-1938*. Translated by Rosemary Edmonds. London: Mowbrays, 1973.
Sophrony, Archimandrite, *Wisdom from Mount Athos: The Writings of Staretz Silouan 1866-1938*. Translated by Rosemary Edmonds. London: Mowbrays, 1974.
Mailleus, P. A. and Stanton, E. S., *The Vladimir Mother of God*. New York: One Fold Books, 1960.
Elias, N. M., *The Divine Liturgy Explained: A Guide for Orthodox Christian Worshippers*. Athens: Astir Publishers, 1974.
Melkite Catholic Eparchy, *The Divine and Holy Liturgy of Saint John Chrysostom*.

Australia: Melkite Press, 2000.

Cross, L., *Eastern Christianity: The Byzantine Tradition*. Sydney: E. J. Dwyer, 1988.

Greek Orthodox Archdiocese of Australia, *Book of Prayers: A Selection for Orthodox Christians*. Sydney: Greek Orthodox Archdiocese of Australia, 1993.

St Augustine of Hippo

Allies, M. H., *Leaves from St. Augustine*. London: Burns & Oates, 1886.

Brown, P., *Augustine of Hippo: A Biography*. London: Faber & Faber, 1967.

Guardini, R., *The Conversion of Augustine*. Translated by Elinor Briefs. London: Sands & Co., 1960.

St Augustine, Bishop of Hippo, *Confessions (c. AD 397-400)*. Translated by J. G. Pilkington. London: The Folio Society, 2006.

St Augustine, *The Rule of, Masculine and Feminine Versions (c. AD 397)*. Translated by Raymond Canning OSA. London: Darton, Longman & Todd, 1984.

St Augustine, *Nine Sermons of, On the Psalms*. Translated by Edmund Hill, O.P. London, Longmans, Green & Co., 1958.

St. Augustine, *The Happy Life*. Translated by Ludwig Schopp. Boston: St. Paul Editions, 1939.

D'Arcy, M. C., Bondel, M., et al. (essays), *St Augustine: His Age, Life and Thought*. New York: Meridian Books, 1957.

Hand, T. A., *St. Augustine on Prayer*. Dublin: Gill & Son, 1963.

Verheijen, L., *Saint Augustine: Monk, Priest, Bishop*. Pennsylvania: Augustinian Historical Institute, 1978.

A New Beginning: Tertullian, Cyril, and Augustine on Baptism. Translated by Sr M. Dominique Slough OC, Sr M. Bernard Fernham OSB and D. Mary Groves OSB. Herefordshire: Gracewing, 1998.

Benedict XVI, Pope, *Church Fathers: From Clement of Rome to Augustine – General Audiences, 7 March 2007 – 27 February 2008*. San Francisco: Ignatius Press, 2008.

Western Monasticism

Cassian, John, Abbot of Marseilles, *The Monastic Institutes consisting of On the Training of a Monk and The Eight Deadly Sins (c. AD 400-435)*. Translated by Fr Jerome Bertram. Oxford: Saint Austin Press, 1999.

Cassian, John., *Conferences (c. AD 400-435)*. Translation by Colm Luibheid. New York: Paulist Press, 1985.

St Benedict, *The Rule of*, translated by A. C. Meisel and M. L. del Mastro. New York: Image Books, 1975.

St Benedict, *The Rule of*, translated by Justin McCann. London: Sheed & Ward, 1976.

Braunfels, W., *Monasteries of Western Europe: The Architecture of the Orders*. London:

Thames & Hudson, 1972.
Benedictine Monks of Subiaco, *Monastery of St. Benedict: The Sanctuary of the Sacred Cave and the Monastery of St. Scholastica, Subiaco.*
von Matt, L. and Hilpisch, S., *Saint Benedict.* Translated by Dom Ernest Graf, O.S.B., London: Burns & Oates, 1961.
McQuiston II, J., *Always We Begin Again: The Benedictine Way of Living.* New York: Morehouse Publishing, 1996.
Leclercq, J., *The Love of Learning and the Desire for God: A Study of Monastic Culture.* Translated by Catharine Misrahi. London: SPCK, 1961.
St Gregory the Great, *Pastoral Care.* Translated by Henry Davies, S.J., New York: Newman Press, 1978.
St Gregory the Great, *Pastoral Practice: Books 3 and 4 of the Regula Pastoralis.* Translated and edited by John Leinenweber. Pennsylvania: Trinity Press, 1998.
Evans, G. R., *The Thought of Gregory the Great.* Cambridge: Cambridge University Press, 1986.
Keep, D., *St. Boniface and his world: A booklet to commemorate the thirteen hundredth anniversary of his birth at Crediton in Devon (AD 680).* Exeter: The Paternoster Press, 1979.
Saint Bernard of Clairvaux, *On the Love of God / De Diligendo Deo.* London: Mowbray, 1982.
Saint Bernard of Clairvaux, *How the Word Visits the Soul.* Translated by Michael Casey, O.C.S.O., Tarrawarra Abbey: The Abbey Press, 1990.
Saint Bernard of Clairvaux, *In the Steps of Humility.* London: The Saint Austin Press, 2001.
Casey, M., *Athirst for God: Spiritual Desire in Bernard of Clairvaux's Sermons on the Song of Songs.* Kalamazoo: Cistercian Publications, 1988.
Daniel-Rops, H., *Bernard of Clairvaux: The story of the last of the great Church Fathers.* New York: Hawthorn Books, 1964.
Anglican Essays with an Introduction by Jean Leclercq OSB, *The Influence of Saint Bernard.* Oxford: SLG Press, 1976.
Cristiani, L., *St. Bernard of Clairvaux (1090-1153).* Translated by M. Angeline Bouchard. Boston: St. Paul Editions, 1970.
Merton Legacy Trust, *Thomas Merton on Saint Bernard.* Kalamazoo: Cistercian Publications, 1980.
Tamburello, D. E., *Bernard of Clairvaux: Essential Writings.* New York: Crossroad, 2000.
Louf, A., *The Cistercian Way.* Translated by Nivard Kinsella. Kalamazoo: Cistercian Publications, 1983.
Matarasso, P. ed. *The Cistercian World: Monastic Writings of the Twelfth Century.* London: Penguin Books, 1993.
Hebron, S. *Life in a Monastery.* Norwich: Jarrold Publishing, 2004.
The Prayers and Meditations of St Anselm. Translated by Sister Benedicta Ward,

S.L.G., England: Penguin Books, 1973.
Shannon, W. H., *Anslem: The Joy of Faith*. New York: Crossroad, 1999.

Celtic Spirituality

Van de Weyer, R., ed. *Celtic Fire: An Anthology of Celtic Christian Literature*. London: Darton, Longman and Todd, 1990.
Ó Maidín, U., ed., *The Celtic Monk: Rules and Writings of Early Irish Monks*. Kalamazoo: Cistercian Publications, 1996.
Bamford, C. and Marsh, W. P., eds., *Celtic Christianity: Ecology and Holiness*. Floris Books.
Adomnán of Iona, *Life of St. Columba*. Translated by Richard Sharpe. London: Penguin Books, 1995.
Allchin, A. M., and De Waal, E., eds. *Threshold of Light: Prayers & Praises from the Celtic Tradition*. London: Darton, Longman & Todd, 1986.
MacDonald, I., ed., *Saint Brendan*. Edinburgh: Floris Books, 1992.
MacDonald, I., ed., *Saint Bride*. Edinburgh: Floris Books, 1992.
MacDonald, I., ed., *Saint Columba*. Edinburgh: Floris Books, 1992.
Wallace, M., *A Little Book of Celtic Saints*. Belfast: The Appletree Press, 1995.

St Francis of Assisi and Franciscanism

Englebert, O., *St. Francis of Assisi: A Biography*. Ann Arbor, Michigan: Servant Books, 1965.
Jörgensen, J., *Saint Francis of Assisi: A Biography*. Translated by T. O'Connor Sloane. New York: Longmans, Green and Co., 1913.
Moorman, Bishop John R. H., *Saint Francis of Assisi*. London: SPCK, 1976.
Moorman, Bishop John R. H., *Richest of Poor Men: The Spirituality of St Francis of Assisi*. London: Darton, Longman & Todd, 1977.
Karrer, O., ed., *The Little Flowers, Legends, and Lauds: St Francis of Assisi and others*. Translated by N. Wydenbruck. London: Sheed & Ward, 1947.
The Writings of Saint Francis of Assisi. Translated by Ignatius Brady, O.F.M., Casa Editrice Francescana-Assisi: Edizioni Porziuncola, 1983.
Carmondy M., *The Franciscan Story: St Francis of Assisi and his influence since the thirteenth century*. London: Athena Press, 2008.
St Bonaventure, *The Character of a Christian Leader, originally titled The Six Wings of the Seraph*. Translated by Philip O'Mara. Ann Arbor, Michigan: Servant Books, 1978.
Hayes, Z., *Bonaventure: Mystical Writings*. New York: Crossroad, 1999.
Armstrong, R. J., ed., *Clare of Assisi: Early Documents*. New York: Paulist Press, 1988.
Stace, C., *Saint Clare of Assisi: Her Legend and Selected Writings*. London: Triangle, 2001.
The Capuchin Reform: A Franciscan Renaissance – A portrait of sixteenth century Capuchin

life / *La Bella e Santa Riforma Dei Frati Minori Cappunccini*. Translated by Paul Hanbridge OFM Cap. Delhi: Media House, 2003.

The Dominicans

Tugwell, S., ed., *Early Dominicans: Selected Writings*. New York: Paulist Press, 1982.

The Dialogue of the Seraphic Virgin, Catherine of Siena, dictated by her, while in a state of ecstasy, to her secretaries, and completed in the year of Our Lord 1370 together with an account of her death by an eye-witness. Translated by Algar Thorold. Illinois: Tan Books, 1974.

Curtayne, A., *Saint Catherine of Siena*. London: Sheed & Ward, 1931.

de la Bedoyere, M., *Catherine, Saint of Siena*. London: Hollis & Carter, 1947.

Foster, K., and Ronayne, M. J., eds., *I, Catherine: Selected Writings of St Catherine of Siena*. London: Collins, 1980.

Ferretti, L., *Saint Catherine of Siena*. Siena: Edizioni Cantagalli, 1996.

The English Mystics

Rolle, R., *The Fire of Love*. Translated by Clifton Wolters. England: Penguin Books, 1972.

Hilton, W., *The Scale of Perfection*. London: Geoffrey Chapman, 1975.

Julian of Norwich, *Revelation of Divine Love*. Translated by Clifton Wolters. England: Penguin Books, 1966.

Furlong, M., ed. *The Wisdom of Julian of Norwich*. Oxford: Lion Publishing, 1996.

Cooper, A., *Julian of Norwich: Reflections on Selected Texts*. Homebush: St Paul Publications, 1986.

Anon., *The Cloud of Unknowing*. Translated by Clifton Wolters. England: Penguin Books, 1961.

Backhouse, H., ed., *The Cloud of Unknowing*. London: Hodder & Stoughton, 1985.

Walsh, J., ed., *The Cloud of Unknowing*. New York: Paulist Press, 1981.

Johnston, W. *The Mysticism of the Cloud of Unknowing*. England: Anthony Clarke Books, 1978.

Crawford, C., ed., *A Mirror for Simple Souls: The Mystical Work of Marguerite Porete*. New York: Crossroad, 1990.

Griffiths, J., ed., *A Letter of Private Direction and other treatises by a fourteenth-century English mystic*. London: Gill & MacMillan, 1981.

Chambers, R. W., *Thomas More*. England: Penguin Books, 1963.

Kenny, A., *Thomas More*. Oxford: Oxford University Press, 1983.

Rhineland Mystics

Boyer, L., *Women Mystics: Hadewijch of Antwerp, Teresa of Avila, Thérèse of Lisieux, Elizabeth of the Trinity, Edith Stein*. Translated by Anne Englund Nash. San Francisco: Ignatius Press, 1989.

Davies, O., *God Within: The Mystical Tradition of Northern Europe*. London: Darton, Longman & Todd, 1988.

De Vinck, J., *Revelations of Women Mystics: From the Middle Ages to Modern Times*. New York: Alba House, 1985.

Gertrude of Helfta, *The Herald of Divine Love*. Translated and edited by Margaret Winkworth. New York: Paulist Press, 1993.

Bowie, F., *Beguine Spirituality: An Anthology*. Translated by Oliver Davies. London: SPCK, 1989.

Olyslager, W. A., *The Groot Begijnhof of Leuven*. Leuven University Press, 1983.

Colledge, E., and Sister M. Jane, O.P., eds. *Spiritual Conferences by John Tauler, O.P.* Illinois: Tan Books, 1978.

Fleming, U., ed., *Meister Eckhart – The Man from whom God hid Nothing*. London: Fount Paperbacks, 1988.

Hadewijch: The Complete Works. Translated by Mother Columba Hart, O.S.B., New York: Paulist Press, 1980.

Jacob Boehme: The Way to Christ (AD 1575 – 1624). Translated by Peter Erb. New York: Paulist Press, 1978.

Devotio Moderna

Devotio Moderna: Basic Writings. Translated by John Van Engen. New York: Paulist Press, 1988.

a Kempis, T., *The Imitation of Christ*. Translated by Betty I. Knott. Great Britain: Fontana Books, 1963.

a Kempis, T., *The Imitation of Christ: In Four Books*. Translated by Joseph N. Tylenda, S.J. Wilmington: Michael Glazier, 1984.

Late Medieval Spiritual writers

Saint Aelred of Rievaulx, *A Letter to My Sister*. Translated by Geoffrey Webb and Adrian Walker. London: The Saint Austin Press, 2001.

William of St Thierry, *On the Nature and Dignity of Love*. Translated by Geoffrey Webb and Adrian Walker. London: The Saint Austin Press, 2001.

William of St Thierry, *On Contemplating God*. Translated by Geoffrey Webb and Adrian Walker. London: The Saint Austin Press, 2001.

de Caussade, J-P., *On Prayer: Spiritual Instructions on the Various States of Prayer According to the Doctrine of Bossuet, Bishop of Meaux*. Translated by Algar Thorold. London: Burns Oates & Washbourne, 1931.

de Caussade, J.-P., *The Sacrament of the Present Moment.* Translated by Kitty Muggeridge. London: Fount Paperbacks, 1981.
de Caussade, J.-P., *Self-Abandonment to Divine Providence.* Translated by Alga Thorold. London: Fontana Library of Theology and Philosophy, 1971
Llewelyn, R., ed., *The Flame of Divine Love: Readings from the spiritual councils and letters of Jean-Pierre de Caussade, S.J.,* London: Darton, Longman & Todd, 1984.
Llewelyn, R., ed., *Daily Readings with Brother Lawrence,* London: Darton, Longman & Todd, 1985.
Matthews, V. J., *St Philip Neri: Apostle of Rome and Founder of the Congregation of the Oratory.* Illinois: Tan Books, 1984.
Steingraeber, J., ed., *Love is Prayer, Prayer is Love: Selected Writings of St. Alphonsus.* Liguori, Missouri: Liguori Publications, 1973.
Erb, P. C., ed., *Priests: Selected Writings.* London: SPCK, 1983.

The Ignatian tradition

The Spiritual Exercises of St. Ignatius: Based on Studies in the Language of the Autograph. Translated by Louis J. Puhl, S.J., Chicago: Loyola University Press, 1951.
The Spiritual Exercises of St. Ignatius. Translated by Anthony Mottola. New York: Image Books, 1964.
Stanley, D. M., *A Modern Scriptural Approach to the Spiritual Exercises.* St. Louis: The Institute of Jesuit Sources, 1971.
Osuna, J., *Friends in the Lord: A Study in the origins and growth of community in the Society of Jesus from St Ignatius' conversion to the earliest text of the Constitutions (1521-1541).* Translated by Nicholas King S.J. Exeter: James Walsh S.J., 1974.
Brodrick, J., *The Origin of the Jesuits.* London: Longmans, Green & Co., 1940.
Hollis, C., *Saint Ignatius.* London: Sheed & Ward, 1931.
Yeo, M., *The Greatest of the Borgias.* London: Sheed & Ward, 1936.

Carmelite Tradition

McCaffrey, E., *Introduction to the Writings of St Teresa of Avila.* Dublin: Carmelite Centre of Spirituality, 1981.
Clare, Mother M., *Carmelite Ascent: An Introduction to St Teresa and St John of the Cross.* Oxford: SLG Press, 1982.
Peers, E. A., ed., *The Life of Teresa of Jesus: The Autobiography of St. Teresa of Avila.* New York: Image Books, 1960.
Peers, E. A., ed., *Interior Castle by St. Teresa of Avila.* New York: Image Books, 1961.
Peers, E. A., ed., *The Way of Perfection by St. Teresa of Avila.* New York: Image Books, 1964.
Rohrback, P., *Conversation with Christ: The teaching of St. Teresa of Avila about personal prayer.* Illinois: Tan Books, 1982.

Counsels of Light and Love of Saint John of the Cross. Introduction by Thomas Merton. London: Burns & Oates, 1977.

Van de Weyer, R., ed., *The Dark Night of the Soul and The Living Flame of Love – St John of the Cross.* London: Fount Paperbacks, 1995.

Venard, J., *The Spiritual Canticle of St John of the Cross (Simplified Version with Notes).* Sydney: E. J. Dwyer, 1980.

Venard, J., *The Ascent of Mount Carmel and The Dark Night of St John of the Cross (Simplified Version).* Darlington Carmel, 1981.

Venard, J., *The Living Flame of Love. St John of the Cross (Simplified Version with Notes).* Sydney: E. J. Dwyer, 1990.

Mary, Sr. E., *Pilgrimage and Possession: Conversion in the Writings of St Teresa and St John of the Cross.* Oxford: SLG Press, 1983.

Nims, J. F., ed., *The Poems of St. John of the Cross.* New York: Grove Press, 1959.

Poslusney, V., *Attaining Spiritual Maturity for Contemplation: According to St. John of the Cross.* New York: Living Flame Press, 1973.

Steuart, R. H. J., *The Mystical Doctrine of St John of the Cross.* London: Sheed & Ward, 1974.

Campbell, C., *Meditations with John of the Cross.* Santa Fe: Bear & Co., 1989.

Ruth, E., ed., *Lamps of Fire: Daily Readings with St John of the Cross.* London: Darton, Longman & Todd, 1985.

Clissold, S., ed., *The Wisdom of the Spanish Mystics.* London: Sheldon Press, 1977.

St. Thérèse of Lisieux: Her Last Conversations. Translated by John Clarke, O.C.D. Washington DC: ICS Publications, 1977.

St. Thérèse of Lisieux: General Correspondence. Volume I, 1877-1890. Translated by John Clarke, O.C.D. Washington DC: ICS Publications, 1982.

St. Thérèse of Lisieux: The Story of a Soul. The Autobiography of, Translated by John Beevers. New York: Image Books, 1957.

De Meester, C., *With Empty Hands: the message of Thérèse of Lisieux.* Homebush: St Paul Publications, 1982.

Oben, F. M., *The Life and Thought of St. Edith Stein.* New York: Alba House, 2001.

Lyne, P., *Edith Stein Discovered: A Personal Portrait.* Herefordshire: Gracewing, 2000.

Sullivan, J., ed. *Carmelite Studies: Spiritual Direction.* Washington, DC: ICS Publications, 1980.

The French School

Bossuet, Bishop J-B., *Letters of Spiritual Direction.* Translated by Geoffrey Webb and Adrian Walker. London: The Saint Austin Press, 2001.

Thompson, W. M., ed., *Bérulle and the French School: Selected Writings.* New York: Paulist Press, 1989.

Bossuet, Bishop J-B., *The Continuity of Religion: From Discourse on Universal History.*

Translated by Msgr. Victor Day. Fitzwilliam, NH: Loreto Publications, 1929.
Lebrun, C., *The Spiritual Teaching of St. John Eudes*. Translated by Dom Basil Whelan, O.S.B. London: Sands & Co., 1934.
Bialas, M., *In This Sign ... The Spirituality of St. Paul of the Cross*. Dublin: Dominican Publications, 1984.
Spencer, P. F., *As a Seal Upon Your Heart: The Life of St Paul of the Cross, Founder of the Passionists*. United Kingdom: St Pauls, 1994.
Klauder, F. J., ed., *Every Day with Saint Francis de Sales: Teachings and Examples for the Life of the Saint*. New York: Salesiana Publishers, 1985.
Fiorelli, L. S., *Spiritual Directory of St. Francis de Sales: Reflections for the Laity*. Boston: St Paul Editions, 1985.
Ryan, J. K., ed., *St. Francis de Sales: Introduction to the Devout Life*. New York: Image Books, 1966.
Quinlan, G. J., ed., *Reflections of Saint Francis de Sales on Living Jesus*. Reflections compiled by Fr Andrew V. Masters, S.V.D. Washington, DC: Fraternity Group, 1999.
Selected Letters of Saint Jane Frances de Chantal. Translated by the Sisters of the Visitation, Harrow. London: R. & T. Washbourne, 1918.
Calvet, J., *Saint Vincent de Paul*. Translated by Lancelot C. Sheppard. London: Burns & Oates, 1952.
Koch, C., Calligan, J. and Gros, J., eds., *John Baptist de la Salle: The Spirituality of Christian Education*. New York: Paulist Press, 2004.
Loes, A., ed., *The Letters of John Baptist de la Salle*. Illinois: Lasallian Publications, 1988.
Loes, A. and Huether, F., eds., *Meditations by John Baptist de la Salle*. Maryland: Christian Brothers Conference, 1994.
Mouton, D., ed., *Explanation of the Method of Interior Prayer by John Baptist de la Salle*. Maryland: Christian Brothers Conference, 1995.
Dempsey, M., *John Baptist de la Salle: His Life and His Institute*. Milwaukee: The Bruce Publishing Co., 1940.
St. Francis de Sales, *Introduction to the Devout Life*. Translated by John K. Ryan. New York: Image Books, 1966.
Vianney, St. John, *The Little Catechism of the Curé of Ars*. Illinois: Tan Books, 1987.
O'Brien, B. J., *The Curé of Ars: Patron Saint of Parish Priests*. Illinois: Tan Books, 1987.

Devotion to Blessed Sacrament and Sacred Heart

O'Donnell, T. T., *Heart of the Redeemer: An Apologia for the Contemporary and Perennial Value of the Devotion to the Sacred Heart of Jesus*. Virginia: Trinity Communications, 1989.

Kerns, V., ed., *St Margaret Mary: Her Autobiography*. London: Darton, Longman & Todd, 1965.
Philip, Mother M., *The Spiritual Direction of Saint Claude de la Colombière*. San Francisco: Ignatius Press, 1998.
Guernsey, D. P., ed., *Adoration: Eucharistic Texts and Prayers Throughout Church History*. San Francisco: Ignatius Press, 1999.
Groeschel, B. J., and Monti, J., *In the Presence of Our Lord: The History, Theology, and Psychology of Eucharistic Devotion*. Indiana: Our Sunday Visitor, 1997.
Groeschel, B. J., Cleffi, G. & Y., *Life in Christ: Meditations from the Oratory of Divine Love*. Huntington, Indiana: Our Sunday Visitor Publishing Division, 2009.
Scheffczyk, L., ed., *Faith in Christ and the Worship of Christ: New Approaches to Devotion to Christ*. San Francisco: Ignatius Press, 1986.
Kern, W., *New Liturgy and Old Devotions: Explanations and Prayers*. Canfield, Ohio: Alba House Communications, 1979.

B1 John Henry Newman

Newman, J. H. Cardinal, *Apologia Pro Vita Sua*. New York: Image Books, 1956.
Bouyer, L., *Newman: His Life and Spirituality*. London: Burns & Oates, 1958.
Dessain, C. S., *John Henry Newman (Third Edition)*. Oxford: Oxford University Press, 1980.
Dessain, C. S., *Cardinal Newman: The Oratory and the Laity. Newman's Understanding of the Oratorian Way of Life and the part it should play in forming an effective Lay Apostolate*. Birmingham Oratory, c. 1971.
Flanagan, P., *Newman, Faith and the Believer*. London: Sands & Co., 1946.

Various Saints

Butler, A., *The Lives of the Fathers, Martyrs and Other Principal Saints. Volumes I – IV*. London and Dublin: Virtue & Company, 1904.
Butler, A., *Lives of the Saints With Reflections for Every Day in the Year*. Compiled from the "Lives of the Saints" by Rev. Alban Butler, with New Saints and Those Whose Feasts Are Special to the United States (New Edition). New York: Benziger Brothers, 1955.
Walsh, M., ed., *Butler's Lives of the Saints: Concise Edition*. Kent: Burns & Oates, 1985.
Farmer, D. H., *The Oxford Dictionary of Saints*. Oxford: Oxford University Press, 1983.
Delaney, J. J., *Pocket Dictionary of Saints (Abridged Edition)*. New York: Image Books, 1983.
Daughters of St. Paul, *Every Man's Challenge: profile of great men and women*. Boston: St Paul Editions, 1974.
Almagno, R. S., ed., *The Saints Always Belong to the Present: A Selection from the Sermons,*

Addresses, and Papers of Cardinal John J. Wright. San Francisco: Ignatius Press, 1985.
Monaghan, A., *God's People? One Hundred and Ten Characters in the Story of Scottish Religion*. Edinburgh: Saint Andrew Press, 1991.
Caraman, P., ed., *Saints and Ourselves: A Selection of Saints' Lives*. Ann Arbor, Michigan: Servant Books, 1958.
Purcell, W., *Martyrs of our Time*. London & Oxford: Mowbray, 1983.
Morris, D., *Beatitude Saints*. Huntington, Indiana: Our Sunday Visitor, 1984.
Aland, K., *Saints and Sinners: Men and Ideas in the Early Church*. Philadelphia: Fortress Press, 1970.
Hoever, H., *Lives of the Saints for Every Day of the Year: In Accord with the Norms and Principals of the New Roman Calendar*. New York: Catholic Book Publishing Co., 1977.
Goodier, Archbp. A., *Saints for Sinners: Nine unusual saints whose inspiring lives have significance for modern men and women*. New York: Image Books, 1959.
Duckett, E., *The Wandering Saints*. London: The Catholic Book Club, 1960.
Sheehan, T. W., *Dictionary of Patron Saints' Names*. Huntington, Indiana: Our Sunday Visitor, 2001.
Ellsberg, R., *All Saints: Daily Reflections on Saints, Prophets, and Witnesses for Our Time*. New York: Crossroad, 2002.
Holböck, F., *New Saints and Blesseds of the Catholic Church, 1979-1983 (Vol 1)* San Francisco: Ignatius Press, 2000.
Holböck, F., *New Saints and Blesseds of the Catholic Church, 1984-1987 (Vol 2)*. San Francisco: Ignatius Press, 2003.
Waugh, E., *Edmund Campion*. London: Hollis & Carter, 1952.
Macklem, M., *God Have Mercy: The Life of John Fisher of Rochester*. Ottawa: Oberon Press, 1967.
Dempsey, M., *Saint Peter Julian Eymard: Champion of the Blessed Sacrament*. Sydney: Blessed Sacrament Fathers.
Peyret, R., *Marthe Robin: The Cross and the Joy*. New York: Alba House, 1983.
Auffray, A., *Saint John Bosco*. Blaisdon: Salesian Publications, 1930.
Ayers, J., *Don Bosco Comes Back*. Salesian Bulletin – Special Edition. April, 1984.
Pascal, B., *Pensées*. Translated by A. J. Krailsheimer. Great Britain: Penguin Books, 1976.
Monaghan, Sr. M. St. Rita, *Monsignor Robert Hugh Benson: His Apostolate and its Message for our Time*. Brisbane: Boolarong Publications, 1985.
Ingoldsby, M. F., *Padre Pio: His Life and Mission*. Dublin: Veritas Publications, 1988.
Flaubert, G., *La Légende de Saint Julien L'Hospitalier*. London: George G. Harrap & o., 1953.
Come, let us sing a song unknown: Prayers of Charles de Foucauld. New Jersey: Dimension Books, c. 1983.

Bazin, R. *Charles de Foucauld: Hermit and Explorer.* Translated by Peter Keelan. London: Burns Oates & Washbourne, 1923.

A Little Brother of Jesus, *Silent Pilgrimage to God: The Spirituality of Charles de Foucauld.* Translated by Jeremy Moiser. New York: Orbis Books, 1975.

Fremantle, A., *Desert Calling: The Life of Charles de Foucauld.* London: Hollis & Carter, 1950.

Lepetit, C., *Two Dancers in the Desert: The Life of Charles de Foucauld.* Kent: Burns & Oates, 1983.

McCreanor, S., ed., *Mary MacKillop in Challenging Times, 1883-1899: A collection of letters.* North Sydney: Sister of St Joseph of the Sacred Heart, 2006.

Wicks, P., ed., *Mary MacKillop: Inspiration for Today.* Croydon, NSW: The Trustees of the Sisters of St Joseph of the Sacred Heart, 2005.

Van Chau, A. N., *The Miracle of Hope: Francis Xavier Nguyen Van Thuan, Political Prisoner, Prophet of Peace.* Boston: Pauline Books & Media, 2003.

Zanzucchi, M., *Chiara Luce: A Life Lived to the Full.* Translated by Frank Johnson. London: New City, 2007.

Spiritual Direction

Laplace, J., *Preparing for Spiritual Direction.* Translated by John C. Guinness. Chicago: Franciscan Herald Press, 1975.

Ashley, B. M., *Spiritual Direction in the Dominican Tradition.* New York: Paulist Press, 1995.

Leech, K., *Soul Friend: The Practice of Christian Spirituality.* San Francisco: Harper & Row, Publishers, 1980.

Guillet, J., Bardy, G., Vandenbroucke, F., Pegon, J., Martin, H., *Discernment of Spirits.* Collegeville, Minnesota: The Liturgical Press, 1970.

Merton, T., *Spiritual Direction and Meditation.* Collegeville, Minnesota: The Liturgical Press, 1960.

Charismatic Renewal

Burgess, S. M., McGee, G. B., et al. eds., *Dictionary of Pentecostal and Charismatic Movements.* Grand Rapids, Michigan: Zondervan Publishing House, 1987.

Suenens, L. J. Cardinal, *A New Pentecost?* Translated by Francis Martin. London: Darton, Longman & Todd, 1974.

O'Connor, E. D., *Pope Paul and the Spirit: Charisms and Church Renewal in the Teaching of Paul VI.* Notre Dame, Indiana: Ave Maria Press, 1978.

Dearn, E., *Christ and Charism.* Sydney: Renda Publications, 1982.

Reichel, A., *The Charismatic Path.* Oyster Bay, NSW: St Francis Community, 2008.

Various spiritual writings

Allchin, A. M., ed., *Solitude and Communion: Papers on the Hermit Life given at St David's, Wales in the Autumn of 1975.* Oxford: SLG Press, 1977.

Ravaz, C., *The Apparitions in Damascus: Our Lady of Soufanieh, Source of Holy Oil, Damascus, Syria.* Damascus: Messengers of Our Lady of Soufanieh, 1997.

Duff, F., *Miracles on Tap.* New York: Montfort Publications, 1961.

Bradshaw, R., *Frank Duff: Founder of the Legion of Mary.* New York: Montfort Publications, 1984.

Uriburu, E. J., *A Hero Today Not Tomorrow: The Life of John Louis Pozzobon, a poor pilgrim and deacon, 1904-1985.* Cape Town: Schoenstatt Publications, 1991.

Anderson, R. and Moser, J., eds. *The Aquinas Prayer Book: The Prayers and Hymns of St. Thomas Aquinas.* Manchester, New Hampshire: Sophia Institute Press, 2000.

Cruz, J. C., *Eucharistic Miracles and Eucharistic Phenomena in the Lives of the Saints.* Illinois: Tan Books, 1987.

Escrivá, J., *The Way of the Cross.* London: Scepter, 1982.

www.ingramcontent.com/pod-product-compliance
Lightning Source LLC
Chambersburg PA
CBHW071840230426
43671CB00012B/2016